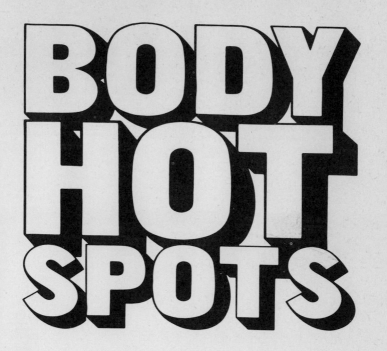

BODY HOT SPOTS

The Anatomy of Human Social Organs and Behavior

R. DALE GUTHRIE

 VAN NOSTRAND REINHOLD COMPANY

NEW YORK   CINCINNATI   ATLANTA   DALLAS   SAN FRANCISCO

Van Nostrand Reinhold Company Regional Offices:
New York Cincinnati Atlanta   Dallas   San Francisco

Van Nostrand Reinhold Company International Offices:
London Toronto Melbourne

Copyright ©1976 by Litton Educational Publishing, Inc.

Library of Congress Catalog Card Number: 75-44118
ISBN: 0-442-22982-8

Manufactured in the United States of America

Published by Van Nostrand Reinhold Company
450 West 33rd Street, New York, N.Y. 10001

Published simultaneously in Canada by Van Nostrand Reinhold Ltd.

Library of Congress Cataloging in Publication Data

Guthrie, Russell Dale, 1936–
    Body hot spots.

    Bibliography: p.
    Includes index.
    1. Body, Human — Social aspects. 2. Nonverbal
communication. I. Title. II. Title: Social
organs and behavior. [DNLM: 1. Interpersonal
relations. 2. Anatomy. 3. Nonverbal communication. 4. Social behavior. HM132 G984b]
GT495.G88   391   75-44118
ISBN 0-442-22982-8

To
Tamia and Owen —
may insides always be more important than outsides

PREFACE

What you are about to read is a new mixture of behavior and anatomy. Together with the study of paleontology and physical anthropology it has merged into a new unified discipline called Human Social Anatomy. It attempts to explain how our bodily appearance influences how we behave and vice versa. For there are some basic biological roots to this interaction, although it has received very little study until recently. It is a book on the re-evaluation of the origins and evolution of our body form that we use socially, and there are many organs which are displayed mainly for social purposes — social organs. Not through any logical design but through oversight and tradition these have not been the purview of the anatomist, nor have they been within the sphere of the ethologist, for one group deals with organ systems and the other with gestures.

Personally, I found the concept of social organs to be an entirely different way of looking at humans, and I think it will be for you as well. So here are some new views about your body and your attitude towards it and the bodies of others.

My many thanks to David Klein, Michael Fox, Valerius Geist and Frederick Szalay for their helpful comments and for many enjoyable discussions. I am particularly indebted to George Narita for his encouragement and editorial expertise.

R. Dale Guthrie

ACKNOWLEDGMENTS

Grateful acknowledgment is made to quote from the following copyright material:

"The Anthropology of Posture" by Gordon W. Hewes. Copyright ©1957 by Scientific American, Inc. All rights reserved.

Human Sexual Response by Masters and Johnson, 1966. Little, Brown and Company, Boston.

The Godfather Papers and Other Confessions by Mario Puzo. Copyright 1972. G.P. Putnam's Sons, New York.

Chocolate Days, Popsicle Weeks by Edward Hannibal, 1970. Houghton Mifflin Company, Boston.

The Living Races of Man by Carleton S. Coon and Edward E. Hunt, Jr. Copyright 1965. Alfred A. Knopf, Inc., New York.

The Winds of War by Herman Wouk, 1971. Little, Brown and Company, Boston.

The French Lieutenant's Woman by John Fowles, 1969. Little, Brown and Company, Boston.

The Cruel Sea by Nicholas Monsarrat, 1951. Alfred A. Knopf, Inc., New York.

With Lawrence in Arabia by Lowell Thomas. By permission of Hawthorn Books, Inc.

Arfive by A.B. Guthrie, Jr., 1971. Houghton Mifflin Company, Boston.

You Can't Go Home Again by Thomas Wolfe, 1973. Harper & Row, New York.

The Informed Heart by Bruno Bettelheim. Macmillan Publishing Co., Inc.

Copyright 1966, 1967, 1968. James Rado, Gerome Ragni, Galt MacDermot, Nat Shapiro, United Artists Music Co., Inc. All rights controlled and administered by United Artists Music Co., Inc., New York, New York. "Hair" in the musical *Hair*.

Games People Play: The Psychology of Human Relationships by Eric Berne. Copyright 1964. Grove Press, Inc., New York.

The Naked and the Dead by Norman Mailer. Reprinted by permission of the author and the author's agents, Scott Meredith Literary Agency, Inc., 845 Third Avenue, New York, New York 10022.

The Salzburg Connection by Helen MacInnes, 1968. Harcourt Brace Jovanovich, Inc., New York.

The Poseidon Adventure. Copyright 1969. Paul Gallico and Matteinata Anstalt. Coward McCann and Geoghegan, New York.

Beyond the Looking Glass. Copyright 1970. Kathrin Perutz. William Morrow & Co., Inc., New York.

CONTENTS

BODY HOT SPOTS

PART ONE: HOW SOCIAL SIGNALS ALL BEGAN

What Our Body Hot Spots Are All About
Social Status and Behavior
How We Use and Show Our Social Organs

1
WHAT OUR BODY HOT SPOTS ARE ALL ABOUT

It was on a subway one day in April, while I was working at the American Museum of Natural History in New York, that this book had its inception. The subway car wasn't crowded yet with the 5:00 p.m. rush, but many seats were already filled. What a fascinating collection: the coiffured lady in front, the red-haired down-and-outer over near the door, and the Wall Street executive swaying with one hand on the hang-loop and the other clutching a folded *New York Times.* My mind was nowhere — just marking time people-watching. There was a beautiful, delicately featured young woman across from me. Her hands were hardly wider than her slender wrists, and her neck was thin and fragile in appearance as a milk-white china vase. I recall thinking drowsily how poorly she would have fared back in those prehistoric days when hard skin clothing was softened by human teeth and kindling was hacked with a blunt stone — where were her beautiful kind then? My mind went on dreamily when suddenly I heard a loud commotion in the next car; then our door slid open with a thunk. There was a pause of disbelief; then we reeled in disbelief. Women cowered against the walls, some dropping out of sight behind the seats. The petite girl across from me swore and looked faint. The men grimaced and shook their heads, but no one spoke intelligible words.

The figure who had just entered the car swayed in a slight crouch, arms half outspread with elbows out. His eyes were wild, shrouded in thick, scowling brows. All he wore was an old pair of army-surplus combat boots.

His black scalp hair and beard fanned out in a curly, oily mess. Either he had been sleeping in a coal bin or he had not bathed for months. His skin was knobby, rough and matted with hair. He had a big erection, purple and persimmon colored, that slapped against his belly every couple of steps as he quickly strutted down the aisle, walking with feet and knees spread to accommodate the lurching of the car. He opened the door at the other end and just as unbelievably as he had appeared, he disappeared.

It was as if the "early man" reconstruction from the museum had been jettisoned ahead into time. He had done nothing, injured no one, but for an instant he had startled — no, terrified — us all.

My wonderings ended abruptly as the train came to a gritty halt, jarring my senses back into consciousness — it was my stop. Walking down the busy platform, I couldn't shake that dream. What if it had really happened? What is there in society that would have created such a response to his appearance? He was indeed the streaking anathema of our secret past and our hidden present, a personification of unspoken taboos about our loves and hates.

That guy in my subway dream had a body like most men, but by letting it go fallow, ungroomed and exposed, it reverted back to the once natural form that we consider vulgar and almost unmentionable. *This book deals with those vulgar and taboo body signals of ours which contain important clues to understanding the roots of our behavior. It is also about noble features and lovely bodies, because there is a basic connection between these different sets of values — the repugnant and the beautiful — which go well beyond the relation of opposites.*

I want to take you on a stroll along the horizon between the familiar, obvious values we share about people's features and the dim underlying biology of our *social organs* which pertain to all animals. Most of the research and popular books about human behavior have dealt mainly with gestures and "body language" and have avoided the delicate subject of the *organs* of communication themselves. Social organs form the essence of our appearance. They underlie our hourly decisions, values, prejudices, gestures, loves, dislikes, weaknesses and secrets about ourselves and other people. *This is not another book about how our evolutionary appearance affects our behavior, but how our behavior affected the evolution of our appearance* — how our physical features have developed to alter social communication.

Until recently it has been difficult to look at human social organs without generating the wrath of racists, anti-racists, women's libbers, male chauvinists, prurient cultists or anti-pornographists, both the political right and left, as well as defenders of the Judeo-Christian ethic. We all have vested interests in our social anatomy. A recent breakthrough, however, has occurred in the interdisciplinary field of "social anatomy." This study of how some specialized organs originated and function in social communication has enabled us to look at humans in an altogether new and rather startling way.

We have always believed that the elaborate decorations of many species evolved primarily as lures to members of the opposite sex. This is in part true, but in a different way than we once thought. For example, have you ever watched a male peafowl display in the spring? It is one of the most remarkable sights in nature. The huge tail is lifted into an intricate fan many times larger than the cock himself. Iridescent blues, greens, and bronzes flash. Wings are held to the side and rustled in a long hiss. But the most interesting thing is the numerous "eyes" that are directed toward the front. Those on top look downward, those on left look to the right, and *vice versa.* So, a peacock displaying directly toward you reveals eyes spread all around the periphery, each watching you like the stare from a picture that seems to follow you around the room. But the backside of this striking display is as drab as the sole of a shoe. *Strangely enough, the peacock usually displays outward from his female; the gaudy plumage he reserves for the view of other males.*

Not unlike the girls who prefer the football captain, the peahen is attracted to the peacock's dominance. Like the letterman's sweater, the cock's tail fan functions to gain stature among males, which in turn attracts the females. Tail fans and letter sweaters are, in a way of speaking, a *threat device* used to intimidate competing members of the same species. This theme carries through the majority of animal ornamentations. The once puzzling array of spots, splotches, stripes, manes, ruffs, dewlaps, elaborate tails, crests, plumes, gaudy color patterns, wattles, inflatable pouches, combs, throat patches, tufts, beards, and many other ornaments seem in their own way to be devices to aid in the display of threat. For when the essentials of animal communication are distilled, the prime ingredient communicated is *social state:* one's internal sense of social position and what is expressed to others.

All areas of the body are not equally important as clues to an individual's social state. There are communication "hot spots," specific body areas with sights, sounds, and smells of obvious prominence, some of which run through all species while others are quite species-specific. This book focuses on those "hot spots" which appear in human beings, and how they became that way.

Social ornamentation generally centers on these zones of information. Sometimes it magnifies and supports the signal, in other cases it shrouds the signal and changes its value. So it is with some of our own features. Not too surprisingly, herein lies the key to understanding what we are doing when we groom and decorate ourselves to regulate our social impact. Why do we snip and shave the hair, paint on artificially raised brows and exaggerated lashes, redden the lips and powder the skin, stocking the legs, and scrub away our natural oils? We'll pursue the biology behind these traditions in some detail.

Picture yourself beginning a new job with a company you admire and would like to remain with. You may spend a significant part of your life in this office. Your future co-workers are watching you — not intently, but with inquisitive glances — and you are observing them. Though your contacts are superficial and your exchanges contain no "real" information ("We're glad to have you with us ... and over here we have Mrs. Fox ... How do you do," etc.), your and their social computers are going wild with information processing — mostly beyond voluntary control or even conscious recognition. Facial lines, color, carriage, accent, movements, expressions are all recorded.

And should it not be so? These people are now important characters in your world and you in theirs. You will be intimately involved in each other's values and lives. Your social state will take on a new form relative to them and theirs to you. The communication of all these things will not be gross — it may be imperceptible. But, by necessity, people are all blue-ribbon, Grand-Prix-class people-watchers. People-watching is required to remain socially alive today, and in the distant past to remain physically alive.

The important signals in our social lives take place in a few milliseconds. The glance flicked across the face or darted at the back of someone who has just passed on the street contains reams of information that we use and record, even though we may not be adept at voluntary retrieval and analysis. What we actually vocalize is only the thin mantle of the complex feelings we communicate to others. And what we look for is not superficial information, but information directly relevant to our own social state and our immediate future actions.

We did not come by these abilities in the last few thousand years. From what we can reconstruct of animal history, they were honed to their present excellence and precision through many millions of years of failure or success in communicating. In the following pages I am proposing that all of our people-watching is a fundamental biological act shared by chipmunks who are excellent chipmunk-watchers, kittiwakes who are excellent kittiwake-watchers, and so forth. We all are looking for the same or similar information, though we use different clues. The information is "how does he relate to me?" — or more precisely, "how does he influence my social state?"

It may appear peculiar at first that the obvious things that other animals see when they watch each other — their color patterns, beards, wattles, and other decorations — have received less study than almost any other part of the creature. But the reasons are fairly clear — one can't plug in a thermistor or make a serial section slide of a monkey's brilliant blue scrotum to see how the color functions. Rather, someone has to sit around for a long time observing monkey behavior. He must have a backlog of comparative knowledge about genitals as social signals, which we haven't had in the past. In other words, many organs — the patterns that strike you first when you look at animals (say, a lion's mane or a deer's antlers) — are *social* organs. They are not amenable to conventional methods of study in biology — the reduction techniques of taking the organ apart and seeing what it is made of.

How do we go about studying our own social signals? Self-analysis is exceptionally difficult. It's tough to be that objective. "The proper study of man is man," but the comparative approach requires us to look further. The concept that man is an organism and has evolved by the same processes affecting other organisms could never have arisen by studying man alone. The fitting of other organisms into a biological scheme forced us, secondarily, to include man.

It was the comparative anatomists who gave us our first in-depth look at man's evolution. Through an elaborate comparison of the living animals and fossils from the past they have been able to reconstruct how the different organ systems arose, and to some degree why they arose and have been modified into their present condition.

There is often something lost if you study a thing as it is without knowing the history of how it came to be that way. You could examine the human mouth thoroughly in relation to its mechanics, development, or pathologies — but you would miss a lot by not knowing a beautiful story behind its origin in the fossil record. Early vertebrates were gill-filter feeders, but in some, the first gill support became modified into a food-grasping jaw. Bony plates shifted or were eliminated. Tiny skin scales were brought into the mouth as hooks to grasp the prey, and became changed into teeth. Their crowns became more complex for crushing and shearing. Harelips were fused and cleft palates sealed. You could never know these things from studying human beings alone.

So there are really two important questions implied by asking, "Why does a biological structure exist?" The *proximate* "why" pertains to the immediate mechanisms involved; then there is the evolutionary, *ultimate* "why."

Why does an Alaskan snowshoe hare moult to a white pelt in winter? Physiologists have shown that it is because the hours of daylight drop below a critical length. The hares can be taken into the laboratory and their coat color changed by exposing them to different periods of artifical light. But that doesn't answer the "evolutionary why." Most people agree that the answer to the latter is that the white coat provides concealing coloration in the snow. The snowy winter environment is the origin of the selection process, and the number of hours of daylight is the proximate control mechanism.

Social organs haven't been easy to analyze on a *proximate* level; our best approach is to look at their comparative *evolutionary* history. Comparative ethology is beginning to do for our understanding of the evolutionary "why" of human behavior what comparative anatomy did for our appreciation of anatomical history. Comparing the behavior of different animals in the wild is a much newer science and several times more difficult than anatomical comparisons. Incomplete though this analysis is, some general outlines are beginning to emerge — enough to see what an utterly fantastic thing our evolutionary story is.

That story is particularly fascinating because it explains why we *look* the odd way we do. There are many "ornaments" which functional anatomists have been at a loss to explain — moustaches, for example. For really the first time we are beginning to see how our behavior — our *social behavior* — so inextricably merges into our appearance, and how each has influenced the evolution of social organs — the parts of our anatomy which function mainly as social devices. More importantly, that story can tell us something about ourselves, why we act the way we do and why we wish to look differently.

Smelly armpits and soft red lips are such emotionally loaded parts of our lives that it will be difficult for us to put aside our cultural inhibitions long enough to examine the reasons why they are that way. At the same time, our intimate involvement with signals from our own and others' organs gives the reason for their existence a deeper fascination. What do we communicate with dilated irises, graying temples, round butts, underarm odors, and colored penises? The comparative evolutionary approach is especially successful in these areas of behavior, where our strong emotional investments make it virtually impossible to look ourselves in the biological face. These areas are not merely affected by subtle personal biases, but form the very roots of rigid taboo systems relating to the function of these organs.

Before plunging directly into a discussion of particular human social organs and how they work, we should be aware of some basic comparative material from other animals. If we were to start with crotch hairs, balding, long noses, and such, before we had a comparative base, we would be less inclined to believe what follows. If the evolution of human teeth from fish scales seems incredible, then wait until we get to the evolution of things like blonds and high cheekbones.

2
SOCIAL STATUS AND BEHAVIOR

Your eyes are deep as the Devon Springs,
Your hair as dark as jet,
Your years are few, your life is new,
Your soul untried, and yet –

Our trail is on the Kimmeridge clay
And the scarp of the Purbeck flags;
We have left our bones in the Bagshot stones
And deep in the Coralline crags . . .

"Evolution," J. Langdon Smith

In the beginning some things were in limited supply, and it has remained so. The story of evolution is how some lines of organisms were able to continue in spite of this fact and be changed because of it. This is true of social behavior as well as of more physical adaptations.

If one could point to a dominant theme in the evolution of social behavior, it would be finding solutions to the problem of distribution of commodities in limited supply – that is, the distribution of *privilege*. Access to these commodities – food, water, mates, nest sites, etc. – is seldom equally distributed among the group. Status has its rewards and is virtually synonymous with privilege. It affects almost every animal's interaction with others and is probably the main force in his struggle to avoid death and to mate.

The more violent signals of rank are ballyhooed in popular literature, but in most species the usual rank signals and responses are more subtle.

They are an ever-present part of social behavior — a tilt of the head, a quick glance held only momentarily, a change in tail position, a few steps, a wrinkle of the nose, a twist of the ear. Photogenic, dramatic displays of mock and real battles are a minor part of social signaling. It is difficult to study a lingering odor on a trail, but such is the new material of the diligent field ethologist.

Success to a particular individual may be measured in a degree of comfort or length of life. But in evolutionary terms, success is the relative genetic contribution to future generations — one's *evolutionary fitness.* Having offspring isn't enough: they must be reared to reproductive maturity and in turn rear their young. Living a long time usually is, but need not be, relevant to fitness. If one lives to be a hundred yet has no offspring, his evolutionary fitness is zero.

Thinking about the how's and why's of natural selection is a more interesting way of looking at biological characteristics than trying to pinpoint their immediate function. You may ask why are you bald? Or why are your nipples so pink? The evolutionary question becomes why, statistically, were balding males and pink-nippled females able to rear more young to reproductive maturity? (We can judge that once in our ancestral line, prior to the appearance of these "fit" problems, no one had bald scalps or pink nipples — by comparing an array of related primates.) So we look for a reason why certain types of scalps and nipples would increase reproductive success. And the same goes for other characteristics used to assist in communicating things that matter most in the lives of animals.

The ability to leave offspring is not dependent on how an animal deals only with his physical environment but also with his social environment. Sexual attractiveness is an obvious advantage; but mainly, evolutionary fitness is dependent on social *rank.*

How did the behavior associated with obtaining privilege evolve? We are beginning to get enough information to piece together some possible answers.

There is quite a bit of evidence that aggression in many species does have an inherited component. Domestic strains of the same species vary considerably in general aggression levels; for example, beagles are low and Doberman pinschers high. The same is true for other domestic species, even for strains of laboratory mice or for farm foxes. One can select for aggression within a strain and get a response — that is, make the next generation more aggressive, and the next, and the next.

The fact that lines of animals generally do not become more aggressive with time indicates that there must be some detrimental aspects of aggression. Very aggressive individuals must raise fewer offspring to maturity. As strange as it may seem at first glance, it is sometimes to one's reproductive advantage to submit and let the other fellow assume the more privileged position. Someday, "maybe next year," that thin-bodied virgin bull moose in the willows will have the weaponry of the big bull with the large antlers and will have all the ladies as well. It may be poor strategy to try to get some of the booty at all costs and not invest a few hopes in the future. Individuals who recognize their inferiority in combat, in most instances, will stand a better chance of leaving more offspring if they admit defeat. They can wait on the sidelines to re-enter competition at a later date when they have grown larger and stronger, when they can establish themselves on a territory earlier, or when higher-ranking individuals have become debilitated or have died. Hence submission can be directly related to an individual's fitness advantage, and not necessarily something done for the public good or the benefit of the species.

Some of the more revealing parts of the evolution of one's behavior regarding status and its anatomical aids lie in the origin of the signals themselves. In the signals of aggression and submission there are some common themes running through the behavior of almost all animal species.

One's social state seems to depend mainly on four major elements, whose importance varies and blends with different species and individuals. These are *confidence, age, size,* and *sex.* In ethological studies these are the recurrent themes that affect an individual's position in the social hierarchy. It is the general rule among vertebrates, with only a few exceptions, that dominant individuals tend to be experienced, large, older males — and human beings are not one of the exceptions.

If it is advantageous to both parties in a conflict to assess their opponent's status properly in reference to themselves, it is not surprising that many displays for communicating social position have evolved. *Displays* are stylized gestures or positions used to communicate pieces of information. Status displays of most vertebrates, including man, take root from the four main themes affecting social status.

If one wishes to signal dominance, the gestures relevant to the real qualities affecting status are used. An increase in animal size is almost universally recognized as a signal of aggression. Height in humans has hidden values far beyond being able to reach the Post Toasties on the top shelf. If one wishes to show aggression he inhales and swells up as large as he possibly can: muscles are flexed, crests raised, appendages extended.

The individual usually shows confidence in carriage and manner. Age and size are developmentally related, but deference is often given to age by the equally large but younger individual. The sex role is also deeply intertwined with social stature and the amount of aggression or submission displayed. Obviously, aggressive signals are the more masculine gestures.

Signals of submission have developed in the opposite direction. To submit, one becomes as small as possible, even making oneself prostrate in many species. Fins are sleeked, crests and appendages drawn near the body. Many which display the back and dorsal crest roll over in a "belly-up" submissive display. In submitting, individuals of many species often regress through the age spectrum, using juvenile utterances and gestures. Notice your different attitudes toward adults with squeaky, adolescent voices and those with a rich radio-announcer bass. A common theme of submission signals is for the animal to act in female role; in some species, both sexes use a copulatory invitation of rump display when dominants approach them.

In many species recognition of these signals of status seems to be "built-in" requiring very little previous conditioning; among others, their lives follow a pattern which makes learning so situationally inherent that it may be difficult to separate the different origins of their behavior. For example, the use of height in human threat for status displays as one necessarily moves through a great part of his physical development — first as a baby, then a toddler, preschooler, juvenile, teenager, etc. — equating height with status, for there is an almost perfect correlation up until reproductive maturity. Little wonder that he carries this attitude into his adult life.

In general, however, human status signals have evolved to be very flexible. A species with so plastic a life history as man would be incompatible with a fixed program dictating a precise format for his social life. But we are not alone in this regard: many if not most species have several ways in which they can communicate status. In the wildebeest, lechwe, and kob antelope, for example, small territories are used in some instances, but in other social and physical environments different expressions of status occur. Territoriality is certainly an important element in human ethology, but it is only a subelement in a vast array of forms of status behavior involving physical acquisitions, knowledge, birthright, group identity, spouse and family, profession, hobbies, tastes, accent, graciousness, and on down a very long list, which is probably headed by appearance.

The evolution of our appearance is not just a study of the old bones of the past: it is a study of the sweep of time to the present. Social selection has not only occurred, it is occurring — it is across the tracks, down the street, next door, and in our own bedrooms. We are accustomed to equating natural selection with evolution, sometime back in the past, but this is not true. As selection is the difference in net-reproduction, and as in no populations, whether humans or boll weevils, do all individuals reproduce equally, a dynamic interplay is going on continuously.

The famous English ornithologist, David Lack, and numerous others since, illustrated how this interplay works. Lack counted the number of eggs in starling nests and found that the clutch size that produced the most young which actually left the nest was neither the large clutch nor the small, but ones near average size. Only in years when insects were very abundant were the starlings with large clutches able to find enough insects to feed all their young well, so that most could live until they were old enough to leave the nest. This is a general principle: those individuals clustering around the middle do relatively more reproducing, while those on the extremes do least; as long as this is symmetrical, no evolution takes place, even though the selection process may be intense. In other words, the opposing selection forces are balanced. But since most things are so inconstant, these pressures seldom remain static for long, but shift and alter with the year and the season, and probably with the hour.

Using this as a background, we can look at the evolution of human social behavior and the accompanying organic social trappings in a somewhat different light. We are only grabbing a passing glimpse at an immensely complex and dynamic process. At this moment your fitness is dependent not only upon your behavior, but upon the color and texture of your skin, your height, ankle thickness, and so on to include your every contour.

If the fundamental theme in the evolution of social behavior is the sorting out of privilege, a close runner-up would surely be the theme of *sexual behavior*, or, let's say, behavior directed toward copulation. If one is to leave offspring, he must necessarily have incentives to procreate. These sexual patterns, like the status patterns, assume quite varied forms in different species. Usually they center on getting the two sexes together. Special calls, odors, or color patterns are used. Many social organs have evolved as a result of these forces of sexual attraction. Many of the organs human beings carry around with them function mainly as sexual attractants.

The young must be cared for in many animals (especially man). Our attraction to children and the need to give them attention become intertwined with sex and status in a beautiful fashion. There are even special human organs which have evolved to assist our child-love. They too have had their effect on adult organs of status and sex.

These diverse aspects of *status, parent-offspring,* and *sexual behavior* show up as dominant themes of our social anatomy — the organs responsible for how we appear to others, or are privileged to make love to them.

3
HOW WE USE AND SHOW OUR SOCIAL ORGANS

Your face, my thane, is a book where men may read strange matters.

Macbeth

The jillions of individual animals who have lived on this earth have usually left their potential life spans uncompleted. The prospects are much the same today and can only continue that way into the future. Those who have been dressed in sombre colors with few frills to attract the attention of the predator or frighten the prey have been able to postpone death's cleaver to a slight degree and be around to hatch their broods, suckle their young, or make it to more than one nuptial season.

But we can't look at only this dimension of animal life — the way many functional anatomists and physical anthropologists have — we can't interpret only how this hair patch or that organ system makes individuals better able to survive and cope with the physical environment (food, weather, predators, etc.). Despite the slim probability and attendant hope of living well beyond reproductive maturity, there are other equally potent pressures affecting an individual's appearance. In most species, an individual's *social relations with other members of the population are a central factor* determining how, and if, he will overcome the physical demands to survive and reproduce. The individual's appearance is an important part of how he interacts with associates. Sometimes the priorities of those social demands override the selection process arising from the need to remain inconspicuous.

If you've never thought about it this way, it may be worthwhile to think of most animals as dressed for a social event. Many fish and reptiles have a very flexible wardrobe. These species have small color cells (*chromatophores*) that can expand and contract. So a species of minnow or lizard have a whole spectrum of instantly available clothing changes. They also use their appendages — fins, gill covers, crests, throat flaps — to modify their social dress. Birds and mammals do the same, except that it is with feathers and hair; their colors are fixed (except for some, including man, who have exposed skin areas that can become colored). Birds and mammals can change their dress dramatically with the season. Some seasons, particularly the rutting or breeding seasons, are full of aggression and disputes about critical matters. A brief thumb through a pocket bird guide or mammal book illustrates the vast differences between breeding and nonbreeding pelages or plumages. Social dress also varies between the sexes, each having a different social role. In addition, dress varies with age in many species. The very young seldom have the same dress as adults, and more often than not there is a special juvenile pelage as well. The attire of the young frequently carries a special status value, and is this not true also in human beings?

In Taku Fjord just behind Juneau, Alaska, I have watched eagles feed on a fresh bear carcass. The adults — white-headed and tailed, with bright golden-yellow beaks, irises, and legs — could be distinguished easily from the drab juveniles. Adults would seldom let another adult near the food, but the more uniformly colored juveniles took it with free license and in some cases even took food directly away from the adults. Niko Tinbergen described a similar occurrence among gulls: the special gray garb of the young gives them a different status within the population of white adult gulls.

In order to picture how social organs function, let's suppose there is a species of animal which fights with its head (either mouth or antlers). In this species, there is a positive relationship among neck size, age, strength, likelihood of winning, and status. Most of the deer family, most antelope and cattle, cats, canids (the dog family), and many primates all fight with the heads in some way or other. Among these different species the older animals usually have disproportionately large necks. A stronger neck gives a fang deeper penetration or an antler more torsion (deer fight by antler-wrestling rather than by clashing). Suppose an individual of one of these species had fought twenty opponents, and of the ten to whom he lost, all had larger necks, while the ten which he had beaten all had thinner necks. He meets opponent number 21, who has an unusually thick neck . . . what is his strategy going to be?

If fights are inexpensive it will probably be to his best advantage to challenge, but if the bouts are significantly wearing or dangerous, it may be better strategy to write the bull-necked fellow off as a probable victor and look for new stamping grounds.

What is to happen, in a situation like the one just described, to a few variant individuals who happen to have thicker hair around their necks than most? In other words, what about a fake big neck? In general it can provide some privileges not normally enjoyed without it — although it can also have the potential of getting you into trouble. If there are two individuals of equal strength, but one has an artificially enlarged neck, with a thick ruff, the latter may have a more menacing appearance and reduce the opponent to submission without fighting. But what if a juvenile is carrying around an artificially thick neck, way out of proportion to the neck size he would normally support? That's bad business! Along the status hierarchy high dominants seldom notice low subordinates, and *vice versa*. It is members of adjacent age classes and nearby status ranks that get most of the static. And here comes little Joe with a big stick but nothing with which to back it up. He loses all his fights; moreover, he continually receives challenges and is intimidated by all of the powerful contestants around.

There are inherent pressures therefore, to correlate threat devices with actual ability. We can see the same kind of principle in our own dress. Professor Higgins wouldn't have put Eliza Doolittle in upper-class English clothes and sent her to the ball before he changed her accent and mannerisms.

It's a beautiful sight to slip up on a slowly moving caribou herd in the late fall and see the neck display of the mature bulls. Their neck manes are brilliant white, contrasting with the dark milk-chocolate-colored body. The long white hairs hang in a tress along the underside of the neck. When possible opponents come near, they show the neck by turning the head at an angle to bring the neck into full display. Yearlings, young bulls, and cows have poorly developed manes, and the older caribou bulls have them best developed. It is a continuum which corresponds with an animal's social state during the rut.

So in addition to being fake weapons (or, in this specific case, fake areas that wield the weapons), social organs serve to dramatize one's social state: age, sex, size, and confidence. In this case they are based on artificially enlarged necks. Though I have mentioned only one character that could have evolved as a threat zone and explained how threat devices (manes) arose to support its signal, I think it represents part of a more general pattern. Many such organs have been modified to strengthen the signals of social state.

Signaling and ornamentation on certain parts of the body are more important than on others: these are our communication "hot spots." These centers are usually the location of important social organs. Some key zones are: weaponry, areas which wield the weaponry, genitalia, locomotor organs, major sensory areas (eyes, nose, ears), and glandular regions. The tighter the lines on an elk's body, for example, the more important the area as a signal source. Other examples of social ornamentation are: false contours which affect signal strength or volume; contrast and attention-getting devices; supernormal signals which increase signal strength; automimicry, or self-mimicry. The purpose of this book is to pinpoint those zones and discuss not only how they came to be, but how the location of these hot spots has affected the social organs themselves.

We can classify the kinds of social threat ornamentation among animals depending on the type of signal they transmit. There are at least four ways in which signals can be affected: (1) false contours; (2) contrasting and attention-guiding patterns; (3) supernormal signals; and (4) social automimicry. I'm sure this list isn't exhaustive, but it will serve our purposes to lay the background for a discussion of the human counterparts.

I referred to the phenomenon of *false contours* when discussing neck sizes and artificially enlarged necks, the ruff or mane. In some animals the entire body is displayed as the animal threatens a potential opponent. The Rocky Mountain goat and the house cat perform this kind of display. The crest along the top of the back is made up of long erectile hairs, which add to the apparent size of the animal. Most threat displays involve an increase in apparent size — hair erection, air inflation, muscle contraction, blood congestion, etc. — and capitalize on increasing the apparent size of the specific organ or body mass. This is basically a signal change affecting signal strength or volume. At this juncture, can you begin to anticipate extending these principles to human beings? A subliminal flash: human beards.

Contrasting patterns and gaudy outlines are an equally common form of threat ornamentation. These probably account for most of the colorful markings of animals. One of the more usual patterns is for the signal area to be outlined in contrasting color (or shade, in the case of color-blind animals); or, the entire area is set off with a contrasting color, like the white mane of the dark-bodied caribou. Wapiti have light colored bodies, usually a soft reddish sandy color; their manes, however, are a contrasting dark brown, especially in older bulls during rut. Individuals of species that are normally viewed from the side by an opponent have a contrasting stripe down the crest of the back — white on black in wild cattle, from which our domestic species arose, or a black stripe on a burro's light body. The expressions of these principles are easy to see in other animals, but what about human beings?

The so-called *supernormal signals* occur in the form of extra-large social organs, i.e. increasing signal strength by increasing the signal amplitude. For example, antlers and horns are used as an estimation of rank in many species of animals. In these species they either grow to gigantic size among the older males, or develop specialized modifications, like filling in between the tines to form palms, thereby increasing the visual effect from a distance; in some species, both things occur.

Social automimicry is a form of mimicry within one's own species or even one part of an organism mimicking another part of the same organism for social ends. One common form is one sex or age class mimicking another. Valerius Geist describes a case in sheep where juvenile rams and ewes have almost identical horn and body patterns. Their social status within the band is much the same and they are treated in similar ways by the older rams. Wolfgang Wickler discusses the mimicry of the female's rump patch in male Hamadryas baboons; the patch has become a submissive display organ where once it was a sexual attractant. Another form of automimicry occurs when a signal coming from one part of the body is duplicated by another part. Wolfgang Wickler uses the example of the convergent colors and shapes between the male mandrill's snout and genitals. The crest down the nose and the penis are bright red, the alae for flaps similar to the prepuce; the scrotum and sides of the snout are robin's egg blue; and the chin and scrotum both have pointed yellow goatees. Both areas are used to threaten opponents. Some species of African antelope have ears resembling their horns, increasing the overall effect of "horns." The American pronghorn has a black hook on the ear tip at about the level of the horn's prong, adding to the overall weapon signal.

It is easy to see these principles illustrated in a caribou's mane or a mandrill's genitals, but can you see them in yourself and your neighbors?

Social organs tend to cluster in predictable areas of the body, in "hot spots" which vary somewhat with the group or species, but which follow several general trends running through most animals, including man. Here are a few of the dominant themes: (1) sensory areas; (2) weaponry and areas wielding the weaponry; (3) anal-genital areas; and (4) locomotor structures.

(1) Most specialized sensory areas are also good transmitters. The reason, I suppose, is that they tell, or did originally, one's associate what kind of information you are looking for or getting. Eyes, for example, are one of the most important signal transmitters. Ears, or, more precisely, mammalian pinnas, are highly mobile and form an important part of mammalian communication beyond their sound reception role. Dog and cat owners are familiar on a grass-roots level with using eyes and ears to read their animals' moods. Nostrils and the mouth areas are other hot spots in mammalian communication. Eyes, ears, nose, and mouth are frequently set off with contrastingly colored outlines or eye-catching patterns. Ears of some species have a tassel of hairs on the tip in contrasting colors, further dramatizing the ear position. Human eyes have elaborate devices to alter the transmitted signal — colored irises, exposed scleras, long lashes, and others discussed in a later chapter.

(2) The presentation of weapons, as in the case of an antler threat, is used by many species of animals. Sometimes they aren't presented to the opponent in the battle position, but to show the most impressive view; for example, Valerius Geist describes a display in mountain sheep wherein the ram twists the head to present the horn sideways. Sometimes weapons are dramatized by contrasting colors, as in the case of many bird beaks. Early deer fought with teeth rather than antlers. A few of the present-day species still retain the black lip spot which gave contrast to the protruding white canine, as it still does today in the Chinese water deer. The human mouth also has not gone unadorned.

(3) Anal and genital organs became modified into social organs because of at least two different reasons. Mammals, one of the group of vertebrates with a well developed smelling apparatus, have used urine and feces as part of the signaling of who was where and when. The actual acts of urinating and defecating have thus become secondary social gestures. Bison and many of the cattle group have a prepuce tassel, a tuft of hair hanging from the foreskin around the penis opening. The tuft is a scent disseminator, but may have a visual role as well, for it is contrastingly colored. Carnivores, meat-eating animals, almost universally have anal glands with which they anoint the feces, giving it a musky odor in addition to the odors of bacterial incubation.

The other type of signal comes from the sexual overtones of different ways of urinating. A 10-month-old beagle pup begins lifting one leg while urinating, instead of using the female squat. Many mammals dramatize their sexual differences in urination posture. Because of the usual differences in social stature between the sexes, genitalia have also become important signals of maleness and femaleness, aggression and submission, and the genitals have evolved specialized social ornamentation only obliquely related to the ancestral copulatory role. Few things harbor as many human taboos as the anal and genital organs.

(4) The appendages for locomotion – tails, fins, wings, arms – also undergo special modifications as a result of their social role. Movements or intentions of movements have become incorporated into many gestures of social behavior. Decorated appendages with contrasting lines and splotches dramatize these gestures. The two dominant themes are coming toward or escaping and going away from. Many have specialized gaits used in approaching-struts or the exaggerated escape leap or "stott." Caribou have a stiff springy gait they use when alarmed, lifting their legs much higher than they need to, flashing their white spots above the glossy black hooves. It is a beautiful sight, enacted on the backdrop of an autumn tundra scene of bright red blueberry shrubs and yellow dwarf willow.

There is a general pattern in nature for status paraphernalia to vary from one subgroup to the next within a species. The balanced pressures of status ornamentation can be affected by numerous physical aspects of a group's situation. The thick mat of hair used by some groups to increase apparent size of some organs or the entire body also affects heat regulation. A desert ungulate couldn't use the same high crest and thick mane as the Alaskan Rocky Mountain goat. Lion manes also tend to be thicker in cooler areas. In some areas, like the Tsavo Park, the male lions are maneless. In areas covered by snow most of the year, body decoration is often sacrificed for a more concealing white pelage or plumage. Hole-dwelling birds can have more brightly colored plumage than birds which nest in exposed places in the fields. The same sorts of varying pressures occur between races and subspecies. Furthermore, most social organs are multifunctional, and a compromise must often be made.

Likewise, the social situation varies throughout the range of the species. Some areas can support dense populations, other areas only a few scattered souls. Optimum social strategy could be expected to differ as well; and so could the accompanying social ornamentation. It has been shown that mountain sheep populations have better developed social paraphernalia (horns, rump patches, etc.) in newly exploited areas. David Klein, working with two deer populations, illustrated how population density and severity of the winter affected selection for body and weaponry size from one population to the next. Undoubtedly, the interrelationships between the diverse physical and social climates experienced by man throughout the world have been responsible for the varying pattern of his social organs — skin pigment, hair texture, armpit odor, eye color, nose size — most of the obvious things which vary among human races.

This brief review of the social organs of other animals can now serve as a sketchy trellis on which the story of our own social organs can grow.

PART TWO: THE LOOK, SMELL AND FEEL OF MENACE

Full Beards and Weak Chins
Odor: The Rankness of Rank
Highbrows and Lowbrows
The Bald and the Blond
The Love and Menace of Hair

4
FULL BEARDS AND WEAK CHINS

Beards, mostly false, were also worn by men of rank. The rank of the individual was signified by the length of the beard. The beard of an individual of low rank was short and square. The beard of a king was equally square, but much longer. The beard of a god was pointed and turned up at the end. Inasmuch as Pharoahs were regarded as gods after death, they too were depicted with curved beards. Merchants, land owners, and upper classes wore beards. The false beards were made of tufts of hair held in place by cords looped back over the ears. Slaves and lower classes were beardless.

— Charles and DeAnfrasio, *History of Hair.*

Throughout human history probably no other social trapping has played so large a role as *hair.* Though the function of hair is complex, one theme predominates — its menacing use to signify rank. Thus, I will use hair as a central thread to introduce several diverse evolutionary themes involving a suite of human social organs used in threat. Out of an evolutionary context, our hair patches are curiously located. Why do we have a little tuft under our arms, a triangle in our crotch, some above our eyes, on our crown, and, among males, this coarse growth on the lower face? Using information from comparative anatomy and behavior, it all fits into a definite pattern of function and location. Each of the five following chapters is devoted to the function and evolution of a different hair patch (and the organs that evolved with each patch): beards, eyebrows, our scent patches, the crotch and underarm tufts, scalp hair, with a final chapter on the social role of hair in general. The origin and function of these hair patches in our communication are quite different, but they have that one thing in common — menace.

In the summer of 1959, on a fossil dig in the upper Brazos in northeast Texas, I grew a beard. Shaving in the field was inconvenient, and it was a good excuse to see what the thing looked like, anyhow. In the late 1950's there were a few beards on T.V. (Mitch Miller was the first, I believe), but there were none to be found in the rural Midwest. If I hadn't realized it before, it became very clear to me then in my travels, that the human beard was no emotionally neutral object. My hitchhiking success was the same as had I been carrying bandoleers of cartridges slung from each shoulder and a knife between my teeth. Drivers speeded up as they passed, gawking in disbelief. In bus stations people talked loudly and derogatorily about me. Some people were considerate, asking what religion it was that I represented. Homosexuals propositioned me in johns and clerks ignored me in stores. It was the same *me* behind the beard, but I was treated like a completely different person.

In the rocks we were excavating that summer were remains of Permian reptiles and amphibians. At that time, about 200 million years ago, no mammal had ever raised a hairy head. But in sediments a few hundred miles to the north of our dig there were bones from later beds that revealed the lives of mid-Tertiary mammals who lived about 30 million years ago. The primitive artiodactyls (vegetarians with cloven hooves), ancestors of the modern deer, bovids, pigs, and giraffes, were still heavy-limbed and thick-bodied. Instead of fighting with horns and antlers, they fought with sharp teeth. As time passed and their descendants evolved into larger creatures, they must also have attacked their opponents with blunt head thrusts to the body with some form of pointed projection on the head. Teeth were still used, but their role was declining in many groups.

Among modern artiodactyls, we can see remnants of these early fighting patterns and can piece together how the animals might have behaved long ago. Not all modern ungulates fight with horns and antlers. In some deer, like the Chinese water deer, the males have long teeth and neither sex possesses antlers. Males fight by slashing at each other with their teeth. And they use their canines in a threat display. The hair on the lower lip beneath the canine teeth is black, setting off the outline of the white fang.

Strangely enough, other deer that have switched from canine fighting to antlers as weapons, such as the majestic European red deer or his American counterpart the elk or wapiti, still retain part of the threat behavior associated with their ancestral canine fighting. These deer still have that black spot on their lips. In some of the American deer, the Virginia (whitetail) deer and the mule deer, the black spot has even expanded to color most of the lower jaw. But even more significantly, wapiti lift their upper lip in a snarl in one of their threat displays to reveal the tiny vestigial canine which in their ancestors was a flashing, wicked scimitar. Opponents, however, recognize the gesture as threat as if the long canine were still there and ready to tear its deep gashes. The ancient, out-of-date weapon is still used symbolically.

If any primate besides man were to attack you or a member of his own species, it would be a biting attack. Non-human primates are virtually all armed with projecting sharp teeth whose main function is to chomp into members of their own species; they have no horns or sharp hooves to use in fights. Invariably the canines of the males are larger than those of the females and in many cases they are so much larger that it is difficult to believe both are members of the same species.

Tooth-baring and mouth movements play an important role in primate social signals — perhaps the most important role. Predictably, the oral area has specialized supporting paraphernalia. It is brightly colored in some, or adorned in contrasting shades. But the major morphological ornamentation occurs in the areas wielding the weaponry — the jaw and jaw muscles.

The two chief themes in these changes are increased contrast and false contours. A number of primate species have contrastingly colored snouts or lower faces. An equally large or even larger number have chin or cheek ruffs contributing to a false contour. That is, they are *bearded*. Old male orangs, howlers, and sakis have particularly large beards. Some, like the male baboon, have immense sideburns, which always remind me of the exaggerated "muttonchops" worn in Europe and North America during the mid- to late 1800's. The mandrill baboon has a blond goatee with a Van Dyke point. The face, and correspondingly the size of the face, are important in primate communication. Beards of various types fuse indistinguishably in some cases with facial ruffs.

Human beings are different from most other primates in our choice of weapons, even though it is only a difference of degree rather than kind. Instead of biting when we fight, we flail away with our arms, objects held by our arms, or missiles thrown by them. I suppose this peculiarity arose in conjunction with the specialization of becoming a rock-wielding predator. We turned the newly acquired methods of the chase back on our fellow man. Since these were several magnitudes more effective than trying to run up and bite him, the whole evolutionary accent on the mouth as a weapon was reduced in our evolutionary line. We can see in the fossil record a reduction in tooth size among our ancestors and their immediate relatives even back into the Pliocene several million years ago.

It is good to point out this dramatic shift away from our primate oral tradition, because it is important in understanding our humanness. But that is a lot of heritage to shake. For almost a hundred million years we have bitten as primates should and served time as non-mammalian biters for several hundred million years before that. Like the antlered red deer who challenges his opponent in the dim light of a German forest glade with a snarl, we fight with our new tools yet can't help harking back to the older ones — as we search for clues to our opponent's social state and signal ours to him. Like the red deer, we still use our teeth and jaws to signal.

A friend of mine once felt extremely self-conscious about his mildly receding chin. He developed the habit of resting his chin in the heel of his hand every time he sat down at a desk or table, pushing outward in the hope that it would make him more prognathous. Another trick was to keep his teeth occluded in an underbite to press his jaw further forward. If his age and the social norms had permitted it, he could have grown a beard, as Abraham Lincoln did during his latter period of office, to increase the apparent size of his jaw.

Bullies the world over jut out their jaws as a symbol of belligerence; it is a gesture understood by people of all tongues and customs.

> "He glared at the schoolmaster. 'Town bred, ain't yer mister?' His beard jutted fiercely, thrust at an angle into the schoolmaster's face."
>
> — Stranger, *Breed of Giants*

People shrinking in horror retract their jaws toward the neck as part of the submission signal, the grimace. The chimp uses the jaw in a similar manner in its displays. Konrad Lorenz refers to humans' sticking out their chins as a vestigial part of our threat display. We often cover up our chins and mouths with our hands when under social stress. Plastic surgeons do a good business inserting silicone artificial chins in people who wish to present a stronger image. In our everyday activities we use chin size in appraising other individuals and refer to *strong jaws* and *weak chins* as if they had some rational relation to people's personalities.

Some types of facial hair and color patterns found among primates, including man: (A) Celebes black ape; (B) Crab-eating monkey; (C) White ear-tufted marmosets; (D) Squirrel monkey; (E) Sacred baboon; (F) Brazzae monkey; (G) Hoolock gibbon; (H) Patas monkey; (I) Red-backed saki; (J) Diana monkey; (K) Congo guenon; (L) Mandrill; (M) Black-crested mangabey; (N) Man; (O) Moustached tamarin; (P) Owl-faced monkey; (Q) Red howler; (R) Red uakari; (S) Orangutan; (T) Gorilla; (U) Grivet; (V) Abyssinian colobus.

In a way they do, of course. The chin is the quickest clue to an individual's sex and age status in an unshaven, unshorn, and unplucked society. One begins life with a tiny smooth round chin, which becomes more prominent with age.

The young (and sometimes the females) of many mammals have an unspoken protection from unrestrained male aggression. This recognition of youth and sex is accomplished by social ornamentation or the lack of it. Likewise, pre-puberty human males and all females have implicit protections from adult male aggressions. It is considered grossly unfair for a man to get into a knock-down, drag-out fight with either a girl or a nine-year-old boy.

At the time of male puberty, chin hair, moustache, and sideburn growth down the jaw become symbolic of membership in adult male ranks. The beard continues to enlarge and become thicker until the mid-thirties. Along in the later thirties and early forties, it begins to gray — not everywhere, just in certain spots; these spots of light hair expand and lighten until eventually in the fifties and sixties the beard is completely white. Chins were accordingly sensitive indicators of relative status among our distant ancestors.

All this changed with shaving. Although shaving seems on the surface to be a rather arbitrary custom to promote comfort and sanitation, it goes well beyond that. Shaving is an alteration of a basic status organ for status reasons. A shaven adult male runs himself back down the hierarchy spectrum so that he can enjoy to some extent the protections given pre-puberty males. It is a gesture of social appeasement — of social facilitation. In general, one interacts more easily with a kid than with a patriarch, for rather obvious reasons. In our modern complex, open society, there are greater advantages accompanying a social posture of cooperation rather than blatantly flaunting one's high position. This factor will emerge as a general pattern as we investigate each character used in human social communication. Or there is a tendency in modern societies to alter one's social organs into more subtle covert signals of rank.

If you look at human beards carefully, you can see that the texture of the beard is very different from scalp hair. The change occurs in front of the ear, at the very zone where the scalp hair of females and pre-puberty males changes to the almost invisible soft velum hair of the cheeks. The beard hair is coarser than the scalp hair and has more kink. Coiling, thick hairs provide loft, creating a more exaggerated false contour than the finer, straighter hair of the scalp.

Also, there is more often than not a slight difference in color between the beard and scalp. On some males with light hair the beard is darker, and there are men with black scalp hair who have light (usually auburn or red) beards.

If the beard originated because it increased the apparent size of the jaw, one might expect that these pressures would result in an increase in actual size. The human chin is unusually large, and I contend this is the reason. The explanations which have attempted to account for our chin size on mechanical grounds — that it gives us greater biting power, allows clear speech, or protects our jaw from breakage — do not jibe with what we know about chins. Rather, the evidence points toward a function similar to that of the beard — a social organ, more specifically a threat device.

Human chins have a forward projection — the *mental protuberance* and *mental tubercles* (a couple of knobs — you can feel them) — which often extends farther forward than the lower teeth. Some living apes and early human ancestors have poorly developed mental knobs. Like the hair growth on the chin, the angles of primate chins vary considerably with age and sex in many species, and especially in human beings. The paired mental tubercles add character to the chin, usually in the form of a dimpled chin, visible mainly in females and pre-puberty males.

It is unimportant to know whether the chin developed before the beard, or vice versa. There is a complementarity in signal. A large jutting chin enhances the effect of a beard, and a prominent unbearded chin gives a signal somewhat similar to a small bearded chin. The large, square jaws of heroes on television soap operas or in cigarette advertisements are a socially acceptable form of menace, without the gross signal of a full, thick beard The male and female models hired to represent types of masculinity and femininity, ugliness and beauty, etc., are sensitive indicators of current values regarding the meaning of facial characters.

It is difficult to believe that in early man the diet of pre-puberty males and females was so different from that of mature males as to produce the gross differences in chin shape. It is not apparent that there are any eating handicaps suffered by a person with a receding chin. Phil Herskovitz discusses a number of criticisms of the earlier theories of chin function and concludes that the chin is an ornamentation. Yet he doesn't go so far as stating the connection between the evolution of jaws as status and threat signals and their role, present or past, as weapons.

The social myths attached to the human chin, and the growth there of special threat structures, suggest it has been affected by selection pressures arising from social interactions. Children the world over protrude the jaw as a gesture of anger and defiance. There are also genetic variations in the expression of skin puffiness below the lower lip. There is a broad continu-

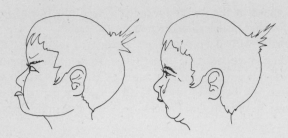

Human beings tend to protrude the chin in times of anger and withdraw it in times of submission. In children the use of the lower lip to augment this display is particularly apparent. The child on the left is pushing out his lower lip in pouting defiance and the child on the right pulls his inward in shame. In personal recrimination adults even suck in their lower lip and bite it.

ous variation in these lip patterns. One such variation, however, was traced through the Hapsburg ancestry and found to be a dominant gene, referred to as the "Hapsburg lip." It is particularly common among Americans of Swedish or Norwegian ancestry.

At the point in human evolution when our ancestors began to swing clubs at one another, the display organs around the mouth began to have less objective meaning. By this time the shift away from the mouth may have had little effect on its value as a signal though the raised arm with the bent elbow and a clinched fist is also an important signal of aggressive intent in humans. Why wasn't the shift away from mouth, jaw, and beard completed? One must remember that the audio portion of our threat still comes mainly from the mouth. Also remember that human beings do go through a relatively short stage in life, from just before one year of age until about one and a half, when the mouth *is* the most important weapon.

The significance of the chin, beard, and mouth also comes out in the actual gestures of aggression. The cheek-slap is a physical expression of anger without injury — an emphatic form of communication rather than a blow intended to cause bodily harm. Women often use it against males as an extreme gesture of displeasure, usually without provoking combat. Between males it has a different meaning. It is the last stage in the threat escalation. In the days of jousting or dueling, a cheek slap with glove on hand was the formal challenge. Striking a blow with the flat of the hand on the ancient weapon of the other individual would have had the greatest intimidating effect. Also, in a serious fight, the first blows with the fist are usually aimed at the jaw and mouth, though other areas (eyes, neck, nose, abdomen and testicles) are even more vulnerable.

Human males with deep voices are considered more masculine. Many men with tinny voices affect a throaty bass. We are well aware of how the voice changes with age, especially at puberty. The male voice loses its pure, feminine pitch and becomes lower, with a squeaky period of alternating highs and lows in the interim. Eunuchs, without male hormones, have particularly falsetto voices.

In our daily conversations, we shift the tone of voice to match the situation. If the person we are talking to is a stranger, the notes are quite low. The way we answer a telephone is a good example of this. Here's a call from you-have-no-idea where or whom. So in a deep, penetrating voice you answer, "Dr. Jones speaking." If it's a good friend calling, one's voice rises several notches in pitch, running back down the age scale and giving a less intimidating signal. The net result is similar to shaving the chin to mimic the shiny chin of a juvenile.

Though vocal cords are not completely correlated with body size (there are some large people with high-pitched voices), there is a positive correlation. Small children, generally, have high-pitched voices. We grow up equating voice tone with age — parents, especially men, having low-pitched voices, younger siblings having high-pitched voices. So as adults, we unconsciously ascribe status to variations in voice, even though we know there is no rational connection. Can you imagine a successful politician with a high, squeaky voice? Next time you hear an argument, listen to the changes in voice tone. The one who is righteously confident will have a quiet, deep voice. Once the argument starts to turn against him, he lowers his voice even further, in desperation. When it becomes apparent that he has lost, but he still continues to support his position out of principle, his voice tone rises in pitch.

Think how differently the church pastor spoke when he met you on the street and talked about things unrelated to the church. There is a special tone preachers and orators use — the sound of high dominance. But this analysis is not limited to a few oddities among us. It's about you and me. It's unnerving, once you tune your ear to pick up these changes, all of a sudden to catch yourself doing it; we do it all the time, but we've become so accustomed to operating this way that it's difficult to analyze ourselves.

Human beings don't differ from the general mammalian pattern in respect to voice quality and rank. Many mammals have voices that vary with age and sex — most primates, ungulates, carnivores, and many members of other groups. In most instances, voice changes are used in status displays.

Loud utterances are important threats among primates, though the sounds, of course, have no direct value in actual fighting (as do beards). Their effect is psychological — it's part of the menacing threat. The human war cry, profanity, or the fencer's *he la* are similar in principle to the lion's roar. There is no rational connection between "Banzai!" and one's ability to shoot straight, yet these cries are not without effect.

The "ruggedness" of the jaws, forehead, and cheekbones of many males is connected to the depth and volume of sound that they can produce. The frontal and nasal sinuses are also social organs; remember that during your next bout with sinusitis. They function mainly as resonating chambers. The selection for deeper, louder voices creates larger sinuses accompanied by a more rugged, knobby face, along with a protruding Adam's apple from a larger larynx, and undoubtedly a larger mouth and jaws.

It is a military truism that traditional weapon use dies hard. Long after the popularity of fully automatic rifles, soldiers continued to carry a bayonet attachment at the muzzle, which converted the gun into a spear, and rifles were heavily constructed to make them useful as clubs. All of this was at the root of the heated M-14 rifle controversy in the 1960's. Biologically, weapon significance and tradition are also slow to change in their evolution. Not only do we still make a big social fuss over the weapon wielders — the chin, cheekbones, etc. — but we still hold a good set of teeth in high esteem, like the flashy but totally unusable sword of the officer.

The tooth, the killing tusk among mouth-killers, went out of fashion in Australopithecine times, both as a predation tool and as an actual social weapon. Among mouth-killers, the display of teeth was one of the more important threat displays; we still carry inherent parts of the primate snarl in our facial signals. Like deer who display useless vestigial canines, we have evolved away from our snarl's having any actual weapon value, but it still has tremendous social significance. The social flash of white teeth is inextricably rooted in our ancestry. But the decline in the value of the canine teeth, and perhaps its social grossness, have reduced it to the level of an incisor — an apple nibbler. Because of the need for more covert threat signals in a highly cooperative society, this ancestral primary weapon might have been the first to go — but it left a legacy. We've lost the protruding canine, but the value of those striking white teeth is still appreciated, as we appreciate the lines of a beautiful chin or high cheekbones.

Among the many forms of cultural alteration of teeth there are gradients between two extremes: (1) an artificial emphasis of the canine, causing an irregularity of the dental line — an ornamentation which attracts attention to the teeth; and (2) a disguising of the projecting canine, a smooth dental line — a general deemphasis of the teeth. Basically, this distinction follows the cultural polarity between menace and appeasement.

There are customs in many cultures which exaggerate the canines. The most extreme of these is *ablation* — knocking out teeth, usually the incisors. It has occurred in some form or other in prehistoric Spain, England, Africa, Asia Minor, Japan, California, Florida, and Alaska. As a rule the upper incisors were the teeth most frequently removed, leaving the two canines framing a gap, much like a make-up for Dracula. Teeth were also notched or filed to points to create a similarly threatening appearance. The Mayas are renowned for their tooth mutilation. Filing teeth to a point was practiced widely, in Africa, Southeast Asia, Central, North, and South America, and among the Negrito pygmies in the Philippines. The inlaying of special stones or rare metals into teeth has been equally widespread. These mutilations were generally associated with high station, puberty rites, or wedding rites — the acquisition of status.

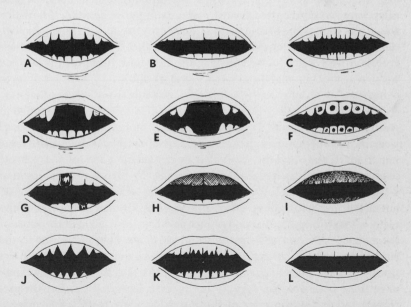

Cultural alterations of natural and artificial human teeth which affect status: (A) protruding canines; (B) even contour; (C) notched incisors which add to the irregular line; (D) ablation of upper incisors; (E) ablation of both upper and lower incisors; (F) inlay of tooth surface; (G) gold cap; (H) painting teeth with red or black dyes; (I) chewing plants which give the teeth a black tartar stain; (J) filing teeth to sharp edge; (K) filing notches in teeth; (L) filing teeth smooth.

The beauty associated with tooth deemphasis, on the other hand has usually been linked with a less threatening signal. The most extreme form is to dye one's teeth black (or red, to match the gums) with a paint, or to chew a material such as betelnut which gives the teeth a natural black tartar. This practice is most common among women (e.g. the Bontak of Luzon or the Japanese and Chinese). It returns the appearance to a baby-like one.

In unaltered teeth there are natural variations of protruding canines and smooth dental lines, or even sawtooth patterns. In most cultures today we admire the compromise of white threatening teeth, but with smooth, even edges — in the same sort of compromising way that a strong chin is admired above either extremes, a receding chin or a gross beard.

The flash of dental white accents, as it did of old, many mouth expressions. Many mammals have what is known as a wide-mouthed "greeting-face" where the corners of the mouth are pulled backward and upward to reveal all the teeth — a gesture much different from a snarl. Ethologists have interpreted this as "See, here are my weapons, but they won't be used against you" (as in presenting one's hand to be shaken in a gesture of friendship — "I could hurt you with this, but instead it is being presented in a non-offensive way"). We have ritualized this in the military "presentation of arms" and the discharge of weapons as salutes.

You have probably seen the "greeting face" on dogs; most household pets use it many times daily. Primates also use it, and there is essentially no difference between this gesture and a smile. The status part of the tooth display is important in both masculine and feminine features. The Balinese even go so far as to file the teeth at puberty to an even profile, as a protruding canine is considered vulgar and ugly.

Most mammals that threaten with their teeth accompany the visual display with an auditory display. They grind and chatter their teeth, especially in what ethologists call defensive threat. We have lost this part of our display, but one can see a vestigial remnant of it in teeth chattering under extreme fear, or in the flexing of the jaw muscles by one who is irritated or nervous (he is grinding his teeth back and forth). We refer to these actions colloquially as "gritting one's teeth" rather than taking action, or as "gnashing of teeth" by the threatened subordinate.

Human beards, then, are part of a suite of anatomical modifications around our ancient social weapon. The evolution of chins, teeth, voice, and beards has changed to modify the signals being transmitted from the mouth. Analogous to the caribou mane, human beards originated as a fake exaggeration of the weapon wielder. Though we have virtually abandoned

the jaw as a physical social weapon, it still is an important signal source —
and so is that chin-mane we call a beard.

Not all human hair tufts function as false contours or to dramatize
weaponry. Some, like underarm and crotch hair, function quite differently.
We use these hair patches as another important vehicle of menace — *odor*.

5
ODOR:
THE RANKNESS
OF RANK

As I walked to the university campus one morning, there were low clouds with a slight mist making odors along the path more pungent than usual. I caught the sweet smell from the geese as I passed the barn, and the penetrating evergreen smell while I crossed into the trees leading to the muskox fence. The muskoxen odors reminded me of cattle lots in the Midwest. My oldest beagle was loose, running a snowshoe hare in the willow thickets on the west forty, her soft baying rolling up through the fog. It's a nice time to let your mind go, without pointing it in disciplined directions. What a vast difference there is between our world views, that old beagle's and mine. She sees the world through her nose; each check of the hare is marked by the changing aroma. What a psychedelic swirl of odor she must sense as she follows the track. It must be like watching from a speeding car on a winding country road — the flick of fence, weathered sign, livestock and changing landscape, all there, but the road our central focus.

It was the first time I had even noticed the odors in a week or more of walking that path. We humans are surely a visual animal — a thousand different sights and sounds had registered, but until today, no odors. One couldn't call human beings a mammal's mammal, because from the very first a mammal's forte has been his nose. In the late Mesozoic, when the first things we can call mammals could be identified, they probably scampered through the night guided by their noses, not unlike some of the modern shrews — who hunt myopically, searching for prey, and keep their distance from others of their kind by recognizing the body humors left behind, and tracking down their sex by the female's estrous odor.

For most mammals, odor is the major social avenue. Unlike birds, which have virtually no ability to smell, mammals communicate in a few grunts, woofs, growls, and whines. As many other authors have suggested, primates are more bird-like in this respect because of their arboreal specializations. Scents in the trees have too much dimension and are whisked away by the breezes, but a climber is carried aloft to see and hear well. The highly colored, chirping monkey is what he is for the same reasons as the highly colored chirping bird — because individuals with effective visual and auditory signals left more progeny than those who still emphasized the odor signals on the forest floor.

The living lemurs of Madagascar are an excellent example of primates that use signals of sound, sight, and smell about equally well. The ring-tailed lemur has two specialized glandular areas, one on the forearm and one in the armpit. In aggressive behavior, the ring-tailed lemur's glands are wiped across the arms, and the huge black and white striped tail is pulled down the forearms, impregnating it with the smell from the glands. The lemur then faces his opponent and arches his colorful tail over his head, quivering it violently so that the scent is disseminated into the air around him.

The tree dwelling primates that do emphasize odor often rub the scent (sometimes mixed with urine) on their hands and feet, transferring it to the tree as they move about. Both the slow loris and the capuchin monkey have stereotyped gestures of anointing their feet and hands with urine. Urine and feces are common scent vehicles; many carnivores have anal glands which add a little musk to each pile of feces. (Interestingly enough, this is the major source of the particularly offensive stench of house cat feces, not the feces themselves.) Mustelids — the weasel family — have extremely well developed anal glands. The skunk group has further specialized these into defensive devices, but like all other anal glands, their original evolution related to their role as a social organ. Some male deer rub themselves with urine, increasing their threat signal during the rut. They have prepuce penile glands which scent the urine; like the cat's feces, the stench is more powerful than the urine odor alone. The dog with the fireplug is an even more familiar example of urine scenting.

There are three parts in this scent display that emerge as common patterns among other mammals: (1) strategic location of glandular areas to aid in odor dispersal; (2) some sort of odor-disseminating device; and (3) a visual accent in the area producing the odor.

In general, the position of the social glands is related to the animal's particular life history. For example, some primates have sternal glands (glands on the chest) to mark trees as they climb. Mammals that use runways or burrows more often than not have glands located on the sides to swipe the vegetation as they pass. Deer have glands on the hind legs that leave a scent on the trail behind them. Pedal (foot) glands are a common mammalian glandular zone.

Almost all glandular areas have elongate tufts of hair to disseminate the odor. In principle they function like an archer's woolen tassel, which hangs from the belt and is used to wipe soiled arrows. The constant rubbing of fiber on fiber, as the archer walks, keeps the tassel clean. The movement of the long hairs of the scent gland on each other wipes constantly and shears the scent molecules into the air as the animal moves.

The function of odor in status displays is not well understood, but what little we do know seems to be sufficient to account for why it arose and how it is used. Much of one's social state depends on being on familiar ground. How often do you get that homesick-little-kid feeling when in strange surroundings without friends or acquaintances near or accessible? When you confront a stranger of unknown social state there is always a certain amount of tension — and the more you have in common, the less strained the confrontation. If he is quite peculiar, the situation is more tense because he may be hostile.

We normally think of visual differences, but the same phenomenon applies to smell. In a tense situation, one sometimes feels even more ill at ease in a building with very strange odors — say, in a hospital, courtroom, dentist's office, or loan office. Familiarity with the surrounding odors breeds a sense of confidence, well-being, a higher social state. Spreading around familiar odors in a place of activity not only marks it as yours — or an extension of you — but also accents the familiarity. Mammals placed in a new enclosure will often scent-mark profusely.

It is easy to imagine how self-specific threat odors evolved. They increased stature; they gave one an edge in a conflict where commodities critical to survival and reproduction were involved. In many species of mammals there is a variaton of intensity of the species-specific odor with age and hence with status. Puppy urine smells quite different from the urine of an adult male dog. Generally, the young have only a slight threat odor or none at all; the strength increases with age, usually undergoing a marked increase at puberty. The change in odor with age complements the age changes occurring among the visual and vocal signals.

We no longer have special glands with which to anoint our territorial boundaries, as our early primate ancestors did. But in spite of our accent on visual and vocal communication, we still have a moderately well developed social scent. We are not too aware of it because of the strong taboos against scent display, which have arisen fairly recently.

We all know what areas of the body social odors come from. You have only to look at the deodorant advertisements. The two main zones are in the axillary region, or armpit, and in the area of the genitals. The underarm deodorant business is a thriving industry. Until lately, any mention of the pubic odors was frowned upon; however, with the relaxation of social restriction on both exposure and discussion of "private parts," there are now deodorants being marketed which are especially for use in the genital area.

Part of what we mean by cleanliness is deodorizing, and a moderately large part of our lives is spent deodorizing to make ourselves more socially acceptable — that is, sweet-smelling *like the immature.*

The chief human stink spot, like the gorilla's and the chimp's, is in our armpit or axilla. There are two types of sweat glands there; one form which produces a briny solution is called *exocrine,* and is similar to the secretion of the sweat glands elsewhere on our bodies. Another type, referred to as *apocrine,* secretes a mucous substance that is eaten by bacteria — their digestive by-products produce the smell. While the exocrine glands function to regulate body temperature, the apocrine are rather attuned to mood. You have undoubtedly noticed that you need to bathe less frequently in a situation where stresses are low — say with the family in a vacation cottage. But as tensions soar before and during social performance, the apocrines spew profusely; in a matter of a few hours the rich aroma generated by the thriving bacteria floats up to signal peers.

To avoid this danger, we jet our underarms with the fizz-can, guaranteed to give protection all day. This deodorant is for the most part a drier plus a bactericide, letting the threat juice flow but remain in its unadulterated form until dry. But the bactericide only lasts so long, and all the while the dehydrated mucus is accumulating. When your deodorant "lets you down," as the ads say, it does so with a crash.

Like the oily glands on their faces, incidentally, the scent-glands of teenagers are also unusually active. It is worthwhile pointing out that our underarm deodorizing by washing can only be done with the aid of soap. The incubated smelly substance is not soluble in water alone. So even if you go for a swim every day, you can still become overwhelmingly smelly, unless you also bathe. But don't waste your time scrubbing under your little kids'

The tuft of hair over the glandular area is used to incubate odors and to disseminate them into the surrounding environment. Often these tufts are contrastingly colored, producing a visual component to the threat signal. Pictured above are examples of scent tufts as found in Fallow deer, a Tree dassie and a Pronghorn antelope. Like those of other mammals, human social glands are located in areas which are easily disturbed by bodily movement. The tufts of hair in the armpit and crotch area are rubbed together every time the limbs move, disseminating the body scent to the surrounding air.

arms to remove their underarm odors; they aren't there. Like pimples and pubic hair, the apocrine of the axilla doesn't come into blossom until puberty.

The armpit is a strategic area in which to locate a scent gland, because it is the area most frequently disturbed by such a dexterous biped as apes. The tuft of hair located there functions in a way similar to the glandular tufts of other species. The tassel rubs and moves on itself to disseminate the aromatic molecules, but at the same time it increases the surface area in that steamy, warm cave, so more bacteria can live and eat faster on the apocrine juices.

Genital odors have a somewhat more complex evolution, but the principle is similar. The "corn-silk" crotch hair functions like the hairy axilla, as a scent holder and disseminator. Again, it is located in a strategic position to be disturbed by movement.

What has happened is that a scent source has also been modified into a visual signal source as well. Evolutionary modifications of this type are common. The hair-tuft glands of many mammals are frequently a contrasting color to their surroundings. The tarsal gland patch of deer with lightly colored legs is dark (moose), and deer with dark legs have white tarsal gland patches (caribou).

The genital area, then, affords the observer with a quick estimate of sexual maturity in an unclothed society, with all the sexual and status implications thereof. Crotch hair probably originated among human ancestors as an odor disseminating spray of hair around the anal-genital area — but once it also assumed a *visual* clue to rank, it extended upward fanning out over the lower abdomen, forming the pubic patch. Unlike the corn-silk axillary or anogenital tuft this pubic patch became more dense and matted, like the hairs of the beard.

The visual role of axillary and pubic hair can be seen in some expression of human behavior in Western society. Women often shave the axillary hair to effect the pre-puberty or early puberty look. In photographs and illustrations designed to arouse erotic feelings or aesthetic emotions about the human body, crotch hairs (and most other body hair, for that matter) have usually been airbrushed or omitted from the picture.

Social odors in other animals are used primarily for status communication, though there are many cases where special odors are used as sexual lures as well. Our human odors from the axilla and crotch arose primarily to give an aromatic accent to status well back in our evolutionary past, and have been retained for that same function. Their offensive character is not inconsistent with other threat signals — when they become concentrated. On the behavioral side, we label offensive and vulgar any dominant who flaunts his superiority in a belligerent manner.

Some of our cultural shifts throughout history have complicated our ancestral use of odor in communication. Our increased population congestion has made body odors more of a problem, and because of this forced intimacy we have ritualized deodorizing behavior. As a result we are less familiar with body odor in our present culture.

As societies became complex enough to place the high dominants in a clean, non-working class, the stench of body odor became somewhat reversed as a clue to status. The non-working *gentleman* could bathe more often and reduce other coarse signals from the past. Status could now be signaled by other things, such as membership in groups and conspicuous consumption. The heavy brow, broad shoulder, and rank smell that stood for success in another era were transformed and became the property of the propertyless, who had to support the delicately clothed, fine-boned, dominant gentlefolk. Hairy genitals and smelly sweat became uncouth. Important threads from our distant heritage, however, still remained: the awareness of genitals from hurried glances in the locker room, joshing at the swimming pool, the guy squeezed up against you in the subway.

The evolution of glands in the genital area is much more complex than those elsewhere on the body. It isn't just the scent of the mammalian body that is important, but also the scent remaining when the animal is elsewhere. In addition to material rubbed directly from the gland itself, the secretions have evolved to anoint various body excreta. The musky odors on urine and feces have been an important mode of mammalian communication. They communicate relative status and estrus condition (when female animals are in heat) but mainly status.

The preputial flap, the foreskin covering the glans penis, and the labial area of the female vulva are common locations of glands that mammals use to taint their urine. Some hoofed mammals have special hair tufts on the prepuce that appear to function in a manner similar to the glandular tufts we have already discussed, mainly as olfactory incubators and disseminators, with visual overtones.

Humans still have glands in the prepuce and vulva areas, though they have long ceased to fulfill any urine-marking function. They do add to the smells of the body, and if not cleansed properly become potent aromatic centers. The preputial flap might even be thought of as a gland itself; the bacterial activity on the secretions is so extreme as to generate a white, cottage-cheese-like by-product.

The ritual of circumcision that has gained almost universal acceptance in the Western world could be thought of as a glandular amputation to eliminate the stinky slime of a key threat center.

There are considerable racial variations, as well as cultural attitudes concerning the quantity and quality of odor productivity among human beings. Orientals in general have poorly developed scent glands, which are large and varied in Caucasoids and Negroids. It is commonly remarked by American soldiers who have served in Asia that native women think they stink. In a syndicated newspaper column, a reader recently asked why Japanese girls had this opinion of American men. The reply was that American men eat more meat, which makes their sweat stink. Yet some Orientals, like the Eskimos, eat mainly meat and do not have the musky underarm odor of Caucasians. We still can't admit to group differences, because that somehow implies inherently different values.

As is true for other organic features of status (like beards and square jaws), the full brunt of the scent signal is offensive; yet in dilute form it is attractive:

> "Like the others, he stank of rancid fish oil, the ointment the braves used before battle. The massed odor, sweeping over the watcher like a visible wave, left his senses reeling. It was a savage odor, old as man himself."
>
> — Slaughter, *Fort Everglades*

> "I recall the scent of some kind of toilet powder — I believe she stole it from her mother's Spanish maid — a sweetish, lowly, musky perfume."
>
> — Nabokov, *Lolita*

In their more subtle dilutions, human body odors are rather pleasant. Many perfumes are derived from musk secretions, but diluted to a level where their resemblance to the odor from our rancid musk glands is difficult to recognize.

So along with the false contours of beards we can add other functions of human hair patches — scent tufts. Next, another use of hair: as a specialized eye ornament to signal status based on size, or more specifically, *height*.

6
HIGHBROWS
AND
LOWBROWS

"... his hunched shoulders and the concavity of his belly which had become his adopted posture, the attempt to minimize or apologize for the height that lofted him so much above his fellows ... he was crouching more than usual in Neveau's presence trying to signal Neveau that their heights should be reversed."

— Hugh Atkinson, *The Most Savage Animal*

In the Prince William Sound area of coastal Alaska, in early winter, the cool air from the mountain snow rolls down the fjords to meet the warm seawater, casting eerie wisps of fog in among the black conifers. The misty rain is incessant, and combines with the gray clouds to produce a ghostly world without color. But if you're willing to climb through the deep moss of the rain forest on up through the tangle of devil's club and alder and leave the lap of the surf well below, there is a sight well worth the effort. Here in the small snowblown meadows scattered between the steep rim-rocks and sweeping cirque bowls is the land of the white mountain goat, which is not really a goat but a furry white relative of the European chamois.

Early winter is a time of both drama and trauma for the male mountain goats; it is the time of the rut. Mountain goats are promiscuous, and the copulatory rights go to the dominant male. Usually, dominance is decided by a stereotyped display, but when neither gives ground, the nine-inch sti-letto horns are brought into action. There are few ruts that pass in any area without some blood-letting, and sometimes even death. This prospect gives the threat display a seriousness not found in some other species, where the most at stake is a battered brow and relegation to subordinate status. One can sense a terror and urgency in the display even at binocular distance.

A billy approaches another, who is with a small nanny band. The two meet and stand head to head. Their heads are lowered, but the backs are thrown high. Every hair along the shoulder crest is held erect as the two stand together like massive blocks of white quartz. Time seems suspended. Then they walk around each other as if around the rim of a prescribed circle. Intimidated by the apparent massive size of his opponent, the challenger steps aside, and jumps back as the incumbent lowers his head in a horn-thrust position. The challenger moves away from the small herd and begins to nibble at the sparse vegetation protruding through the snow. One realizes that an important social issue has just been settled — this time, at little immediate expense to either party.

Although the particulars of this display vary considerably among animals, there is somewhat the same kind of information exchange running through many different groups. The goats were displaying their respective *size.* An even better clue to the opponent's stature, if one doesn't have the time to assess each area and contour at leisure, is a quick glance at his *height.*

The high crest of hair running along the mountain goat's back dramatizes his display of height. Crests along the neck, shoulder, or sacral curve are common among mammals. Sometimes they are limp and can be raised in threat (for instance, in dogs), but in other groups, such as the mountain goat, they are always partially erected.

Our most familiar experiences with crests or hackles are with dogs and cats. Watch your dog as he begins to bark at a passerby. Even in the short-haired breeds the hair along the ridge of the back becomes erect. (Rhodesian ridgebacks are a breed in which it is permanently erected.) Coyotes and wolves have a special colored tuft on their shoulder-crest that is erected in the threat display. A housecat fluffed-up, hissing, and advancing sideways toward another cat erects the hair along the top more than in any other area.

Height displays centering on the back and especially on the shoulder crests have not only resulted in specialized hair patches, but in more meaty structures as well. Social anatomy is not always just skin deep; sometimes it is bone deep, figuring into the sculpturing of an animal's framework. The bison, for example, has a shoulder hump built up on bony supports. The humps of the old world camels and zebu cattle (sometimes called Brahmas in North America) have a fleshy hump without bony support. More often than not, these specialized height-display structures are contrastingly colored.

We think of body shape as being purely related to how the animal interacts with its physical environment (swims, runs, slides through holes, etc.), but there also seems to be a social component. Species with a broadside display have become flattened on that plane. Pan-fish are almost a study in two dimensions, while the warthog has a frontal, face-on display and accordingly has a very broad, flaring face.

The social organs for the display of height are intimately associated with the particular pose that is used. In many species (such as foxes, seals, and many antelope) the head-high display is performed with the muzzle stretched upwards. Several kinds of markings dramatize and accent this gesture. One is the white throat patch so common in head-high displayers. As the head is lifted, the white underside of the chin is exposed, further adding to the signal that a height display is being performed and is to be heeded. Crests on the head are common among birds and also among primates. Apes stand on two legs, further dramatizing their height. Gorillas even have a large crest of hair on their crowns which is erected in threat.

We are no exception to the trend in these other species: we also have varied organs associated with our height displays, just as deer have throat patches and dogs have hackles. Height displays are important in our behavior; they permeate our daily lives, our cultural values, our vocabulary of hierarchy, our clothes, our dates or marriage partners, and our body itself.

Being physically above another person gives one an almost inherent social advantage. A judge's platform, an emperor's chair, a minister's podium, or a teacher's lectern are frequently constructed so that the person has his head above the audience, as much to increase his authority as his visibility.

There seems to be a basic biological component to our reactions of physical position. Hazlett, observing contests between hermit crabs, found that the crab elevated slightly above another had a significant probability of becoming the dominant. The South American vicuna (a gangly camel) has a habit of standing on a tall tussock to gain height when it displays a head-high threat. The vicuna's fights are attempts to lower the opponent's head by neck-wrestling. In much the same way, human fights are often rituals of lowering the opponent's body by throwing him from his feet or pinning his shoulder to the ground.

In his book, *The Silent Language,* Hall made the point that we come to accept our sub-group gestures to be so normal that we often offend people of other sub-groups inadvertently by using the same gestures of communication to them, for whom our meanings are entirely different. This same principle applies on a larger scale to communication between our species and others. To many mammal groups that use a height display, an upright, two-legged posture is a signal of threat; but of course, this is the usual mode of human locomotion. So when we approach members of these species, we are not *consciously* transmitting a threatening signal, but it is interpreted as such.

Heini Hediger found that a human can be much less offensive to kangaroos by walking in a bowed position. Since his observation, zookeepers the world over have had an easier time in the kangaroo pens. Another ethologist, Eibl-Eibesfeldt, has remarked that sea lions can be intimidated "by virtue of human's superior height." A vertical head-high posture is also an important first part of the threat display of most bear species. I have two shy female arctic wolves. They are much bolder when I am sitting, and quite wary when I'm standing. My small son is a delight to them; they show no trace of caution with him.

Fewer physical aspects play so important a part in our social lives as height. When a boy five feet two inches tall asks a girl of five-eleven for a date, he puts her in a bind. On one hand she recognizes the status nature of height and is uncomfortable with the physical arrangement of taking the role of the dominant; yet she also recognizes rationally that individual worth is poorly correlated with height. Her more immediate feelings are repulsion and guilt. In a highly mixed society, like that in the Western world, where superficial status signals play a major role, a very short man and an exceptionally tall woman are in an awkward social position even if not together. You can see our values about height in statements like, "She was tall, almost six feet, but her grace and smile had a softening effect" (Paul Gallico, *The Poseidon Adventure*).

But it isn't only the unusually short or tall who feel the impact of the status value of height; it is all of us. We talk about *rising* to meet the challenge, not taking it *lying down*, her *highness, one-upmanship, condescending, looking up* to someone, *being above* that kind of behavior, walking *tall*, feeling *low, upstanding,* giving a *boost* to the ego, the social *ladder*, the *lower* classes, *haughty, hauteur, stuck-up, high* society, lording it *over* someone, *head* of the class, bringing up the *rear*, being on the *bottom* — even the terms *stature* and *status* themselves relate to height.

The inherent connection between height and status in our lives can be found deep in the pattern of human development. *First*, we live pretty much on a common substrate with the rest of our species. This we share with most of the apes, but not many monkeys. Arboreal, or tree dwelling, monkeys have a poorly developed height form of threat display because the presence of another above him has no necessary relevance to his absolute status. In addition to all the "folks" being on the ground — a common baseline for judging height — there is *secondly* an important relationship between status and age. In a group where knowledge, experience, and strength are part of the social hierarchy, status cannot but be related to age. Just ask any 10-year-old child.

The correlation between age and status is especially apparent in animals like ourselves where there is a long period of development before reproductive maturity. The better part of one's first two decades consists of looking directly at peers, down at subordinates (*under*classmen), and up at those who are dominant. So we arrive at our adult height thoroughly conditioned into regarding height as a direct clue to status. And in varying degrees we react accordingly to everyone we meet and they to us. In essence, a short man is treated more like a juvenile than a taller one is, all else being equal. Since being treated like a juvenile denies him his just status, he is likely to make a compensation.

The stereotypes of the tall, dumb hick and the short, cocky tough are exaggerations of what is basically a real phenomenon. In order to be successful if one is deficient in a threat-display component, one has to compensate by exaggerating other aspects. In the case of the short man, he often becomes hyper-aggressive — by creating or conveying an image of high sexual accomplishment, driving himself to excellence in a status profession, or being a fast talker.

Such behavioral compensation, by one who is socially handicapped in obtaining status, is in my opinion a much more useful principle in understanding behavioral irregularities than, for example, an "Oedipus complex." It is a familiar feature of the *nouveau riche* — the drive behind Robert Ruark's hero in *Poor No More.* It is an almost universal character of women competing in what is traditionally a man's profession. Indeed, professional women with high aspirations in a field where a strong masculine bias exists often exhibit in remarkable detail almost a "small man" syndrome.

But this principle of status compensation has its opposite counterpart. Tall men, with their decided status edge, are almost apologetic about it.

> "Henry did not realize how big he was until he stood up; he was six feet three or so, and he stooped and looked a little ashamed of his height, like so many overgrown men."
>
> — Herman Wouk, *Winds of War*

Generally if someone has a position of high stature in one area, the pressures for status are likely to be less in others. As an example, there seems to be little competition among academic types over what sort of automobile one drives; whereas among assembly-line workers, where professional excellence is difficult to distinguish or isn't revered, a new, powerful car carries more status value.

Height also plays a role in our carriage. When we are feeling confident and dominant we walk straight and erect; when feeling dejected and "low" we slump and slouch. Like most species which use height in threat display, we use some form of decreased height as a gesture or symbol of appeasement. In a ritual way, we bow, curtsy, kneel and prostrate ourselves before dominants. We lower our height customarily by removing headgear (or saluting, a ritualized reach for the cap brim) in front of superiors, or in front of those whom we do not wish to offend (women, elders, etc.). Coming "hat in hand" is a symbol of appeasement.

The use of height for purposes of status has other repercussions throughout our behavior. It affects our gait and the corresponding social values we apply to gaits. In a marching column of men, the taller are placed in the front and seem to be mechanical toys — the torso relatively rigid and the head on a constant plane. But as one nears the end of the column where the shorter men are, one notices an undulating vertical movement of the rows and a pronounced pelvic waddle. In order to keep in step, the shorter ones must stride farther relative to their size and rotate their upper torsos more. The effect produced is a vertical bobbing of heads and an agitated bearing in the last rank.

These same differences in gait are noticeable when several people are walking down the street at a leisurely pace, even though there is no necessity to keep in step. However, a small person usually combines a long stride with a faster step to keep up with his taller associates. Carriage and gaits have become secondary social signals.

In finishing and modeling schools, young girls learn to modify their gait and posture by carrying books on their heads. The desired movements are fairly short to medium steps, little agitation of the torso, and a movement of the head in a horizontal plane. Deviations from this cause the book to jiggle off. These movements are essentially the natural movements of a taller person. Dwarfs are often used in comedy parts because their disproportionately short legs exaggerate the hip swing movements of a shorter person. It is relevant to the height issue to observe that the pity we feel for dwarfs has little to do directly with their growth pathology, but for their social disadvantage.

One would not at first guess that the social uses of height have affected the evolution of our brow gestures. Most monkeys have a "high brow" threat, as they look "goggle-eyed" directly at their opponents. Men and the apes, on the other hand, have a "low brow" scowl.

Apes who live on the ground, in contrast to arboreal monkeys, have evolved important displays because of their radically differing heights due to their upright posture. Over the long period of juvenile development, a young ape or boy looks up to adults, that is, raises his eyes and brow, and he is looked down upon with lowered eyes and brow. Brows up is an admission of smaller size — younger age — i.e. the juvenile or subordinate signal. Brows down symbolically relegates the associate to a subordinate or younger class (looking down on someone).

The hairy eyebrow is a social organ that accentuates these signals. There are several telling pieces of evidence pointing to its function as a communications ornament. The eyebrow undergoes a marked change during puberty. Small children have poorly developed brow hair, and what little of it there is is usually a fine light velum. If it serves some physical function, as physical anthropologists have suggested (like keeping the rain out of the eyes), one would expect the need to be as great among the young as among adults.

There are also prominent sexual differences in brow hair. Males usually have longer or thicker brow hair. Though there is some overlap between the sexes, females rarely develop the coarse, heavy "John L. Lewis" type of eyebrows.

The hairy brow patch seems to function as a contrast line, giving the signal of brow position greater clarity and emphasis. Though this is undoubtedly the main social function of brow hair, it doesn't account completely for age and sexual variations.

Disproportionate brow hair development among older males seems to provide a false contour to the underlying bony brow. This brow ridge was an important sexually distinctive character of our early ancestors. It seems to have a role in the threat display, among primates, of permanently accentuating the lowered brow. As we shall see, it also has a role in obscuring optical signals. Even to us, the exaggerated, protruding bony brows of an old male gorilla connote awesome intimidation. Hence fiction writers portray it as a dangerous beast, even though it is a rather shy vegetarian. The thick row of hair across the brow ridge in older human males gives the underlying structure a more permanently lowered appearance.

Unlike the bony brow ridge of our ancestors, which was a rather "fixed" social organ (like permanently erected hackles), the false brow of eyebrow hair provides much the same signal, yet it is mobile enough to run through a broad range of social signals. Unlike the beard, which only contributes to dominance, the human hairy brow can communicate the extremes of intense aggression or of fear, and, when combined with other facial movements, many other emotions.

The popular habit of modifying the eyebrows cosmetically adds some insight into their function and evolution. Eyebrows are important organs of beauty, as the inscription from the Egyptian *Book of the Dead* proclaims: "Thine eyebrows are twin goddesses who sit enthroned in peace." Cosmeticians pluck the low-brow and paint on a higher arch of the high brow to give a fixed air of attentiveness and receptivity. In a sense, this creates a stimulus of mild subordination. In much the same way that they carefully pluck any chin or moustache hairs to reduce the signal of aggression (masculinity), women cosmetically thin their brows, giving them a more juvenile appearance.

Women also remove the hair directly above the bridge of the nose (the area physical anthropologists refer to as the *glabella*), because any indication that the brow ridge runs continuously across the face smacks of extreme masculinity and caveman coarseness. The separation of the bony brow ridge or hairy brow into two disconnected arcades is a character of juveniles, females, and fine-featured males.

The chin, though basically a weapon display, also seems to be affected by a kind of height. Kids see mainly the lower half of adults' heads and adults see the top part of juveniles' heads, especially during a confrontation. Lifting the head to protrude the jaw toward *peers* gives kids and adults alike the same picture they received from taller folks when they were young. This eyes-down, raised-face gesture has become the cartoonists' standard of aloofness; snooty, nose-in-the-air, stuck up.

Erectile shoulder hackles are one of the main mammalian modes of increasing height and enlarging outline. Chimps and dogs both erect them in threat — especially in the form of threat referred to as defensive threat (attempting to ward off an attacker). We don't use this gesture anymore, but have a remnant of its ancient wiring, which still persists. Eibl-Eibesfeldt has referred to it as a "shoulder shudder." It is a contraction of the skin muscles in the back along the middle of the shoulder blades toward the crest of the spine. This vestigial hackle display is triggered when we hear an eerie sound, learn of an especially repugnant incident, barely miss an accident.

Colloquially, it is a "shiver up and down the spine." In its milder form, a wave of hair erection creeps along the fuzz up the spine, for that "creepy sensation."

Height displays permeate many of the subtle gestures we make toward one another. Kummer observed that among baboons who are embracing each other, it is not always the larger animal who lets its chin rest on the nape of the other, but the one of higher rank. The one of lower rank plays the role of a young animal and rests its head on the chest of its companion. Similarly, if a human couple are walking arm-in-arm or holding hands, it is the man's which is uppermost. In animal copulation, it is the male's prerogative to mount on top.

Height definitely influences clothing styles, particularly hair and head dressing. The history of the hat is intertwined with increasing apparent height and stature. As in putting on a pair of high-heeled cowboy boots, many feel an ego lift in donning a high hat. Turbans, bearskin hats, crown-plumes and others all add status by adding height. The modern officer's cap reminds one of a false-front building with its forward-sweeping crest as an artificial extension of the forehead.

"High society" events are often marked in Western culture by women's styles which accentuate height: hair piled high on the head, high-heeled shoes. When a woman relaxes from the status struggle, her action may be symbolized by "letting her hair down." Curly or kinky hair in some human sub-groups gives loft to the hair, increasing apparent head size and body height, as does the hair-whorl of other sub-groups in a somewhat different way.

If most of our humanness is connected to the evolution of our two-legged or upright stance, then one can make a good case for height displays being a critical element in the evolution of many uniquely human features. Our invasion of the predatory niche depended upon the use of hand weapons — a weak "carnivore" using wit and rocks to kill, instead of tooth and muscle. As many authors have recently stressed, being a primate predator provided the necessary combination for becoming the thinking primate.

As in animals that use a broadside display, the frontal display of bipeds shows off the whole body mass. Attention is pulled to the belly or chest rather than the side. It is more than accidental that one of the trends among bipeds is belly-to-back flattening.

The success of a two-legged animal that uses its arms in combat is roughly correlated with the mass of the upper torso, shoulders, and arms, all else being equal. It is not surprising, then that this area would be used in threat. Flattening of the chest increases the *apparent* if not the real body mass.

Kangaroos, a non-primate group of bipeds, have also undergone some chest flattening. The males fight mainly with their forelegs. They flex their chest and arm muscles as part of their threat, just as we do, further increasing the apparent massiveness of the chest and shoulders. The gorilla has a relatively flat chest that shows off his torso, and he slaps it for both visual and sound display (similar in principle to a sneer being accompanied by a growl). The inhalation of air to expand the chest is a dominant part of the human expression of either pride or offense (two occasions when we use our threat display).

As the forelimbs became more important in aggression, the two-legged stance was struck not only in fighting but also to present a more formidable appearance in height and breadth as part of a threat. The contemporary "knuckle-walking" primates also resort to the bipedal stance in displaying threat. Thus, the breakthrough that was produced by freeing the forelimbs may have occurred hand-in-hand with the evolution of our threat display pattern. Much of our humanness stems, in part, from our particular mode of aggression.

In Konrad Lorenz's discussion of the human communal defense reaction (one's response when the Alma Mater is played, or when the flag passes by), he observes that "a shiver runs down the back, and, as more exact observation shows, *along the outside of both arms* . . . The arms are raised from the sides and rotated inwardly so that the elbows stick out . . . the head is proudly raised and the chin stuck out." The shiver, of course, is the "goose pimples" from the vestigial response of hair erection. In the chimpanzee and gorilla this intimidation posture is still important as a threat signal.

The chimpanzee has well-developed hair on the outer surfaces of the arms, and it is erected during the threat display. Gorillas have the best developed shoulder and lower arm manes of the apes. The mountain gorilla, in particular, has spectacular hair development of the lower arm; the hair flows out sideways at right angles from the body axis and is brought into full display in chest slapping.

It is probable that arm hair once played a more important role in our own threat display than it does now. This is also true of hair on the chest. Chest, arm, and leg hair seem to function in a similar manner to chin whiskers, in increasing the apparent size of the organ on which they grow and in drawing the opponent's attention to that area of the body. Gorillas, and some men, have shoulder hair crests on the back and shoulders, rather like biological epaulets. As in most other display organs, strong sexual and age differences in hair emphasize the opponent's degree of social dominance.

It is difficult to overemphasize size and height as factors in the evolution of our social organs. It has also been vital in governing our impressions of others and, of course, in determining our own self-confidence. And we can now begin to see how hair is related to our values of size and height. Little wonder hair is an emotionally loaded subject at any age.

7
THE BALD
AND
THE BLOND

Scalp hair also has had some history as an organ of height display, most obviously among gorillas. But the evolution of scalp hair in human beings is more complex. There are three outstanding features of scalp hair that I will try to account for: its color, its texture, and its absence — balding.

Is it really true that gentlemen prefer blonds? Our ancestral scalp hair color was black, with brown variants in many sub-groups, judging from related primates and the general distribution of human hair color throughout the world. Among human sub-groups having shades of brown adult scalp hair, there is almost invariably an increase in pigmentation with age. Most people recognize that just because you have a towheaded child, it doesn't at all mean he'll be blond as an adult. In a community with a number of brown-haired adults, there will be a statistical association of hair color with age groups, similar to the correlation of size with age. Like a short adult, a blond adult will carry some subordinate signal element.

Apparently, blond adults are a comparatively recent human innovation, and they originally came from a relatively small part of the world. Human beings appear to be at the same stage of blond-brunette evolution as the gibbon *Hylobates lar lar*; having come from a dark-haired ancestral stock, we have substantial hair color variation, within which there are opposing sexual preferences. (Just flip through the magazine ads and see how infrequently a blond man is shown with a dark-haired woman.) Yet we haven't reached the sexual stage (represented by the species *H. concolor*) of all blond females and all dark-haired males. In one human subspecies (the Australian aboriginals) there is a striking age gradient in hair color throughout the entire population. The young are dark of skin and eyes but have exceptionally blond hair. This darkens with age until it is black or a very dark brown.

We can separate movie sex-goddesses into two types: the babyfaced sort and the dominant kind. Generally, the babyface neotenics (childlikes) have blond hair which, of course, complements the signal. Women, in cultures where it is accepted, are fond of bleaching their hair. Like thin-arched eyebrows and "made-up" eyes, blond hair gives them a child-like air, that is, the social posture of an attractive subordinate.

It is no news to anybody that scalp hair affects social posture. Millions upon millions of dollars and man-hours are spent annually modifying scalp hair so that people can present a better social face. Culture-specific alterations and whims of style tend to obscure some rather fundamental themes permeating our values about scalp hair. In fact, when examined carefully, the cultural modifications support to a great degree the natural signals already present.

The actors of ancient Greece used a black wig for the villain, blond for the hero, and red for the clown or fool. According to Kathrin Perutz, "light hair is usually the wife, heroine, princess, maiden in distress or Doris Day, dark hair is for women, mistresses, or more aggressive heroines." For example, Salome is always pictured with tendrils black and tightly curled, not too dissimilar from pubic hair. Yeats saw the special attraction of a blond beauty:

> Never shall a young man
> Thrown into despair
> By those great honey-colored
> Ramparts at your ear
> Love you for yourself alone
> And not your yellow hair.

In order to investigate the biology of scalp hair patterns, other than color, we have first to take a brief look at other primates. From the extreme use of facial hair as an enlarged fan around the face, such as is found in the saki monkey, Goeldi's marmoset, and the crab-eating monkey, there is a complete spectrum of specializations into dorsal crests, brow bands, cheek whiskers, and chin whiskers. The moor macaque and the drill are two species that have all, or most, of these specializations. It is difficult not to argue that the scalp hair functions mainly as an organ of intimidation in primates. The head hair on the gorilla forms a prominent crest along the center line from front to back. The crest is erected, when the animal is threatening, by pulling the skin down in a forward direction over the scalp.

Scalp hair doesn't seem to be a protective "hat." The thickness or length of the hair on the head doesn't seem to be related to the amount of time spent out in the sun. Baboons living in semi-open situations have short hair on top of the head while some monkeys living in dense forests have a thick mat of scalp hair.

There are a number of scalp hair patterns in primates. Some have hair fans, like open taxicab doors, with a part in the middle, giving the head an appearance of greater breadth (e.g., the golden marmoset). More commonly, the head hair is arranged as a middle crest. Many have crests of different color from the rest of the head hair. The macaques, gelada baboons, and the drills have dark crests on light backgrounds, while Geoffrey's marmoset has a white crest on a darker background.

There are some sexual differences in scalp hair among the primates (the males generally have more) but not as many as in the case of the beard. If the primate scalp hair has functioned only as a threat device, then one could expect more scalp hair among males. But humans and a few other primate species do not fit this pattern; some men have almost no scalp hair at all.

Among human beings, and a few other primate species, it is the female who has the full head of luxuriant hair. Men's hair tends only to be somewhat bushier, in some caucasian groups. Human females often repudiate their attractive femininity by cutting back their hair near the stylish male length (for example, suffragettes, flappers, lesbians, high-powered business-women, nuns and Orthodox Jewish brides).

Do our scalp patterns reflect an overall primate trend? First, we are kind of similar to the other primates in having a poor correlation of hair thickness and length with different climates. For example, the African Hottentots and Bushmen occupy one of the sunniest places on earth, yet their hair is arranged in little peppercorn tufts scattered over the scalp, exposing the naked skin in between, much like the very young of more northern African tribes. So one might begin to suspect that human scalp hair may also function as a social organ — as per primate tradition.

Our balding isn't peculiar to ourselves. It is found in several primate groups — apparently having evolved independently in all of them. The South American uakari monkey balds with age even more completely than human beings. Male uakaris generally become more bald than females. Among the African monkeys the stump-tailed macaque males bald with

Balding is not an uniquely human phenomenon. Several other species of primates also bald and, as in humans, it is more common in adult males than among females or the young. Shown above are the Chimp, Man, Uakari monkey, Stump-tailed macaque, and the Orang.

age. Among the apes both the chimps and orangs experience balding, but the trait is highly variable among chimps — occurring more notably with age and more so among males than females.

Because of our particular attitudes toward aging we are accustomed to think of balding as a deterioration process — a symbol of senility, a by-product of a general decline. Interestingly enough, this attitude prevails even among physicians, gerontologists, and physical anthropologists. In a culture that worships youth as ours does, it probably couldn't be otherwise, but there is more to balding than being a symptom of senescence. Among those other balding primates it seems to be a social badge of privilege, that is, an organic symbol of status. Its evolutionary history among human beings once followed this same pattern and became even more exaggerated.

But how can we reconcile these two divergent primate patterns: some species using a thick mat of erectile scalp hair, and others a bared skin, all for a similar signal? I think there are several lines of evidence pointing to a plausible answer.

Prosimians — the early primates — and virtually all living primates are without foreheads. The brow is the highest point that you see when the animal is facing you. The main avenue available to expand the apparent size of the face is to top the brow or scalp with a crest of erectile hairs. Among apes this is especially apparent in the gorilla. Old males have a long erectile scalp crest, which adds several inches to their stature.

One of the general trends among primates, however, has been to remove the hair from the face. A naked face amid head hair attracts attention and greatly facilitates communication by allowing for skin color changes and obvious skin wrinkling, which are at least hampered by the hairy covering. Changes in the skull which expand the braincase or lower the brow ridge to form a forehead offer a new surface for skin exposure.

Among the species with well developed foreheads, there has been a switch from the use of hair to the use of skin. As has so often been the case when one threat device is substituted through evolution for another, the old device becomes a symbol of femininity or pre-adolescence, a symbol of those of low social stature. I think this has happened to human scalp hair (as well as uakari monkey scalp hair).

Why exactly should the forehead and scalp be bared in threat? Again, the other bald primates provide some interesting insight into our own balding process. Skin color is of utmost importance in uakari monkey communication. The entire face turns brilliant crimson as the skin is distended with blood when a monkey is threatening. Somewhat the same thing is true with the stump-tailed macaque. Like the uakari monkey, mature macaque males have a network of large, spongelike, cavernous vessels just under the surface of the skin on the forehead and scalp, that can be flooded with blood under the stimulus of certain emotions.

The forehead also displays skin texture. As males of all primate species tend to have coarser hair than the females, among many of them the exposed skin areas become more granular, pitted, and irregular with age. In the forehead area, texture seems to be an important part of the display. An old male macaque monkey has a particularly greasy dome. The stump-tailed macaque monkey has a well-developed sebaceous (oil) gland system on the same areas of the face and the forepart of the scalp as man does. In this species there are sexual differences in this character, suggesting that the organ has other functions than keeping the skin from drying out. Secretions from this gland are more abundant at puberty in human males than females, and remain so throughout life. The human forehead, scalp, and face become quite greasy if these oily products are left to accumulate.

Like the uakari monkey, humans redden with age or anger, and the function appears to be primarily a social signal. Facial reddening does in fact carry important information and serves no other physiological function. As the blood vessels of the face flush, the skin reddens, the angular vein which runs upward from the bridge of the nose is especially distended and has been referred to as the temper or anger vein.

Exposed foreheads accomplish several things. (1) They increase the area for color and skin position displays; (2) they increase the apparent area of the face; and (3) they magnify the changes in skin texture with age.

But there is a fourth function that is perhaps the major explanation for human balding.

There are two fundamental, instinctive things every baby primate must know. It must be able, from almost the very beginning, to hold tightly to the hair of its usually arboreal mother, and it must be able to nurse. Somewhere in that complicated inborn neural switchboard, these two circuits have not been kept completely separate.

Terence Anthoney's work on the development of adult sexual behavior and grooming, starting from the babies' nursing and hair fondling in baboons, has told us a lot about ourselves and our attitudes toward hair. When the young are weaned they still retreat to the security of hair fondling. Growing out of these associations, hair grooming later in life takes on an important role as a socio-sexual gesture. Thus baboon hair is not only an organ to regulate body temperature and to threaten with, it is something to be loved.

Human babies are like baboons in this respect: they like to run their fingers through their mother's hair when they nurse. But our human nakedness leaves little hair to fondle. Babies cannot easily fondle crotch or axillary hair, and women have very little facial hair. All that remains is scalp hair. Developmentally, this is where humans get their *love* for hair — not all hair, just scalp hair. We associate it with sex and tenderness. It is denser, finer, and longer in females.

If mothers have very short hair or if babies are nursing from bottles, their little hands reach up to their own heads, coiling and twining their own hair. More commonly, they substitute a soft "velum" blanket for the missing maternal hair. Even well after weaning, some use a nipple substitute — the thumb — and fondle their mother's or father's hair when they are tired or insecure. A puzzled or frustrated man uses the same gesture in a scalp hair stroke or moustache pat, not to displace his anxiety, but to retreat in a subtle way to the security of an earlier age. Baboons and humans alike are conditioned early in life (and perhaps with some genetic guidance) to love scalp hair.

Indirectly because of our nakedness, scalp hair has changed its signal role. No longer is it a coarse erectile crest used to signal threat. Its role has shifted from an emphasis on male dominance to an organ of child-female interaction. And as an extension of the latter, it has become part of the allure of female attraction.

What has this done for the male scalp? It has reversed the selection pressures for status opposite to long tresses — a bald head. One identifies a full head of hair with femininity and youth. The actors who are chosen to play the roles of very young men in movies or on television frequently have an unusually low hairline, so that the forehead is reduced to a narrow band of skin. This is also true of the "baby-doll" actresses. People with this kind of hairline look younger than their age.

The status signal of the high forehead is obscured by our current accent on youth. Head shaving is a common phenomenon among many tribes and often is done only by males. Interestingly enough, it is sometimes performed in a manner which exaggerates the natural balding patterns. For example, the South American Yanomano shave the crown of the head, leaving a wreath of hair. Scars from battle are exhibited in this manner. Another South American tribe, the Tchikrin, pluck all facial hair, even in small children. The men, especially, have their hair plucked back from the forehead to the crown or hair whorl area. It was a common practice during the 1800's for Chinese males to shave the forehead well back to the top of the head and then braid the remaining hair in a queue.

At the present time Western cultures are caught in a pinch between the adulation of youth — which is responsible for our holding low hairlines in esteem — and our continuing respect for status and the high forehead — which retains an element of nobility or at least an aristocratic mien. The superhero males of the comics almost invariably have a high hairline.

The most common type of pattern balding is for two naked arches to expand upward from the brow, leaving a strip of hair along the midline. Even on non-balding foreheads, these lines sometimes come together to form a sharp "widow's peak." This pattern presumably arose from an upward movement of the double-crescent hairline which rims the brows of the other primates. These double arches baring the upper temples seem to carry a signal of stature even when diluted into a double scallop hairline, non-balding pattern, such as is found in women. The straight line pattern has a more juvenile character to it.

Virtually every human sub-group has some form of pattern balding, but there are extreme variations in onset, rate, and patterning. Some combine the bald spot with the double arch, and others, especially in the Eastern Mediterranean area, have a line-of-march which moves backward across the head with age. Similar patterns are seen in other primate species. Some macaques, chimps, and some baboons seem to expand the balding zone backward along the medial line, a pattern sometimes seen in humans.

In the distant past, the gloss of a bare scalp became the badge of leadership and dominance, whether it was the greased plucked head of the Yanamano or the oily, scraped scalp of an Ainu, Jew, Chinese, or Saxon. It is mimicked unconsciously by shiny metal helmets in many cultures.

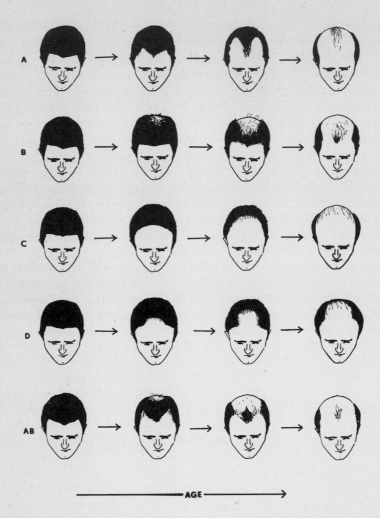

Human balding occurs in several patterns. These sometimes occur together or separately and occur at different frequencies. Some noteworthy patterns are: (A) Double point, forehead recession, widow's peak; (B) Monk's spot (usually A and B occur together; they are common in many European countries); (C) Line-of-march, common in the Mediterranean countries (e.g., Albert Einstein); (D) Single point forehead recession, common among Orientals (e.g., Mao Tse-tung).

Why then do we have so many hangups about baldness? Probably more people have been duped by "hair-growing" elixirs than by any other ineffectual cosmetic. Any man's magazine on the newsstand contains advertisements for secret formulas and special treatments to bring back lost scalp hair. Hairpieces and wigs are commonly used by men to cover the bald patches and receding hairlines. One of the newer alternatives, made possible by plastic surgery, is the grafting of small pieces of hair from other parts of the scalp onto thinning areas, to recreate permanently one's earlier hairline. Recreating the hairline of a 20-year-old is a retreat to the courtship age. We live in a society which bases most status evaluation on one's potential courting currency; that is the secret behind our reverence for youth.

The evolution of human scalp hair has followed this pattern: first it was an erectile threat crest, then strangely, it began to shift. Balding became the threat ideal, and a full head of soft hair was what we clung to as babies — a symbol of maternal-sexual security and attraction, like a round, warm breast. But recently the evolutionary bent has looped into an even odder twist. The symbols of age and status are in disfavor, even repugnant. Now it is the mature male who mimics the post-puberty vigor of youth that has become our ad man's ideal. More than any of the other organic epaulets of the past, the threat value of the very high forehead and its exaggeration, the bald scalp, has been debased. And like the Confederate dollar, there is something uncomfortably humorous about its continued existence.

8
THE LOVE AND MENACE OF HAIR

"She asked me why, I'm just a hairy guy,
I'm hairy noon and night, hair that's a fright,
I'm hairy high and low
Don't ask me why, I don't know."

— from the song "Hair" in the musical *Hair*

I would like to attempt to answer the question posed in *Hair*. You will find little mention in textbooks or symposia volumes of the fact that hair functions as a social garment. Yet that is one of its main functions.

Mice who skitter among the dark moon shadows beneath thick mantles of herbs have a monotonous gray-brown pattern concealing them from mouse-eaters. Their main contact with fellow mice is through dank scents left on stems by the trail, or the droppings sprinkled on the mouse path. There are dozens of species, yet experts have to cut them open or look at teeth or resort to such tactics as counting teats to identify them. At first glance, all of the species seem to be made with the same cookie-cutter; most of the important differences are inside.

This isn't true among a lot of other animal groups, particularly the ones that depend mainly on visual signals — most birds, primates, hoofed animals of the plains, clear-water fish, and lizards, for example. These species have resplendent colors and flashy patterns, particularly the reptiles and fish who can change their skin into brilliant reds, blues, and yellows in myriads of pattern permutations.

Unlike fish and reptiles, mammals have few bare patches of colored skin. Their social garments are coats of hair. Hair is mainly what they see of their fellows and it is this hair that must carry the signals of love, seniority, youth, aggression, submission, and sex. Hair ornamentation is their trapping of rank — tall crests down the back of the neck, manes that flow from around the head and neck, tassels and tufts, splotches and spots, lines and stripes, colorful tails and faces, contrasting genitals and ears, wooly thighs and hairy chins. Some of these specialized hair areas are erectile to super-normalize the signal or add false contour; other areas are dangling, ever-present symbols, like a goat's tresses or a lieutenant's parade plume. Hair is a warm, many-tangled tentacle in which bacteria can digest the body sweat and produce the salty stink of a social aroma. We hate for hair and love for it.

While still in your mother's uterus you were cloaked in a fine soft hair called *lanugo*. It is usually shed well before birth — perhaps a vestige of some hairier day in our ancestry. At birth and during the first few years of our lives we are not naked — not hairless. Babies and children have almost as many hairs as adults — or, for that matter, chimpanzees and orangutans. The hair of the young, however, is very soft and almost invisibly fine; anatomists call it *velum* hair. Velum hair gives bare skin a soft powdered texture, considerably softer looking than bare skin itself. It is smooth to kiss and stroke. It is what we want to cuddle, nuzzle, care for, protect and love. Soft, velum-coated baby skin is our standard of inoffensive child-like beauty. And for that reason, it is the coat many men want women to wear.

The ends of most social hierarchies (there are a few special exceptions) can be characterized by the baby or newborn at the protected low end of the spectrum, and an older male at the high end. Hairiness is associated with most of the more important components of status — sex, age, and size. It is easy to see why, in the locker room, a hairy body is nothing to be ashamed of. In a society that must emphasize cooperation and de-emphasize direct serious competition, excess hair may be too gross for most tastes, because it is a symbol for rough masculinity. If the best key to physical prowess among humans is the amount of body hair, the corollary is the more body hair, the greater the intimidation. And one's success, his evolutionary fitness, in a highly organized society may depend on how well he cooperates, not how much he intimidates.

So here is the same human tissue — hair — used to represent the entire spectrum of status; to invoke love and care for the baby, and yet to give the dominant a more intimidating image. This, I believe, is what underlies our antithetical feelings about hair. As babies, we suckled and fingered our mother's soft and fine hair. As parents, we pat the soft hair of children with tender affection. As lovers, we run our fingers through each other's scalp hair.

But at the same time there is that other curly hair we cover or remove. Women spend considerable time grooming and cleaning their scalp hair to add to its display, but in most of our culture shave their underarm and leg hair and remove their trace of moustache, if it exists. Men do a similar thing in cropping the beard back to where it is nothing like the full, 20-inch natural organ.

The hair on the head and body have thus taken on a quality above and beyond their original function — to give a false contour or to incubate and disperse an odor. It now possesses visual beauty and vulgarity, but these are just extensions of the original biological signal.

But we don't love all hair: just some. The lady at the ball with her elaborate curls and coiffure decked with jewels and gold netting would be repulsed if the man next to her whipped down his pants to display his body hair. The hair which is referred to in the song "Hair," "hair that's a fright," doesn't have the qualities of baby hair: it is smelly, coarse, and greasy.

Old male stump-tailed macaques, a predominantly ground-dwelling monkey, have an inordinately well developed sebaceous or grease-producing organ. In these monkeys there are striking age and sexual variations in hair character. Old male macaques have dirty, greasy hair. Emanual showed that sebaceous secretions are also more abundant in human males than females at puberty, and remain so throughout life. The difference in greasiness parallels the change in hair texture and amount.

Like old male macaques, our hair would be dirty, dandruffy, and greasy if we didn't wash so much. Most washing is a social appeasement gesture to rid ourselves of the adult grease and smells; its sanitary value is pretty much a myth. Washing grooms our scalp hair back to its childlike powder fluff, just as shaving creates a pre-puberty effect.

Many sub-cultures throughout the world have adopted the custom of oiling or greasing their hair. Like the wearing of false beards among the ancient Egyptians, this seems to be an increase in status signal by adding artificial exaggerations of threat paraphernalia. The Congo natives use castor bean oil, while New Zealanders favored shark oil. The Polynesians used pia gum from the coconut tree, and Tahitians, coconut oil itself. Egyptians concocted their pomades from six different kinds of animal fat. Grecians also had special hair mixtures. The more blatant male-female distinctions between the post-Gibson Girl era and the pre-bobby-soxer era were marked by the greasily pompadoured man — the early Clark Gable look. Now, however, male styles have shifted toward the feminine. Both sexes wear their scalp hair with "that natural" (natural for a pre-puberty juvenile) "lustrous, squeaky clean sheen."

If indeed our present social grooming of hair came about because of the increasing need for a low social profile in order to function well in an intricate open society, it is not difficult to understand the rebellious upsurge of bizarre and exotic hair, with accompanying dress styles. It is symbolic of an objection to the "organization man" kind of existence, where lives are run and determined by rigid norms beyond our control.

In a closed folk society of simpler, more sedentary days, one knew his position. Full beards, wooly chests, and rancid odors reinforced the lines of authority by giving a rather awesome or even fearsome visage. In present-day society we come in contact with many strangers daily, yet seem to have dragged the old fear of strangers along with us. We continually must appease and be appeased, to reassure that we are "friendly" and to be assured that the other guy is a "friendly" too. The ungroomed, hairy hippie of the 1960's, though symbolizing something that most were sympathetic with, inadvertently used a basic threat device appropriate only in a much different setting. So instead of pacifism, naturalism, and love, to many he symbolized greasy, hairy King Kong in the dark alley – a stylized antisocial stranger dressed to intimidate all folk. It may have been a better idea for the flower children to become more childlike, but that was impossible because the establishment's elaborate grooming rituals had already returned us to a very childlike appearance.

The polarity of values about hair is particularly apparent when we look at the kind of garments we wrap around ourselves. The velum of children and Lolitas is mimicked in soft velvety material and downy furs. Rabbit, lynx, mink, sable, fox and muskrat are traditionally women's furs. Men sometimes use wooly sheepskin, wolf, and bearskin, but seldom don the softer materials and furs except in societies where men are feminized. In aristocracies, for example, gentleness is displayed to separate members from the coarse lower classes. At times in the past men have resorted to powdered wigs of long, light velum hair to match their silks and velvets. The blouse was tied at the collar to conceal the curly chest hair, and the tie has continued as part of formal dress today.

In its partially groomed state or in special situations such as at the beach, coarse hair can add status under our present value system. A clean, well-trimmed beard is not very offensive, rather it adds some years to one's appearance, carrying with it a subtle increase in stature. Daniel Freedman and his students at the University of Chicago tested undergraduates on their response to beards. Generally, men with well-groomed beards were thought to look older; females responded with comments like "more masculine and mature" and felt more feminine toward them. Freedman also refers to the phenomenon of beards affecting individual distance; people are willing to stand nearer to a beardless man while conversing than to a bearded one.

All this should not surprise us, because threat devices give status, and human beings are to a great extent attracted to one another by status. It's not the only component of social and sexual magnetism, but it is undoubtedly an important one. There are elements of status to which we often are not attracted: status achieved by belligerence or gross flaunting of power, hypercompetitiveness — a "poor loser," "lording it over someone," "taking advantage." At least in Western societies, letting one's natural status ornamentation develop to its fullest extent does go beyond the limits tradition (and perhaps the necessity of forced intimacy in elevators) allows.

To contend that our smell and threat hair was selected in evolution because of its sexual magnetism is only half true. Coarse hair was selected for because it gave a clear signal of our status, even though there was a large component of *offense* involved. Status must have been the main theme of our hair patches, judging by how other threat-sexual lures function in other organisms. Those females who favored the dominant males left more genetic material behind them because of the differential privileges incurred by association with them. At the same time there is the counterselection pressure favoring the behavior of those men and women who are attracted by the markings of the young — because they give their children more intensive care and attention. In a social situation where adults must rely on mutual care and attention, it may be the more baby-like appearance that is genetically most successful.

In the next section I will shift emphasis toward the organs of sexual attraction. The evolutionary crosscurrents between attraction and status are so intertwined that, to a great degree, it is a continuation of the pattern of love and menace we have seen in hair.

PART THREE: THE ANATOMY OF SEX AND BEAUTY

9
THE NOBILITY OF HIGH CHEEKBONES: THE BIOLOGY OF BEAUTY

"Every morning I look in the mirror and thank God for my high cheek bones."

— Suzy Parker, supermodel

One of the most fascinating unsolved problems in biology is the evolution of beauty — aesthetic appreciation. Because it is such a complex and abstract emotion, one finds difficulty in identifying such things as outward signs of artistic enjoyment in other species. So any evolutionary sequence is hard to come by. What I have done in this section is to offer a few ideas about how some aspects of our aesthetic sense evolved.

The part of aesthetics I am concerned with here is that which underlies human physical beauty. There seem to be two major biological elements. These are undoubtedly affected by the times, cultural context, and one's particular psychological bent, but they form the basic ground plan nonetheless. They come from the two basic elements of our social interaction — (1) sexual attraction (*copulatory lures,* if you will), and (2) badges of status.

Badges of status consist of two opposing pressures, which at first seem antithetical but are in complement. They are (2a) our love for the dominant and (2b) our love for the subordinate. We love dominants for the security they give us. They can be relied upon for protection or to make difficult decisions. We are attracted to subordinates — infants, pets, or extreme underdogs — who need our care and protection for the security we can give them, which in turn increases our own self-esteem.

These status-associated, aesthetic attractions seem to be derived from the parent-child bond and the child-parent bond. In social-hierarchical terms, we translate these relationships, respectively, as parent-dominant and child-subordinate. Together with the sexual-copulatory attraction, these complete the primary social attraction pattern of parent-child, child-parent, and parent-parent. The underlying ingredients of sex and status are blended and intertwined among all three bonds.

The biological source for these bonds comes from parents who had an (aesthetic) attraction to infants, especially their own, and were able to rear more children well than parents without such attraction. Children, of course, had to develop a respect and reliance on the adult in order to function and survive. Both of these are fostered by the increased requirements for parental care in an animal like ourselves; we occupy a very flexible niche, which necessitates a long learning period. The sexual attractions increase fitness, of course, by offering the occasion to produce offspring. Courtship and pair bonding seem, however, to be a blend of both status and copulatory attraction.

Factors of sex and status affect our own features and model our values concerning our fellows. Let's look at them one at a time — first, the love of dominants.

Desmond Morris has suggested, and I agree, that dominance is why we have gods, superman heroes, etc. We find some satisfaction in *not* being the alpha, the dominant, and in having him to revere and lean on. A dominant has the privilege but also the responsibility of decision-making. Our reverence for dominance extends beyond human behavior into the physical image of one's stature.

Yet there is a compromise. To be revered for dominance one cannot be so dominant in his behavior as to be overbearing or belligerent; he must tone down the blatant threat to an indirect signal of superiority, to be socially appealing, yet not so subordinate as to invoke the child-parent (infantile) emotions. A mousy man may present as bad an image as an overly aggressive one.

The same is true of one's physical features. There are differences between the sexes in the optimum balance point along this scale. As we have seen, a full, greasy, ratty beard is too overt for most societies, whereas a man with a shaven, strong, square chin is revered (the signals are essentially the same; it is the amplitude which has changed). Movie queens have dominant chins, not so square as to look masculine, but bold enough to be a signal of status. Let us look at cheekbones as an example of how our values about them have been derived from a fundamental biological theme.

An artist would find in the faces of Raquel Welch and Katharine Hepburn the *haut monde* essence of nobility. Their common quality (along with other admirable features) is the protruding cheekbones flaring outward from beneath the eyes. One who frequents the pages of fiction is familiar with the esteem in which high cheekbones are held in character portrayal. John Steinbeck in *The Winter of our Discontent* describes his *femme fatale*: "Her chin was fragile and deep-cut but with plenty of muscle in the cheeks and very wide cheekbones." High cheekbones, for vague reasons, have the flavor of aristocratic beauty. They are as necessary as the rugged square jaw on the face of a stylized superhero. In fact, they are so exaggerated in cartoon characters that one would have to be an almost pathological variant to actually possess such features. Like artificially extending the length of a model's legs, the cartoonist overdramatizes the cheekbones to the point of caricature. It is interesting to note that in the male the upper margin of the beard does not encroach on the cheekbones, but rather complements the line of the cheekbones.

But why do we ascribe social value — personality characteristics — to a protruding bone on the face? Why should such a fixture be so important as to influence your choice of mate and even affect the election of people who will govern your fate?

I believe the answer cannot be found by trying to penetrate deeply into our psyche, nor are there any clues in the dusty annals of history, nor even in human prehistory. In this case, we must look to nonhumans for comparative material.

As we saw earlier, the evolution of social paraphernalia is sometimes based on physical areas that wield the weaponry. Deer look at neck sizes of their opponents for fundamentally the same reason that men in the locker room note thick chest and arm muscles. But deer and men have in the course of their evolution shifted weaponry. The ancestors of both once fought with their mouths, and now deer use their necks to twist and push with antlers, while men use their freed upper limbs to swing clubs and throw objects.

Deer were once similar to their relatives, the pigs, in their weaponry. Pigs fight with their teeth, attempting to slash the opponent's body. Among the pigs who have well developed fighting teeth and ornate head displays, there is a tendency to display frontally, that is, to confront the opponent face to face. The bush pig and warthog have expanded their head-on profiles sideways, thereby giving a more imposing image.

The muscles of the jaw originate on the side of the skull and on the underside of the cheekbones (technically called the *zygoma*). In essence,

Examples of cheekbone development and ornamentation for display. *Top row,* left to right: an Entelodont, an extinct pig-like creature, an early man (Australopithecine), a Warthog, a Forest pig. *Bottom row:* Baboon, Orang, and two types of human beings showing different degrees of cheekbone development. The living pigs on the top row have fleshy artificial cheekbones, the orang has expandable pneumatic ones and the baboon has false cheekbones in the form of cheek ruffs.

then, these are the counterpart to the wrestler's biceps or the deer's neck muscles. In pigs the jaw muscles wield the weaponry. There are tooth displays among pigs (weapon displays) and judging by the accompanying paraphernalia there are also displays of the jaw and cheekbone. There are several independent examples of animals in which the cheekbones have expanded well out beyond the muscular area, sending a bony wing out on either side in a bigger-than-life flaring cheekbone. One of these is among the extinct New World peccary, among specimens as yet undescribed in the American Museum of Natural History. Another is among the pig-like entelodonts, extinct cloven-hoofed mammals. Another is among living pigs. Both the giant forest hog and the warthog have artificially enlarged cheekbones, in part fleshy and in part bony. In the forest hog there are well developed, contrastingly colored facial "warts."

In the case of the "social chin," I argued that the human chin and chin whiskers evolved as an artificial enlargement of a weaponry display area (at least an important ancestral weapon, the mouth). The same is true, I believe, for the flaring cheekbone. Look at some of the massive cheekbones in the reconstructions of early man. These guys don't look much like Raquel Welch, yet I contend that the dominance signal that we still associate with high cheekbones is one of our ancestral social organs. Jaw muscles were once a real indication of fighting ability. In the faces of Raquel and the superheroes, we are seeing a modified version of that old label of stature. I doubt if our perception of and response to this signal is built-in; probably it is an inherent part of our social development in the same way that we learn to associate chin size with social status, but that makes the bond through time with the Australopithecine children (who had to learn its social significance) no less rigid.

Because adults have gotten away from biting one another, for the most part, as a means of settling social issues, cheekbones and chins have theoretically become esoteric clues: but in fact we perpetuate their ancient threat value in a modified form as a symbol or regality (that type of beauty stemming from social stature).

At the other end of the pole is our attraction to subordinates — our protection and love of children, pets, and soft, furry little things. This has been responsible for our physical regression to youthful appearance (neoteny, in technical terms) particularly apparent in women. Infantilism in women is attractive to men because it befits men's social situation. Men are the traditional and biological dominants, however repugnant this may be to the Women's Liberation movement. A burly Amazon may excel in business management, but statistically it is the more infantile women who attract men.

Of course, we are talking about a point along a scale between two opposing loves. Looking "babylike" probably isn't the best of all strategies. One must at the same time present a childlike image and broadcast subtle (not mannishly blatant) threat signals, which in their dilute state are the revered symbols of rank. We can illustrate this with movie stars. Actresses such as Debbie Reynolds, June Allyson, Tuesday Weld, Hayley Mills, Shirley Temple, and Mia Farrow have appeared attractive by combining many infantile signals with an adult (sexually mature) symbol. Other actresses, such as Raquel Welch, Grace Kelly, Ingrid Bergman, Marlene Dietrich, and Katharine Hepburn also have infantile signals, but they project a stronger mixture of subtle adult status symbols: not so coarse as moustache fuzz or heavy brow, but dominant chins, jaws, mouths, foreheads and cheekbones. Humbert Humbert expressed this duality:

> My world was split. I was aware of not one but two sexes, neither of which was mine: both would be termed female by the anatomist. But to me, through the prison of my senses, "they were as different as mist and mast." All this I rationalize now.
>
> — Nabokov, *Lolita*

Sexual attraction is to a great extent independent of this status spectrum. For example, one can combine full lips, big busts, broad hips, nar-

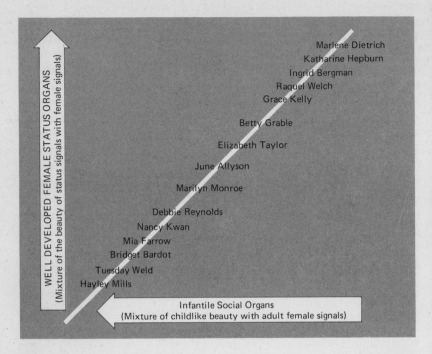

A hierarchy of present and past Hollywood beauties (in their prime) ranked in relationship to the origin of their appeal. Some depend on a more neotenic (childlike) signal and others on a status signal. None are at the extremes of superdominant (tough bitch) or extreme subordinate (flighty nellies). Note how the ornamentation of sexual attraction is somewhat independent of these two different types of beauty. Bridget Bardot, Marilyn Monroe, and Raquel Welch are all well endowed, yet are in quite different places along the hierarchy range. The latter is what gives the "sex kitten" or "femme fatale" character to their sexual attraction.

row waists, etc. (the sexual attractants) with or without the status features. Sex kittens such as Bridget Bardot, Marilyn Monroe, "Candys" or "Lolitas," and virtually all the Playboy foldouts are sex "babies," with virtually no status features, whereas Raquel Welch, the early Mae West, Marlene Dietrich, Sophia Loren, and Lauren Bacall are more "dominant sex," more aggressive in their social physique, all the way from noble to tough. The young Elizabeth Taylor is somewhere in the middle of the hierarchy spectrum, though probably at the head of the column in sexual beauty.

There is the same hierarchy spectrum among actors. Humphrey Bogart, Burt Lancaster, Anthony Quinn, Marlon Brando, and Paul Newman are well suited for roles as the dominant male; whereas Anthony Perkins, Tony Curtis, and Jack Lemmon play a more subordinate image. Yet handsomeness runs through the whole spectrum. In males, this is determined not so much by copulatory attraction as by the proper blend of hierarchy signals — the "leading man" face (say, Paul Newman). It is to some extent a mixture of feminine characters with masculine ones.

I suspect that one's personality dictates where, in his or her opinion, beauty lies along the hierarchy spectrum. If a woman has a need to mother a partner she will yearn for an Anthony Perkins type, and if she wants a protector more than anything else, she will want a man like Charlton Heston or Burt Lancaster. The same goes for a man's choice of young women. If one is somewhat insecure about his ability with women, he will lean toward the more diminutive, childlike sort. Men who want to "marry

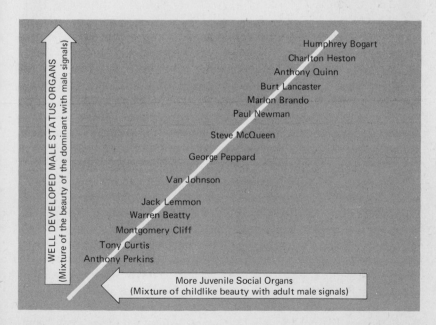

A hierarchy of actors past and present (in their prime) which the Western world considers as being handsome. All have well balanced features and none are at the extremes of "superdominant" (a repugnant villain-tough) or a "subordinate" (Casper Milquetoast). They do, however, spread along a spectrum of mixtures between two types of appeal to women. Women who, most of all, need someone to lean on will favor those further upslope, while women who, most of all, need to "care for" will have their preferences further downslope.

up," to get rewards in sharing spouses' status and having someone to complement or add to their own stature, will be attracted to the larger, more angular — in effect (excluding the copulatory lures) more masculine women. This is a somewhat simplistic view, of course, as first appearances are only one element in courtship.

Courtship gestures and paraphernalia among animals are similar to the ones used in threat (that was why gaudy bird feathers were once thought of as just sexual lures). There is even an almost inherent selection pressure for this combination. A female who picks a male from the upper end of the hierarchy scale could be expected, statistically, to leave more offspring than had she picked a male from the lower end: status has traditionally been associated with privileged access to limited commodities — health, food, shelter, etc. The relationship is more obscure in the other direction — a male choosing a female of high status — but it is still there. Here, direct sexual (copulatory) attractions play a major role, but they are also enmeshed with the status component. Who at the time could have approached the status of the World War II sailor who had dated Betty Grable?

One's spouse or date is not an insignificant part of one's own status. Why is it that the teenager has trouble asking for his first date, or a fairly experienced fellow fears asking a beautiful girl for a date (palms perspiring, throat dry)? Is it because he is intimidated by her rather than because he is overcome with anticipation of copulation?

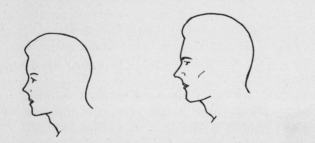

A spectrum of male beauty from moderately neotenic (left) to a craggy dominant (right). All might be considered handsome by the use of two different values — love of respected dominant and love for childlike subordinate. All are of the same age. Notice how much more prominent the features are on the man at the right — eyebrows, nose, chin, cheekbones, forehead exposure, etc. However, the eyes and lips are much tighter. Some women prefer to mother a more boyish man and others wish to be protected by a more rugged-featured, coarse dominant.

A spectrum of female beauty comparable to the one for males. The one on the left has more childlike features — small chin, small upturned nose, rounded forehead, large lips, eyes and eyelashes. To the right, elements of masculinity creep in — strong cheekbones and chin, high forehead, prominent nose, thinner eyes and mouth. All may be beautiful, but in different ways — the variable is in their status signals. Some men may be intimidated by the one on the right and others may feel the one on the left too dependent.

What then is ugly? Ugliness in human physical features seems to be a factor of either distorted, overly exaggerated social organs (in either direction but, as it turns out, mainly at the upper end of the scale), or social organs disproportionately developed. Dominant noses are all right with dominant chins and foreheads, but a mixture makes one look peculiar — *the net signal is garbled.* Even if the signals are balanced, one can go to extremes, though — gargantuans with a ten-inch jaw span and heavy protruding brow aren't going to get many dates, nor will Casper Milquetoast.

Beauty may be in the eye of the beholder, but nature sets the guidelines — whether it is a prairie chicken choosing her cock on the display lek or a young man girl-watching on 54th Street.

Our organic heritage affects not only values about ourselves and other human beings, but about inanimate things and other species of organisms. We have neotenized several dog breeds (Pekingese, for example) to fulfill our unsatisfied brood-care feelings. And in several species, like bulldogs and giant Great Danes, we have selected for a more threatening signal. In so doing we have made use of human childlike and superdominant features. In the Pekingese there are a snoutless face with a rounded forehead, petite features, and small overall size — but big eyes. Bulldogs have undershot jaws, protruding canines, and broad chests. Great Danes are of extremely large size with deep voices.

We characterize the slit-eyed alligator as secretive and evil. Birds of prey (e.g., eagles) have become national emblems almost solely because of the determined, dominant look the super-orbital crest gives their eyes. Who would want an eagle emblem with quail eyes? We think of fish as being emotionless because of the "fish-eyed" look. (Many people who enjoy fishing wouldn't think of hunting creatures with more human-like modes of communication, say, oral and facial expression; fish communicate through olfaction and color change mainly, which are removed from human empathy.)

The lines of the female body — mainly her social organs — affect our aesthetic sense about automobiles, gazelles, Arabian horses, dogs, furniture, landscape contours, etc. Wasp-waisted sports cars with teardrop butt-shaped fenders have real sex appeal, especially to teenage boys. The trim legs, smoothly sloping hindquarters and long graceful necks of gazelles remind us of women. Some of the beauty of fleet horses also stems from their resemblance to human curves, both the trim limbs of women and the bulging massiveness of men. There is a lot of hidden love of the human body in equestrian admirers.

The trim waist and bulging breast of the greyhound and the femininely clipped poodle are not unrelated to the female form. And it doesn't take a sex-starved sailor to see women's lines in French and English furniture. Scrolling attracts the eye because it copies and repeats the curve of the hips, waist, hair tendrils and breast. Some scenery elicits the same response. Gunstocks, hot rods, racing boats, artistic pottery or abstract sculpture are often referred to as *sexy*; a Martian wouldn't notice the resemblance to a human female's lines, but his search-image is not so finely honed as ours.

We are also intrigued by mixed tints of blues and reds, the old primate skin-display colors. There is a little bit of food and sex in the sunset. Much of our common art values relate to the values regarding social organs: the feeling for line and color — values between darks and lights — round eye-like designs which grab and hold our own eyes — the power of vertical "height" lines as opposed to the inoffensiveness of horizontal lines — coarse and smooth textures — deep booming sounds and high-pitched ones — smooth melodies and sharp noises — musky odors and sweet flowery smells — gentle curves and sharp angles — the weakness of small size and the power of large. There is a lot of biology blended into, "Ah, my dear, how handsome you look tonight!"

10
THE PHALLIC THREAT: GIANT PENISES AND SIMILAR THREAT DEVICES

"Why with the functioning role unquestionably established should the functional role of the penis have been shrouded so successfully by 'phallic fallacy' concepts? This, indeed, is one of the great mysteries of biological science."
— Masters and Johnson, *Human Sexual Response*

No other anatomical structure shows the behavioral crosscurrents between sex and status more clearly than the genitalia. One might think that the primary copulatory organs would be used only in displays of copulatory attraction, when in fact they are intimately linked to the biological signals of social status. In these next two chapters we can look at how genitalia are used in social interactions and how these uses have, in turn, changed the appearances of the genitalia.

There is no aspect of human existence which is more emotionally loaded, carries more taboos, and dominates our mythology more than genitalia. Comparative ethology is rich with clues as to why this should be so.

A review of the general themes of mammalian hierarchies shows that sex membership is an important element, with mature males at the top of the scale. The characteristics of "maleness" that signal mature males' status are the main centers of his status communication, even to the point where, in several groups of mammals, females have evolved mimics of male genitalia for social ends. If a quick check for the qualitative signal of sex is important in status, one can see where qualitative signals can blur in quantitative ones. A signal of maleness which is larger or more conspicuous than those of most other males might easily be interpreted as more male — more dominant.

In some characters this principle carries directly across from qualitative to quantitative meaning with real worth. For example, if in a group of antelope the presence of horns signifies that the individual is a male (where females are hornless), by the size of the horns an antelope can tell how "male" his opponent is. There are many species where the horn size gradient among males does influence the outcome of fights — the larger horns giving more momentum to the thrust. In these cases a male seeing "horns" not only gets information as to sex, but also probably stature within that sex.

What area of the mammalian body would be more subject to being a source of direct information about sex than the primary sex organs — genitalia? It is in this area that a fundamental sexual difference obviously exists in all mammals. Unlike horns or fangs, one would think that genitalia are not weapons to be wielded in a status bout — but indeed they are. It is an easy progression, if one is equating male genitals with social position, to equate larger genitals with higher status. Male squirrel monkeys threaten each other with their erections in a display labeled a "penis duel."

In the ethological literature there is common reference to male hoofed animals getting penis erections as part of the intimidation ritual. It is seen in threats or fights between buck deer of almost all species, and is very common among antelope. Erection and threat occur together commonly in many of the monkeys. Understandably, it was once quite a puzzle for naturalists to see an erection in the context of anger; now we know it to be a general theme.

A colleague of mine recalls that, at the swimming hole in his boyhood days in the rural South, the nude swimmers were called either "bank walkers" or "quick divers" depending on their degree of puberty progression. The tiny penis of the prepuberty male undergoes a dramatic change in size as the pubic and upper lip fuzz begins to coarsen and darken. The bunched prepuce, which gives the prepuberty male's flaccid penis a miniature "coke-bottle" shape, stretches back around the expanding glans. Statues of warriors probably say something about the oft commented upon sexual attitudes of early Greek males: amid those bulging Charles Atlas muscles, showing under the massive breastplate, is a diminutive prepuberty penis.

Though the sexual clinicians, Masters and Johnson, tell us that the female's satisfaction is virtually independent of the man's penis size, males all over the world are concerned about it. It is not an overt part of our daily interactions, because we take great care to cover up and taboo our organs

The maturing human penis goes through several stages, marked especially by the onset of puberty. Before puberty it is a small "coke bottle" structure with the foreskin or prepuce gathered in a fold beyond the glans. As the penis grows the gathered foreskin disappears and the prepuce allows the tip of the glans to protrude beyond it. In conditions of extreme fright or cold the adult penis reverts to the prepuberty form.

so they are not as they once were — a usual part of the ancient social display of personal confrontation.

Yet genitals are still important social tools beneath all those draperies of civilization. Especially during that trying time of puberty, males compare and judge. A slow developer or one naturally unendowed may be marked for life psychologically in self-confidence or assertiveness — either by compensating by aggressive activity in other areas, as in the Napoleon complex in shorter men, or simply by receding socially. Self-doubts about sexual prowess go much deeper than male-female satisfaction; rather, they are tinged with that same squirrel monkey penile duel. There is a large male-male social component — that is, relative status.

But at the same time that we cover up our real genitals, we have consciously or unconsciously incorporated phallic symbolism into our social paraphernalia — canes, swagger sticks, dangling neckties, staffs, scepters, batons, maces, truncheons.

The combination of (1) the fact that the penile display is an important part of the intimidation display of other primates, and (2) the knowledge that penis size is important in many societies and subcultures today as a symbol of status, suggest that the penis had a significant role in human social organization and communication in the past. I believe this may be the solution to the problem posed by Masters and Johnson: "Why with the functioning role unquestionably established, should the functional role of the penis have been shrouded so successfully by 'phallic fallacy' concepts?"

If indeed we have such basic biological values relating to the role of the penis socially, one might suspect that there has been some selection feedback affecting its anatomy.

One of the most striking things about primate genitalia is their vivid color. Signal "hot spots" are usually demarcated by contrasting hues or bright colors. In African monkeys, the glans tends to be red and the scrotum blue. Sometimes the penile shaft is white. Male genital displays in the vervet monkeys have been referred to as the "red, white, and blue display." In most other groups it is a mixture of these colors, red from the scarlet of the red blood cells showing through the skin and blue (from the melanin pigment colors transformed by the epidermis), forming purples, persimmon, violets, lilacs, and pinks. Some have an eye-catching contrast derived from different intensities of melanin, whether almost completely absent or in deep concentration.

Our own genitals are more pigmented than the surrounding areas, markedly at puberty; but the kinship with our simian relatives can best be seen during erection. Masters and Johnson describe the "plateau phase" of erection as having a marked color change: "The male response is an increased purple cast to the coronal area of the penis." In contrast, male Alakaluf Indians in South America have deep blue genitals even in a flaccid state.

The anatomical specializations of the penis for social signaling are not limited to color. Morris brought attention to something which had received casual comments for some time: the human penis is much larger than it functionally needs to be to accomplish internal fertilization. In comparison to the rest of the apes, it is very thick compared with the pencil-like penis of, say, gorillas and chimps. Morris proposed that this giant organ was selected for because it stimulated the female clitoral area more than a slender simian rod would have, thereby giving more satisfaction to the female and further strengthening the pair-bond. This may be partially true, but I suspect the inordinate size of the male genitals is rather a result of selection pressures originating among males, because of its influence on social stature.

There are a number of pieces of evidence for this. The size of the normal flaccid penis can be reduced further by severe physiological and psychological changes, indicating that even in its non-erect state it is under some tonus by vasocongestion (constriction of the blood vessels). Male Miamin of New Guinea, and some tribes in South America, even wear artificial penis extensions to further increase their masculine appearance. Penis size varies among different human subgroups, as do other social organs. For example, some Negro groups maintain a flaccid penis size nearer the erect state than do Caucasians.

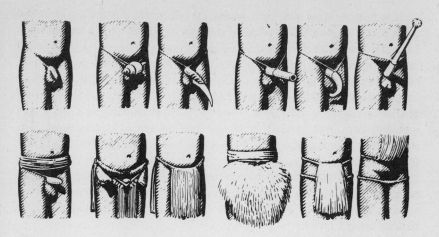

A variety of genital ornamentation found in different tribes throughout New Guinea.

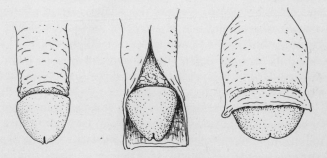

Various forms of penis alterations to affect status – as a weapon permanently un-sheathed. From left to right: circumcision as found in some Western cultures; South Sea Island Mangaia's superincision; and an Australian Aboriginal urethral split.

It was a tradition among the Australian aboriginals to split the penis down the urethral slit so that it ended up as a broad flat band – kind of like cutting a garden hose along a seam and flattening it out. One of the puberty rituals of the South Sea Islanders from Mangaia involves "super-incision" deep down the top of the penis so the foreskin hangs down in a drape, leaving the glans exposed. It used to be done with a sharpened flint, but now the leaders prefer straight razors. Like the widespread rite of circumcision, these leave the glans exposed so even a flaccid penis carries some status — as a weapon permanently unsheathed.

Unlike the rest of the primates, we have an erect posture which provides an increased exposure of the penis to public view, continually reminding other individuals of its size. This may explain why the giant penis is, among primates at least, uniquely human. Because of our unusual posture, it is impossible to approach another individual without performing to some degree a genital display (with both intimidation and sexual overtones). I would argue that the covering of the genitals is not so much to conceal a sexually attractive organ as it is to cover an organ that is intimidating, in addition to, or maybe because of, its sexual significance. I believe I am monitoring general sentiments correctly by saying that pictures of genitalia away from the excitement of the sex act are more offensive than pleasurable.

The common guinea pig which kids keep as a pet is a native South American rodent with an unusual genital display. The males can lower or withdraw their testes from within the abdominal cavity. In a threat display directed at other males, they raise their rears and flick the testes into the colored scrotum. Among some male macaques, when an individual is approached by a monkey quite his senior, the testicles may even retract temporarily through the inguinal canal, leaving an empty fold of skin where the large scrotum once was.

There are some indications that human erections of penis and testicles were also once a part of a threat display. In our era, the human erection and testicular swelling with threat has almost vanished in the adult male. Anger in babies, however, still produces these changes. Adults do tend to undergo penis and testes contraction, however, in times of fear or extreme subordination. We still have the potential for testicular enlargement; in the middle stages of sexual excitement human testes enlarge, sometimes doubling in size.

The males of many primate species choose comfort postures — ways of relaxing — which seem to display their genital equipment to its fullest. There is a remarkable similarity between the comfort postures chosen by human males and those baboons sitting out there on a bare anthill, or monkeys in tall shrubs. It is mildly verboten for a male to heist one leg up and place his foot on the chair though this is quite comfortable.

In *Body Language,* Julius Fast analyzes leg-crossing and its importance in social signaling, but doesn't refer to its origin. It is a genital cover-up — just opposite of the straddle-legged slouch posture. Leg-crossing is a symbolic gesture of hiding the naked self.

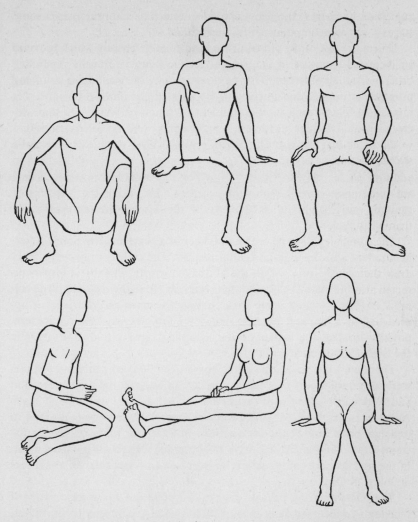

Human comfort postures — ways of relaxing — appear to differ between the sexes. Males tend to use the legs-apart postures more frequently than females. These same sexual differences are found in other primates who use a penis display as part of their status signal (after Hewes, 1957).

It is not difficult to imagine how, in a closed folk society (the context of much of our evolutionary history), subtle differences at puberty could play a role in later relationships. I don't mean to imply that girls had no say in who wasn't a desirable boy to date, but they were surely influenced a great deal by the stature a boy had among other boys. One has only to look at how frequently the team captain dates the pretty cheerleader, the homecoming queen, or some analogous pairing. Also, a woman plays a definite role in the man's self-image. Some of the psychoses men with small genitals have must derive from their fear of disappointing a woman — not necessarily in her orgasmic satisfaction, but just in her getting a man with smaller male organs that might be incorrectly interpreted as less masculine.

Males who brag about their sexual exploits or must continue to fly from "flower to flower" are not so much superendowed with sexual drive as they are deficient in masculine self-image; that is, deficient in status in their own estimation. Often these are small men, men with small genitals, men conspicuously lacking in other organs of status, or men with some major social handicap. The phallic threat has rebounded on them.

11
THE FEMALE LURE: RUMPS AND LEGS

A few years ago, I was hunting sheep alone on a steep hogback ridge in the Wrangell Mountains. The crest was only a sheep trail wide. To the west the ridge broke away into precipitous rimrocks, unmanageable without serious mountaineering gear, but to the east the steep talus swept downward into a smoothly carpeted basin. I could see 27 mountain sheep in all that basin, and there were some middle-aged and young rams not far below, oblivious to my presence. They were too exposed for a stalk so I waited. Some rams were feeding quietly and others were bedded down facing the valley floor. There was some social bantering and displacement from bedding sites as the afternoon wore on.

Then I saw the strangest sight. Two animals were copulating. Impossible — rutting season was four months away. I swung the spotting scope over on the two animals; the ewe was bending her back to allow the ram to penetrate. Then something definitely looked wrong, for a moment I didn't see it — but there it was. The ewe wasn't a ewe after all, but a young ram — both were rams.

It wasn't until a year later, after Valerius Geist's work on mountain sheep behavior had been published, that what I had seen that day took on meaning. The young subordinate ram was assuming the female's copulatory posture as a ritualized display of subordination; and by mounting him, the dominant ram relegated him to the status of a mere ewe. Here was status-sex in its most diagrammatic form.

Male sexual organs signal dominance. The evolution of sexual signals coming from the female are quite different. They have a large component of attraction, though man's subordination gestures and social organs of submission arise from female reproductive parts.

Throughout most vertebrates there is a general rule that the female has the *copulatory* lures well developed and the male the *threat* organs well developed. There are some exceptions to this; for example in some species the sexual roles are switched due to some mechanical quirk of polyandry or nest tending. Human beings, however, go along with the basic rule. Kathrin Perutz, in her analysis of beauty, stated it better than any anthropologist:

"Love traditionally follows a beautiful woman as it does a powerful or successful man . . . Men's fashions are used to announce his affluence and taste, not to attract sexual partners. Femininity is associated with curls and lashes, blushing cheeks, alabaster brows, and ruby lips, but masculinity is shown by action."

There is a beautiful story behind how females came by their copulatory attractants and what they are. We know them well, they are part of our daily aesthetics, but that's just it: they are so close to us that it is difficult to stand back and look at them objectively. Using principles from other organisms we can get some insight into our own emotions and values — how we are similar and different.

A sweep across the primates reveals two basic themes relating to sexual attractants. The first and most obvious concerns the primary genitalia and the area around them. The second is not so apparent: it relates to our mode of development of sexual behavior, the majority of which in primates stems from nursing. Let me take these up in detail, one at a time, though they are in fact related.

First, the female's vulva region is the "hot spot" of attraction in most mammals. It is often contrastingly colored or enlarged in heat and is a major odor-producing area. In addition to producing local odor, the glands also scent the urine. What an annoyance to have a pet cat in heat: she wants to dribble her urine all over the neighborhood, and if she can't get outside, then she does it all over the house. Many, if not most, ungulates and carnivores scent their urine in heat so that not only does the vulva region smell, but everywhere she has been recently tells the story "Here I am; come on if you want me." Judging from the behavior of males, the sight is attractive and so is the aroma.

I think the female's vulva, as the visual target area for copulatory attraction, has been responsible for the evolution of rump patches. The vulva colors or the colors around the vulva expand across the whole butt, carrying a stronger signal that *"there"* is the sexual end. Females of many species have a rump display which mainly functions as a sexual presentation. Among many species it has taken on a secondary meaning of submission, because it is used to remotivate an aggressor into a sexual mood.

The gesture of rump presentation can easily be modified into a submissive gesture, which transcends the original sexual differences. Males can then "present" their rears to other males in appeasement and females can "present" to other females. There is an entire gradient representing this evolutionary series among different mammals. The whole behavioral spectrum of rump patch evolution can best be seen in the primates. We now have more information about the behavior of this group than any other mammalian order. In some lemurs rump presentation is only made by females during their estrous peak. However, in the chimp, rump presentation is made by the female to males at any time, not necessarily when she is fertile, apparently as a signal of submission. The common langur uses the rump presentation as a submission signal in both sexes. Females commonly present to other females as well as to males. A further step in the evolution of this gesture is made in some groups by their using the rump presentation as a greeting or reassurance gesture, such as in the hamadryas baboon. Many greeting gestures arise out of submission signals, whereby both individuals show there is no hostility toward the other.

Among mammals with poor color vision, rump patches are light or cream colored. Apparently this color is an expansion outward onto the flanks of the white underbelly color that normally comes up near the anogenital area. Among primates, however, who have excellent color vision, the rump patch is often naked (except in some lemurs, where it is white), and usually a brilliant vermilion, purple, blue, or lilac. These rear swellings grow larger than usual in zoos and are familiar to every zoo-goer. They also enlarge in size when the female is in heat — a flashy visual advertisement of her state. It is interesting that our nearest living anthropoid relative, the chimp, has the best developed rump patch of almost any of the primate groups, and we do not — though we certainly must have had some gadget back there in the past.

We do, however, focus on that area as a center for sexual attraction. Reference to the buttocks is equivalent to copulation in our slang. And it is not surprising that special organs have evolved to complement that signal. The swollen buttocks of the European paleolithic carvings and the

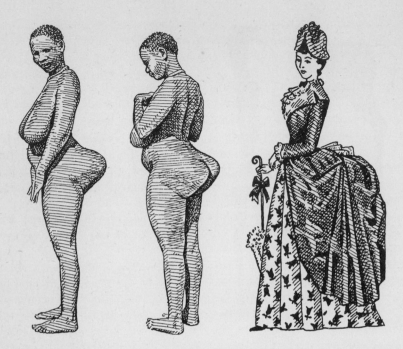

A female Bushman illustrating a posterior protrusion of the buttocks (steatopygia). The bustle of an earlier era in Western cultures seems to have served a similar function (after Wickler, 1967).

presence of steatopygia (excessive development of fat on the buttocks) among the Bushmen, Hottentots and South Andamanese suggest that greatly enlarged rears may have been the original human condition. In general we have shifted to a teardrop ideal, away from gigantic bulges toward a more sideways "broad" outline. The thread of this ancestry keeps returning in such forms as bustles.

Buttocks still play the major role in sexual attraction — even though the usual copulatory approach is forward, face to face. The groin area is erotic, but still not as much as the rear. The rear is the last thing to be disrobed in modesty; if it were just the vulva which had to be hidden it could be easily done, but someone with a bare bottom is considered nude. Rationally it appears peculiar — why should a structure that we sit on become an erotic zone to pinch and fondle? But the primate pattern tells the story:

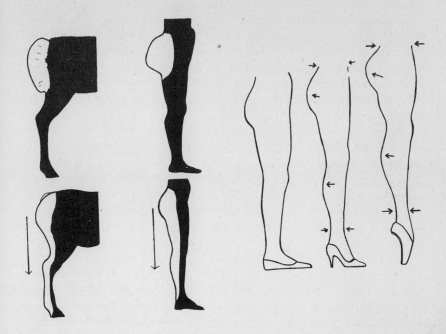

Rump patches of most animals are expansions of the female sexual signal out onto the rear. In some mountain sheep the rump patches fan out to cover the entire rump and pass down the posterior part of the legs. The human zone of sexual attraction also spreads out from the genitals to the buttocks to make the buttocks a sexy thing. Like the mountain sheep, it passes down the posterior part of the legs to include thighs, calves, and ankles. The white portion in the illustration of the human female's legs sets off the main erotic zone. The lines of the buttocks, thigh, calf and ankle have a native sexual stimulation, but this can be increased with high-heeled shoes; the curves are exaggerated when the heel is lifted. These curves are particularly apparent in a ballerina's toe stance.

it is the copulatory zone, where one approaches if he is male and what one presents if she is female.

Rump patches in other organisms aren't limited to buttocks, however, but flow down the back of the leg like dripping cream to reach the heel. This is especially true of the sheep. From the rear view the whole posterior is a sexual signal. So it is also with humans. The buttock region is the focus of sexual attraction, but the erotic zone flows down the back portion of the leg from the thighs' backside, the knees' backside, over the smooth lines of the calf, to the ankle.

Such a standard is scarcely ideal, of course, because it has no rational bearing on copulatory readiness, expertise, or anything else; we are just following the pattern of our ancestors, both the last generation and ten thousand generations ago. What a crazy animal we are! A woman with a pancake bottom just doesn't come across — like the man with a receding chin, she doesn't have the social paraphernalia we require; yet she may be ideal in every other respect.

The other area of sexual attraction is tied up with nursing. It is concerned with a transference of the maternal-child attraction to a sexual attraction between adults. Our attraction to members of the opposite sex has to come from someplace, and our sense of oral and genital satisfactions begins to be built in the early child-parent relationship. Though not a directly comparative work, one of the most stimulating discussions to be published on this subject recently was Terence Anthoney's work on the yellow baboon.

The baboon infant's main activity in its first few weeks is nursing, that is, sucking. A closely related gesture (and apparently a derived one) is lip smacking, which is a sucking smack in the absence of a nipple. Older infants sometimes do this toward nipples they are not allowed to nurse. When the young are small, nearby females lip-smack in their faces while grooming the mother, just to enable them to be close to the newborn. The mother also lip-smacks the genital area of the young. After she lip-smacks the penis for several seconds it immediately becomes erect. As the infant grows older it embraces rather than trying to nurse. If the female is in estrous she frequently presents her rump to him and lip-smacks over her shoulder. The infant mounts (an infant's grasping reflex), thrusts, and sometimes achieves intromission.

Lip-smacking is also associated with greeting. Oral grooming seems to have developed as a means for juveniles to remain near the females and gain some of the nursing security without being driven off when attempting to nurse. Instead, they lip-smack the hair. Later in life the lip-smack is used toward peers to show amity and to allow them to be near one another. All of these gestures (nursing, lip-smacking, erection, mounting, grooming, and greeting) become interconnected as part of the socio-sexual development of the young.

Why should we associate breasts — the mammary glands used to feed young children — with adult sex? There is no rational association unless one begins to understand the developmental aspects of general sexual stimulation. Nursing and the gestures derived from it contribute to the development of adult values and behavior, among them sexual stimulation.

Nursing and the gestures derived from it contribute to the development of adult values and behavior, among them sexual stimulation. We have some sort of a breast fixation. It is our first experience with lost security (a rubber nipple substitute in the breast vicinity seems to have the same effect). Like yellow baboons, boy babies get erections while nursing. Why have the erotic acts of cunnilingus and fellatio developed? Kissing and nuzzling are curious erotic gestures, yet they are all takeoffs on nipples and nursing.

Pink nipples, pink tongues, and pink penises all thrive on a common signal. Why is French or soul kissing regarded as an upper-story form of copulation, known to bring orgasm from either party? And why do men and women alike consider nipple-sucking an erotic form of precopulatory play? Because it's actually quasicopulatory. It's where they were first stimulated sexually. The Oedipus urges have a biological undertone. Through our parents we prepare ourselves for life competitively and sexually. In the prepuberty years, long before we learned of the strange goings-on after puberty, our nervous system was gearing up our values of physical love, about using genitals and lip-smacking our bed partners in years to come.

Though the origins may be dual, we cannot talk about just two separate entities, then, the breasts and buttocks, but the whole developmental syndromes that involve many parts of the body — noses, lips, tongues, nipples, penises, and so on. Nose to nose, nipple to nipple, tongue to tongue, and genital to genital, the wiring is all interconnected as two sexes stand together. Themes of lilac-pinkness, stemlike projections, and sucking begin to assume broader behavioral significance outside their original functions.

Interestingly enough, the wiring is such that it can easily get crosswired into homosexual activity, because the development of sexual reward is much the same in both sexes. It is the status — the hierarchy — component which plies the sexes into their sexual compartments, and it is here where the wiring of heterosexuality can easily be shorted.

We aren't baboons and don't go around sucking baby genitals, you'll say. But almost all the script is there and we do very similar things. By we, I mean the Western world. Some tribes in New Guinea have a tradition of the female lip-smacking the penis of the male baby. It is not foreign to human nature to make *direct* associations between infantile nursing and copulation.

We do some strange things in the heat of sex, or even better yet in the fantasies of early puberty, and if you stop to analyze them for their own inherent worth, they are as idiotic as elbow banging or heel rubbing for kicks. But immersed in the milieu of our primate background, our modes of love-making take on a special meaning.

Females have different selection pressures on their physiques than males, for a multitude of reasons. One of these is that a woman must carry a baby in her womb and be able to pass it through a portal in her pelvic girdle. So among most mammals the female's pelvis is quite differently constructed than the male's.

Among human beings, the wider birth opening in the female's pelvis necessitates a slightly wider pelvis than the male's. The erogenous character of this pelvic region is also reinforced by the proximity of the erogenous buttocks. The hips are much wider than they "need" to be. Many svelte-hipped women give birth with no more difficulty than some with wide hips.

Actually, hip width is not so simple a thing as it appears. It relates to both the width across to the upper bony flange (the ilium), the head of the upper thigh bone (the femur), and the fatty deposits which cover them. Women vary considerably in these measurements, and they are often disproportionate. For example, a woman with a narrow ilium width and wide femur span has a teardrop droop to her hips. One with a narrow femur span and wide ilia has an inverted triangle form with "shelf" hips. Both of these areas expand rapidly at puberty, making a gangly teenager into a true "broad." The buttocks undergo some swelling at puberty, complementing the expansion of the entire bottom area.

The breasts also blossom at puberty, along with the chest and shoulder width. However, women do not experience the dramatic shoulder and chest broadening seen in general among males at puberty.

The female waist, strikingly enough, undergoes no perceptible change in dimension at puberty. Actually, from the age of about six or seven the waist seems to stabilize. The major fat depots are away from the waist in most women, so that even though she is gaining weight, a woman's waist changes less than other areas like the thighs. Men, however, have a major fat depot in the "spare tire" area, and the waist is one of the first areas to change when fat is added.

12
THE FEMALE FIGURE: "BROAD WHERE A BROAD SHOULD BE BROAD"

The expected picture of the female figure in its post-puberty condition is an hourglass shape. There are those who find repugnant the idea that women's wasp-waist character has been produced (evolutionarily speaking) from their differences in attractiveness to men. That man's whims have influenced their appearance is to them degrading; but, indeed, this is a general biological principle which in human beings has worked both ways.

A man's first clue to female sexual readiness is the figure outline. A beanpole means prepuberty, a 30-24-30 is a signal of age eligibility and there is an immediate spark of attraction to a man as his eyes scan for more information. However, a super signal of 40-24-40 gets a super response. All else being equal, someone with those measurements would attract more glances than someone who was merely eligible.

What does the wasp-waist have to do with it? Nothing directly. It is like the stripe down a burro's back: it emphasizes contour. A tighter waist dramatizes the chest and thighs, which is what makes a 33-17-33 as attractive as a 40-24-40 — probably more so, because of the decreased intimidation of smaller size.

The muskox probably illustrates best the principle of *contour modification* as seen in women's wasp-waists. Though in muskoxen it has to do with an exaggeration of threat paraphernalia instead of sex lures, the same principle still holds. One of the main threat display zones of the muskox is the big shoulder hump, but the top of the rump is also displayed to some degree. Both are elements of a size-height display. To enhance the dark shoulder and butt humps, muskoxen have a white saddle which visually scallops out the middle or lumbar area of the back. And since most of their social conflicts occur in fall when snow covers the ground, the white "cosmetic" shading gives humps a more awesome height and massiveness.

It is revealing to compare the differences in men and women in the fat depot patterns immediately beneath the skin — the *subcutaneous depots,* as they are called. These especially include the upper thigh and particularly its lateral or side portions. Women talk about being "hippy" — meaning "fat" — a derogatory connotation in a society that puts emphasis on being youthful, mobile, trim, and athletic. Men, on the other hand, tend to accumulate excess fat in a roll running immediately over the crest of the ilium. Pants won't stay up on heavy-set men — belts are made to cinch over the hipbone, the ilium.

I believe that women's fat depot patterns have been selected to accent natural sex-attractant contours. Maybe that's why many men think skinny women never look very sexy. There is, of course, a lot of cultural specificity about the degree of obesity which is considered attractive. Cultures where food is accessible and plentiful generally tend to admire hard leanness, which indicates one has leisure for sporting activity. When food is scarce, however, obesity carries with it a signal of privilege. Right now obesity is out of fashion, but a *little* fat helps to round out bosoms and buttocks to accent curviness.

Girdles firm the bulges in the buttock-hip areas and make them look young, yet gently, naturally, rounded. Girdles give a signal of a *young* lass, not a flabby matron. The same is true for bras. Breasts begin rather high on the chest and are moderately firm, protruding slightly sideways, but with age, especially after being suckled, they begin to sag and droop. Bras tighten them up and pull them back high on the chest, and at the same time round them out into the conical shape of the youthful breast.

Both Bushmen and Hottentot maidens have breasts which are unusually high on the chest, actually up near the collarbone or clavicle. This general group is especially child-like in many features; some of the reasons for this will be discussed later.

There is a shift away from the posterior bustle "shelf" type of buttocks to the broad, flatter look, which has apparently taken place from the Paleolithic to the present. Interestingly enough, the Orientals generally have wide hips but flat bottoms; this is especially true of some American Indian groups. Athabascan girls are especially broad-hipped, but have virtually no buttocks at all. Many African groups have individuals with well-developed buttocks and thighs, resembling steatopygia. These probably represent some past interracial mixture, as the archaeolgical record reveals that the Bushmen-Hottentot (Capoid) group once dominated most of Africa and have been pinched into a relic area, replaced by more dominant groups. The shift from the posterior shelf to broad hips has probably been subtle, for both have been functionally responsive to the same phenomena.

Movements of the hip and butt area have had a considerable role in human erotica — because they are stylized versions of the copulatory thrust. In the mid-50's Elvis Presley got away with what would earlier have been regarded as obscene gestures of back-and-forth hip wiggling, and in more recent years rock dances concentrated on the hips and their movement. The Polynesians must be the epitome of hip-wigglers, for they have developed it into a fine art in dances and in lovemaking. Many societies around the world use it in some form or other in erotic dances. High heels, as Desmond Morris pointed out, exaggerate movements of the buttocks, because women dramatize their sensuality with their gait.

Gestures also play an important part in copulatory attractants in other species. Pussycats in heat have the habit of crouching on the floor with their genitals swung up in a "lordosis" back bend, tail up and aside, ready for a phantom entry. At the same time they softly tread in place, giving a soft purr-rrowl — it gets to be kind of disquieting when performed in the middle of the living room floor for several days straight. My point here is that *bumps and grinds* call attention visually to the main zone of attraction, thereby strengthening the signal.

Why else at a beauty contest do they parade the girls around the judges for their evaluation? Note in those instances how often the contours are outlined as much as possible with a bathing suit (they aren't going swimming) and *high heels*, which are in no other social context worn with bathing gear.

13
AUTOMIMICRY:
BIG BOOBS,
RUBY LIPS AND
PENDULOUS NOSES

In the dank morning heat of Malaya a little fly has already visited several flowers, but the next will be his last. Though it appears to be a flower in every way, he has in fact alighted on a praying mantis in disguise, and in a heartbeat's time the mantis has gobbled up the fly and folded its artificial petals out again to wait for another visitor. In Thailand a lantern fly is about to be pecked by an insectivorous bird, but at the last moment the fly jets away, not in the direction in which the bird was prepared to make its aerial correction — the damned thing flew away backwards! For on the rear it has artificial eyes, antennae, and proboscis, and in reality it was flying away headfirst.

These are examples of the evolutionary adaptations of mimicry, of looking like something which you are not. Zoologists for years have understood some of the principles of mimicry of other species or objects, as in the case of the mantis and flower, but there is another form of mimicry which is just beginning to emerge in our understanding of evolutionary patterns. It is quite different from the usual type of mimicry. The little lantern fly can serve as an introduction to this form, yet it still shows the similarity in principle to other forms of mimicry. The lantern fly, in fact, just mimicked himself, but backwards. The head looked like the tail and *vice versa.*

Mimicking parts of oneself or other members of one's own species has been referred to as *social automimicry*. There are four main kinds of automimicry: (1) parts are shifted artificially to other areas (as in the lantern fly, or in snakes that have tails that look like their heads); (2) a duplication elsewhere on the body of characters from other areas of the body, a convergence sometimes of two different characters on the same signal theme (like the peacock who displays many stylized "eyes" making himself more intimidating by possessing all those "stares"); (3) replication in the immediate vicinity, like "eyestripes" scattered around the real eyestripe; and (4) and (5), one age class, or sex mimicking another (juvenile rams have horns and body contours almost indistinguishable from those of females, so to dominant rams both are in the same status category of socially non-offensive).

Even the latest textbooks in evolutionary theory make little reference to the concept of *automimicry*. It is so new its implications are yet to be realized. For why mimic yourself when you are already you? But two heads are indeed often better than one. If an eye stripe or spot is intimidating, what then is the effect of two? Maybe not double, but perhaps more than one. If, say, tails are important communication organs, and a tipped tail carries a stronger signal of tail position, what about a tail with an adjacent ring in contrasting color, and another, and another, until there is a striped tail? That is how tail striping may have evolved. In essence, then, you can be just like yourself, only more so!

There are some cultural counterparts of automimicry that might make the concept more intelligible. Shaving is a form of automimicry, where we duplicate the signal from another age group — a more juvenile age class. Automobiles are an important status symbol, hence threat tools. As many have pointed out, autos are giant creatures, extensions of the driver — headlights as eyes and the grill a gaping jaw of shiny teeth. The coming of the dual headlight was hailed as an automobile salesman's windfall — it almost doubled the threat value. The most threatening type of car is the "cherry-dome V-8" — a police car. Many officers have taken to putting two red flasher lights on top, and several I have seen had two sirens. These are all forms of automimicry.

How does all this affect us? We don't look like flowers, nor have our heads and tails reversed, nor do we have dual headlights; but we do exhibit, along with many other primate groups, some excellent organic examples of automimicry.

One of the categories of automimicry I mentioned was the mimicry of one age class by another. Human beings have done this as much or more than any other organism. All forms of social neotony (an evolutionary regression into a more youthful appearance) fall into this category.

Men have the same taboo against striking a heavy blow that would harm a woman as they do against striking a child. This is reinforced by the general similarity between women and children in skin texture, hair distribution and texture, voice pitch, and many other body signals. A more neotenic (small and childlike) woman generally has a wider range of males with whom she can mate, and a larger and more masculine woman, fewer. The male attraction to the baby-face is just that, an attraction from one age-class extended to another.

This type of automimicry — at least the argument for it — is not difficult to picture. The other forms of automimicry are a little more difficult to portray and assess, but they are nonetheless there and are important elements in our everyday body signals.

Desmond Morris argued in *The Naked Ape* that breasts are buttock's mimics, and arose because we have shifted our mode of copulation from "aft" to "fore." Rather than mounting from behind in the ancestral way, we usually go about it face to face. He argued that we simply moved our sexual fetish of double rounded curves to the front; hence, the gigantic breasts which are much larger than their mammary function warrants. I agree with his general conclusion, but for somewhat different reasons. I think the preceding two chapters add some insight into the interrelation between breasts and buttocks. The latter are the primary erotic zones; the former are erotic because they are inextricably involved in the development of our copulatory behavior — nursing, sucking, and so on. The two organs converge behaviorally into a sexual image; by making them do so *physically*, automimicry has strengthened the signal of sexual attraction.

We are not alone among the primates in the convergence of breasts and buttocks, as both Desmond Morris and Wolfgang Wickler have pointed out. Another terrestrial primate, the Gelada baboon, has some otherwise unaccountable resemblances between the buttock and breast areas. The nipples are vermilion and lie adjacent to each other like the red labia; a pink hourglass skin borders this, which in turn is separated from the surrounding hair by a white pearling of a skin fold, amazingly like the rump patch pattern.

It wasn't until the braless "natural" look came into vogue that human males became generally aware of the resilient breast mobility accompanying body movement, and its attention-getting role, very similar to swinging hips and buttocks.

Morris has proposed that lips are female genital mimics. To some secondary degree, they may be, but first and foremost they are blood-flooded, exaggerated nursing organs. A woman with lipstick, rather than

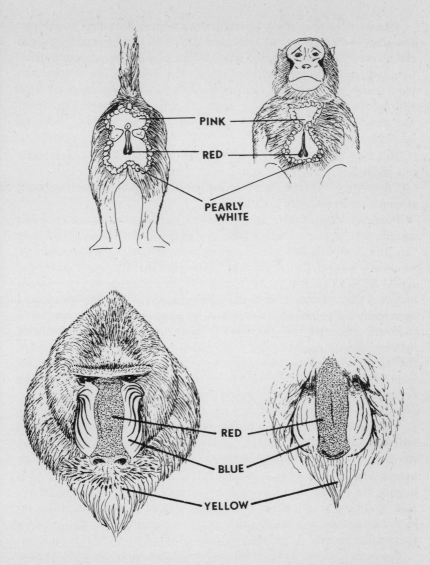

Breast and buttocks automimicry in the Gelada baboon. There is a pink-hourglass feature rimmed by white pearlings of skin. The vulva is bright red as are the nipples. The latter are close together, mimicking the outer lips of the vulva. In another form of automimicry in animals, the male mandrill uses a facial and genital display in threat, and there are remarkable physical similarities between these two structures. Humans also have different organs of automimicry, such as lips, which serve as important elements in our everyday body signals.

Children's lips are redder and proportionally larger than lips of adults. Large red lips on an adult are a mimic of "baby lips." Coloring the lips red with lipstick artificially strengthens this child-like signal (in the same way rouge mimics the youthful rosy cheek). Some women with small lips paint out past the lip to artifically enlarge its appearance. Some other cultures even tattoo supernormal sized lips over the mouth.

Some variations of human lip form are: (A) full lips; (B) thin lips; (C) lips showing "trim" of skin line; (D) expanded trim; (E) large thick lips (Zulu); (F) Cupid's-bow lips, more common among females than males; (G) New Zealand Maori scar trim ornamentation; (H) Ainu scar-tattoo lip exaggeration; (I) lip scar-tattoo from North Formosa; (J) waxed lips with red lipstick; (K) false contour constructed by putting lipstick on outer skin.

having a flashing vulva, has a child's distended nurser. And a tongue stuck through the lips in a "French or soul kiss" is at the same time a nipple and a penis. They have converged into a common pattern. Sticking one's tongue out at an opponent is intimidating, like a dilute penis display, but in early courtship it is a sexy gesture.

Those of us who gawk at *Playboy* foldouts or garage calendars are familiar with the degree of variation in female areolas, the pigmented area around the nipple. On some it is huge; on others it covers a small spot around the true nipple, and on others still it is distended as if the whole areola were nipple. I believe that the areola's function is a false nipple, an exaggeration of a real structure, a super-signal — not to children, but to adult males. Listen to Coon's description of Bushmen girls' breasts:

"The usual pubertal form of the feminine nipple, with its swollen areola, is exaggerated among Bushmen girls; to the extent that the nipples look like bright orange balls loosely attached to the breasts, a startling sexual attraction that wanes after the first baby has been suckled and weaned."

The mandrill has brilliantly colored genitals which have taken essentially the exact pattern and color combination as the mandrill snout, his primary fighting organ — the flaring, nostril-shaped prepuce and yellow scrotal goatee, the red penis shaft similar to the central red snout, and the scrotum and sides of the muzzle the same cobalt blue. The proboscis monkey is apparently one of the species which uses a penile display, but it also erects its male elongate snout in threat. Snouts and genitals have one important thing in common: they are both used in threat display. It is not unbelievable that these subtle duplications of visual threat patterns could have taken place in humans, with the glans being represented by the enlarged soft tip and the scrotum by the oval swollen alae.

Among many people the urethral slit is represented by a vertical nose-dimple. Curly thick eyebrow hair (similar to pubic hair in texture and color) is placed at a fortunate spot at the base of the nose. Perutz refers to plastic surgeons having noted penis-nose association in psychological feedback following "nose jobs". Whether the intimidating qualities of a large nose come from the long association with the mouth, or as a duplication of a sexual threat, or whatever, they do appear to exist. The nose changes size and shape with age — being a flattened little pug in the young and tending toward bulbousness and magenta color with age. The significance of the "flared nostrils" accompanying the frown (notice the difficulty in moving either nostrils or brows separately) and the villain's long, warty beak in cartoons are recognized by everyone as *offensive.*

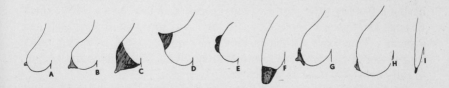

Nipple, areola, and breast forms differ according to individuals and races. Some examples are shown above: (A) medium breast with small areola and small nipple; (B) medium sized areola; (C) exceptionally large areola; (D) pert erect areola and nipple; (E) inverted nipple in high placed breast; (F) sac-like nipple and breast; (G) undercut areola with posterior constriction (Micronesia); (H) acute case of hypermastigdia; (I) deflated breast with pendulous nipple (Australia).

Not only does the vertically dimpled nose tip look suspiciously like a genital opening, the cleft chin seems to be an even greater exaggeration. This may sound a bit far-fetched, but one is at a loss for other more plausible alternatives. In an Italian poem by Uberti, its functional puzzle is well expressed:

> "I look at her white easy neck, so well
> From shoulders and from bosom lifted out;
> And at her round cleft chin, which beyond doubt
> No fancy in the world could have design'd."

But listen to the description of one of the young lady-killers in *The Godfather,* by Mario Puzo:

> "His face was that of a gross Cupid, the features even but bow shaped lips thickly sensual, the dimpled cleft chin in some curious way obscene."

Also, the parallel features of beard color and texture and pubic hair color and texture may not be fortuitous. They both are generally darker than scalp hair, coarser, and coil more, at least among Caucasians.

The graying patterns of human beards also fall into a kind of automimicry, which I referred to in the evolution of tail striping. The patches of gray radiate around the head in an alternating pattern, one on each side of the chin tip, another at the angles of the jaw, one above the ear on the temple, and still another at the forehead in the area of the "widow's peak," producing a swirl of variegated lights and darks.

Just as a mandrill has a theme of vermilion, cobalt blue, frosty gold, and black as its socio-sexual theme, we have hairy-lilacness running through human social organs. The organs of status are not easily separated from the organs of copulatory attractions; just the same as for behavior there are strong cross-currents between sex and status, love and aggression, attraction and repugnance.

PART FOUR: THE ORGANS OF SOCIAL REVEALMENT AND CONCEALMENT

14
THE OPEN
AND
CLOSED HEART

"Very few Victorians choose to question the virtues of such cryptic coloration; but there was that in Sarah's look which did. Though direct it was a timid look. Yet behind it lay a very modern phrase: come clean, Charles, come clean. . . Ernestina and her like behaved always as if exhibited in glass. . .They encouraged the mask, the safe distance. . ."
— Fowles, *The French Lieutenant's Woman*

In many ways we have the social strategy of an armadillo. Each of us walks around in his own individual shell, allowing only slender peeks at his inner softness. The tough crust protects us from our competitors in much the same way the armadillo's shell wards off enemies who would destroy those tender inner parts. We take our opaqueness so much for granted that the small patch of inner skin which we customarily bare to close associates becomes magnified in our own mind as self-disclosure. To know or share one's love with someone is to spread that patch of exposed "you" wider, but it remains at most a large crack.

How much we expose ourselves socially is metered by our experience, but the machinery and the parameters were given to us by our distant ancestors. Social strategies are a big part of the evolution of behavior. How one approached an unknown social situation has surely been one of the fundamental determinants of how many genes he contributed to following generations. By necessity, one must operate differently toward family members, peers, subordinates, neighbors, and enemies. Among the exceedingly complex characters of these relationships, perhaps the main element is how much of his inner self one discloses or conceals. One has a spectrum of aligned strategies stretching between personal transparency and complete obscurity.

The evolutionary selection for social *concealment* has been underplayed in the past and remains a fairly well hidden part of our self-view, but neither should we overlook the selection pressures for self-revealment. Opening up to others is the main element in the social bond in all its forms. The wonderful attraction of a child is his open, free expression of feelings. Anyone, by exposing himself to another, allows that person to touch and control, to some extent, his destiny. Mutual exposure establishes the need for trust, and at the same time, curiously, a threat — for if broken on one side the trust can immediately be broken on the other. A tattletale's story is immediately countered by "Oh, yeah, what about when you. . ." The forced intimacy of matrimony exposes the partners to a view through the shell's crack "for better or for worse." And divorce carries the social and personal stigma that the one "getting out" didn't like what he or she saw.

Though couched in human terms, the general principle of these social strategies seems to be a broad biological one, spanning the behavior of most animals. Communications biology has been built on the advantages of signal clarity. There is, however, another whole sphere of signal modification which we might call anti-communication: the signal is transmitted but is deliberately obscure. One gets the best insight into the character of this phenomenon by studying social paraphernalia. Though much social ornamentation strengthens the signals being transmitted, there is an equally large portion of ornamentation which obscures the signal or falsifies it in some way.

Because of its greater unknowns and hence potential for disadvantageous social experience, a signal stripped of direct personal involvement is often a more potent display than otherwise. Such a signal contains *less* information but enough to raise expectations. People often write letters to strangers, whom they plan to visit, for reasons of social strategy. But the absence of personal involvement makes them threats. Joe Blow walking in the door unheralded may be merely a derelict who has lost his way. What does a fox feel when, out of his normal rounds, he strikes a scentpost of another fox with the salty musk scent of urine still hanging fresh in the air? I can imagine it is akin to that formal letter of introduction, or the glance at an engraved calling card. The flame of self-doubt burns higher on a lean mixture of little information and lots of imagination.

Some animal species are very self-revealing, others self-concealing. In many species of animals, such as bears and foxes, only the basic elements of mood are transmitted. These animals are rather asocial individuals which spend little time with members of their own species in the wild and the strategy of self-concealment has frequent rewards. The wolf and the mountain sheep are, on the other hand, quite social species and have little to be gained by being too socially obscure.

The gestures of an animal meeting a stranger of his kind are cautious. He does not quickly communicate his feelings openly and may even *displace* them in an unrelated gesture, such as eating. Most initial social displays are not offered to provide the optimal amount of information, but rather to provide a mixture of clear information — to the displayer's benefit — and obscure signals. It is irrelevant that the latter may not be beneficial to him.

Social ambiguity, achieved through such organs as moustaches and manes, seems to be used in five situations where: (1) Life styles preclude an intimate knowledge of one's neighbors. (2) Tradition or historical context is such that an acquaintance with one's peers isn't well developed. (3) Low density of population prevents intimate and prolonged personal contact.   (4) Social structure does not tie individuals to herds of well-known associates.   And (5), a rather special case, the population becomes so artificially dense that one has to cut off signal transmission to function.

Many small predators fall into these categories.   For example, a fox's or badger's given life style is solitary hunting.   More often than not the signs of one's neighbors' presence are encountered often, but actual contact is infrequent (which in part results in No. 3).   Because of their mode of life, such animals' densities are seldom high in comparison to, say, herbivores.

Wild sheep and many primate groups, on the other hand, reject social ambiguity.   One grows up in a herd or band knowing everyone around, and there are usually a number of members always nearby.   These groups usually carry badges of rank and the status of each is recognized, if not personally, at least by his rank paraphernalia.   In a social situation where there is almost continuous contact, communication clarity is selected for. Without clear information one would be in a constant state of attempting to interpret his social state and never have any time for living.

Many authors have referred to the present human trauma as a disintegration of our earlier band or tribal social structure as our numbers and mobility have increased.   We have the evolutionary background of a sheep and its concomitant social transparency, yet we are becoming more like foxes in our brief, shallow contacts with continuously passing strangers. So, in contrast with our position in the tribe, where we slid along the concealment-revealment scale only to a slight degree, now we swing back and forth violently.   We may also settle on single strategies which are inappropriate much of the time — like becoming foxes and never revealing ourselves at all to our spouses, friends, and children.   Violent swings result in spasmodic social bonds, and an inflexible stance results in flimsy ones.

Some advise us to "let it all hang out" and become completely transparent (mostly in reaction to parents who were "foxes").   The possibilities are interesting, but I doubt personally if we can pull it off.   It takes too much courage.   We are foxy for reasons.   Taking off one's social shell means complete exposure to being hurt.   Keeping bad thoughts about associates concealed is what keeps us functioning.   If our souls were complete windows, relationships might be far more difficult to achieve.   Most of us can look forward only to fishtailing around somewhere in the middle of the spectrum.

Situation (5) could be called the "downtown effect," where the intensity of new social contacts is exaggerated so far beyond what our evolutionary history has modeled us to cope with that we cut off most of our signal transmission. One sees this in a zoo or animal research enclosure where densities are built up unusually high; individuals will try to ignore others by hiding in corners or brushing past without acknowledgment. This behavior eventually feeds back into the evolution of the design of social organs.

In addition to those five situations where social ambiguity seems to be used most, another deserves separate treatment. Generally, if one is well up the social scale, one can afford to become *aloof*. By giving a signal of unconcern and independence, the transmitter communicates that there is no doubt that he or she is the dominant. Aloofness is symbolized among human beings by drooping upper lids, tight lips, a protruding jaw and a raised head (snobbishness).

Someone with a subordinate frame of mind cannot chance either an overt threat posture nor aloofness, but must protect himself by clear signals of "no offense." Among human beings, social nervous tension (feelings of insecure social state, we might say) produces exaggerated motions, louder and more talking, and usually more social exposure. There is a tendency in us to equate twitchy, flexible mouths or eyes, the mobility of which facilitates communication, with weakness. Puppies are open and expressive, old dogs sober and aloof. Adults in the presence of children tend to be more serious (unless actually *playing* with them) than they are among still older adults or among peers. This is a common behavioral trait among many animals — subordination tends to result in more open communication.

Children reared in homes with lots of love and a modicum of permissiveness are much more open than adults. Interestingly enough, greater openness is also a characteristic of absolutely rock-bottom social classes. The essence of the American Negro's "soul" may derive partially from the once childlike status values in the rural South. So whether you are roaming the woodlands with bushy tail or waiting to catch the 5:10 p.m. train to Westchester, you must make decisions about social strategies of revealment and concealment. If you are as opaque as you can be, you may avoid trouble and gain some privileges, but then again you may miss some important information or a potential friend. If you "let it all hang out" you may gain closer relationships or, since closeness involves exclusivity, at least more acquaintances, but if you really tell all, it may catch up with you. "We really don't want Randolph for a new director — he told me himself that he cheats on his income tax and married Marge mainly for her social position." At one extreme you would never make friends, and at the other, you stand to alienate them all by being so truthful.

Seldom, if ever, do we approach these extreme strategies, but we feel their effects on a fairly gross level. The sentiments that we refer to as *respect* and *friendship* can be thought of as euphemisms for the polarities of *dominance* recognition and *submission* for the sake of alliance. They come across primarily as self-concealment and self-revealment.

High respect and friendship often seem mutually exclusive. One usually numbers *true* friends only among his social peers. A radical change in social state that gives one of the pair a disproportionate control over the other's future inherently changes the base of the friendship. Many of one's closest bonds are formed in school years among classmen. At that time upperclassmen, lowerclassmen, teachers, and administrators are all "other." One is allied with peers because of a common plight.

People who aspire to high leadership roles are almost inevitably social foxes; though the mannerisms of social facilitation are there and well oiled, the lid is down tight. What an epitome of social ambiguity the smooth politician is! He can survive an hour-long major TV network interview, with pointed questions coming at the rate of one a minute, and never give any real answers, yet leave us all satisfied that he has said something. What he has carefully shunned is self-revealment.

We are all born with certain limitations in our social strategy because of the limitations (or facilitations) of our social organs. Someone born with a tight-lidded eye, bushy brows, and pencil-thin lips is not allowed physically or socially to be as transparent as someone born pop-eyed and big-mouthed.

One sometimes hears the accusation that a person is "hiding behind his beard." The hair around the mouth covers up the critical expression zones, giving the wearer a *mask* of stoicism. A moustache and bushy eyebrows do something similar, as do squint eyes. They decrease the likelihood of a submissive or "scared" face being recognized. When we talk about "saving face," we are really talking about concealing weakness, either on the face or in some other way to which the metaphor applies.

An obscure signal, therefore, sometimes insulates or buffers both ends of the status spectrum. In species that have evolved ritualized displays to establish hierarchical position, an individual has the opportunity to back down slightly and still not "lose face" with himself, and to conceal his status position (other than the fact that he is subordinate) from his competitor. At the same time, the dominant recognizes the most important immediate concern — a submission signal — and is reassured of his own dominance. Opaque signals coming from the dominant can also give status merely by being ambiguous. These forms of behavior, of course, result in accompanying anatomical changes.

In comparison to other organisms, human beings have evolved a fantastic freedom of communication, no doubt due, in biological terms, to our reliance on learned behavior and to our occupying an extremely flexible niche. Yet in any discussion of the flexibility of our communication we often forget that, more than any other creature, we have the ability to edit and modify (obscure or falsify, if you will) the transmission of our feelings. We may give one signal while feeling just the opposite.

Precision has been selected for in human communication to such an extent that it forms a striking chasm between us and other organisms. But communication precision is almost independent of the openness, the transparency of the communicators. High-fidelity communication does not necessarily mean *open* communication of our emotions. Precise communication means the ability to convey the ideas one *wishes* to convey, (which are almost invariably different from what is going on inside).

In other organisms, communication is by far less controllable. An ethologist watching a monkey is more likely to be reading signs of real emotional state than an observer at a cocktail party. Yet we haven't become masters of our own communication by a long shot. One feels a blush coming on and thinks, "If I could just stop it," yet the blush blooms forth all the redder if one tries to intervene.

Revealment and concealment superficially go in and out of vogue. During the 1950's the emphasis was on the "cool approach" — play your cards closely and don't show emotion. Remember Marlon Brando? Much of this changed in the 1960's. The *zeitgeist* shifted toward exposure — "Learn to live with your hangups by sharing them," "Rather forthright than uptight," and so on. On balance, it would seem better to err in the direction of too much exposure than too much concealment. The concept of modern psychiatry is behind such a strategy.

In any event, the evolution of our visage has been affected by these varying benefits of enclosures and disclosures. What we see in ourselves and our fellows is a product of the shifting strategies of the past. In the following chapters we will discuss two critical areas: the eyes and the mouth.

15 GOGGLES AND SHADES

"One morning I was in the tent with Lawrence when a young Bedouin was hauled in charged with having the evil eye...Lawrence ordered the offender to sit at the opposite side of the tent and look at him. Then for ten minutes he regarded him with a steady gaze, his steel-blue eyes seeming to bore a hole into the culprit's very soul. At the end of the ten minutes, Lawrence dismissed the Bedouin. The evil spell had been driven off!"

—Lowell Thomas, *With Lawrence in Arabia*

We customarily think of the eye as a signal receiver, but it has an equally important role as a signal transmitter. It is easy to edit and modify the spoken language, but the eye language is a true window to the soul, through which shine the real meaning of the other person's intentions and attitudes. For eye signals are to some degree autonomic or almost automatic and do not lend themselves to voluntary control.

Our daily lives are full of examples that illustrate how important eye signals are, and how difficult they are to manipulate voluntarily. Social confrontations (such as asking for a date) are more easily settled by phone than in person. We lose quite a lot on the phone in the subtle signals of varying emotion that can be perceived visually.

The uses of eyes in human behavior are complex and poorly understood: they are rather difficult to study because they are so close to our everyday experiences. Nevertheless, similar patterns can be found among other organisms through the help of comparative ethology.

The stare is undoubtedly a dominant theme. It is mildly threatening to hold the gaze of an associate. The social blink or fleeting glances away from the eye are used to moderate its effect. Someone who refuses to meet your gaze is being usually appeasing, but this interpretation varies somewhat between cultures and subcultures.

The lower-status animals of a social troupe often spend more time looking in the general direction of the *dominant* than he does in theirs. Daniel Freedman has referred to this fact as a *fearful watchfulness* on the part of the subordinate and a sort of *disdain* on the dominant's part. Freedman's experimental work with children showed a similar trend, as have ethnographic field studies. Sheinfield's work with street gangs on Chicago's West Side, for example, showed that the leader never looked at the lower status males; though subordinates watched the leader, neither they nor strangers dared stare into the eyes of the dominant males.

Your first introduction to eye-power was probably the childhood game of "stare-you-down." The rules are simple — only two could play, and you stared into the eyes of your opponent until one person lost by blinking or averting his gaze. It took more than the ability to withstand dry corneas to win; you had to steel yourself emotionally to receive his gaze and to deliver yours. The contest was similar in many ways to a power grip handshake contest. You were giving and receiving at the same time like two balanced forces — any slip in your giving meant an increase in his. It was as if his stare was doing something to you physically. Its effect was as real as a pinch or cut: it was the age-old drama of social confrontation.

We carry our eye values into our feelings about other species. Folklore gives snakes the mystic power to stare a bird out of a tree; and we call the two unblinking black beady dots on white dice "snake-eyes". The glaring stare of snakes arises from their lack of moveable eyelids; unlike other vertebrates, they can never blink. I suspect that much of our attitude toward the penetrating eyes of snakes arises, from our anthropomorphizing of their lack of a social blink. They transmit a signal of arrogance.

The eye's role as a signal transmitter originates from its function as a signal receiver. In order to gather information about an associate or opponent one must point the eyes toward him; consequently, he can read in your stare that you are acquiring information about him, perhaps for some precipitous act. Breaking off social communication by averting the gaze is recognized as avoidance, unlikely to be followed by action.

To stare or not to stare was, however, only the beginning of a long and complex theme in the evolution of eyes as signal transmitters. How do the non-sensory uses of eyes and their associated social organs function,

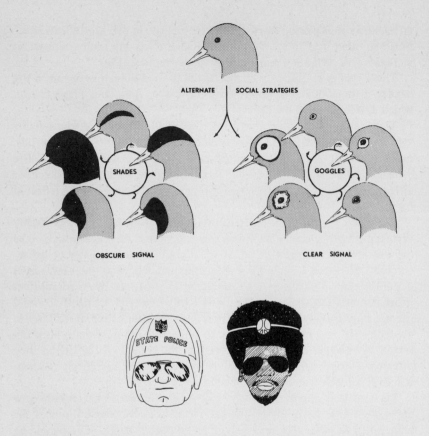

In animals and humans, there appear to be two main alternative social strategies – self-revealment and self-concealment. These basic strategies can be seen in the forms taken by eye ornamentation and in its social uses. There are a number of different forms, but they tend to cluster at two poles – those that exaggerate the eye, referred to as the "goggles effect," and paraphernalia that obscure the eye, which may be called the "shades effect."

Sunglasses, either silvered or stained, have a social effect. They obscure the optical signal being transmitted, allowing one to hide his weaknesses and transmit a steady, aloof image.

and how have they developed? These questions relate to the two basic poles of social strategy – whether one is an Arctic fox, wildebeest, Hottentot, or Sioux Indian. The two poles, as we have seen, are *self-revealment* and *self-concealment*. They accomplish much the same result, but they are different ways of getting there. One is appropriate in one life style or situation, the other in a completely different one. They are both strategies to increase social advantage and, ultimately, net reproduction.

These strategies show up in the social uses of human eyes and in the display paraphernalia of modified skin, bone, hair, and pigmentation which develop around the eye.

They take the form of what I have called the "goggle" effect and the "shade" effect. The goggle effect is a dramatization of the iris, sclera, lids, or surrounding features to contribute to an open social signal. The "shades" effect, on the other hand, is characterized by a concealed eye, or at least by an obscuring of its position or of the emotions being reflected by it.

Let's look first at some comparative aspects of the goggle effect. Many vertebrates have special anatomical features around their eyes which make the eye more striking. One of the most common is a brightly or lightly colored iris. From a comparison of different living vertebrates it looks as if the iris was originally dark to protect the retina, but in numerous lines it became more lightly pigmented or brightly colored. A brightly colored iris not only makes clear the direction and character of the stare, it is also used directly in an iris display. Both birds and mammals have been observed to contract their pupils (increasing the surface of the iris) as they threaten an opponent, and to dilate the iris when submitting. Human beings apparently use this same involuntary signal.

Eckhard Hess illustrated how people in a more submissive, attentive, or appeasing mood have dilated pupils. He showed two illustrations of the same girl, one with the pupils inked in to appear larger. The people he interviewed found the one with the enlarged pupils appeared more attractive, warm, and attentive. The fundamental role of iris changes is, of course, to regulate the amount of light hitting the retina, but it is also obviously that of a transmission device.

A very dark iris gives the impression of an infinitely dilated pupil, a warm attentive signal.

Light irises, because of their greater ability to dramatize pupil diameter, are often thought of as cold on a face with otherwise self-concealing features, but on a child they are angelic, dramatizing his openness.

The women's magazines (Vogue, Glamour, Redbook, etc.) more often than not choose models with light irises, probably because women see them as having *character* — as complex people capable of complex expression. But the girly magazines don't want character and involvement with their models; they usually choose brown-eyed pinups. As Perutz points out, "The girls look available, show what they've got and invite masturbation. They are no one's ideal."

Primate irises, like those of wolves, sheep, and cats, for the most part are not highly colorful. They are just light. The lightening can take several forms: light green, blue, and brownish tan. In some human beings there is a darkened border around the light iris interior, which adds a striking concentric edge-effect to the white background of the sclera. But when it comes to iris color we are bested by many other groups. Some, particularly birds and fish, have brilliantly colored irises — deep crimsons, lemon yellows, bright orange, or even pure white.

Other eye modifications besides iris color reveal the inner person. Humans are unique among primates in the degree of sclera, or eye-white, exposure. Though Jane Goodall does show some chimps with moderately exposed white scleras, most non-human animals are beady-eyed, with lids that hug the iris edge.

Why should human beings have such naked, bulging eyes? I believe the answer can be found in social uses. It is easy to tell almost exactly where a person with big, exposed scleras is looking, even though he may be on the other side of the room. One can tell if he is looking at your eye or your mouth — a tremendous feat when you realize it is done by calculating the position of two round dots on two round balls, of which you can see only a thin slice. Increased scleral exposure, according to this theory, not only increases the precision of the signal but also increases the breadth of communication. As in most increases in communication breadth, the potential here for self-revealment seems to be disproportionately distorted toward the submissive end of the spectrum. In much the same way that hairless upper lips and mouth areas bare of moustache express more weakness, large, exposed scleras mean sensitivity and attentiveness, or, more basically, submission.

This interpretation accounts for differences in eyes along sexual lines. Generally women have more exposed scleras than men; the most exposed are almost always in women. Cosmeticians are aware of the sclera's importance and so darken the immediately adjacent zones of the eyelid, further emphasizing this optical signal. Shading the surrounding area also adds to the same effect.

Spectacles or goggles tend to do the same thing. They provide more concentric rings around the ones that are there naturally. Witness the current fashion of "aviator" sunglasses for women. They can give a person an air of "directness" by exaggerating his or her gaze, especially if worn by someone of purportedly high stature. It is interesting to note how many men in esteemed positions — statesmen, dictators, business moguls, judges,

Humans have a number of optical ornamentation patterns. Most primates and other mammals have an unexposed sclera (a). For example, in some instances it is exposed and colored white around the iris (b). But the classic exposed white sclera is a human pattern (c). Sometimes the iris is lightly colored to dramatize the degree of pupil dilation (d). There are variants which have a dark border around the light iris (f), adding a considerable concentric effect to the direction of the stare. In some races (e) the scleral exposure has been reduced by folds of skin giving the eye a "slit" effect.

and experts of all sorts — choose heavy, dark-rimmed glasses.

But like any ornamentation which increases signal *clarity,* eyeglasses push the signal latitude in both directions. As well as adding to intimidation when used by the dominant, they also emphasize subordination when used by the subordinate. When worn by a solemn leader, eyeglasses add class and stature as he socks you with his stare. In the other direction, glasses earmark one as someone with an optical defect — something you expect on hoary judges or scholars, but not young fillies or the bully down the block. So when worn by a sissy (remember Superman in his Clark Kent disguise?) glasses aid in the portrayal of subordinate status. The 1960's "left-mod" movement, rejecting the establishment's covert optical display reverted in its taste to thin, wire-rimmed spectacles.

Among Caucasians (particularly in Iberia and North Africa) and Eastern Indians, there is a tendency toward an increased amount of melanin in the skin surrounding the eye. This natural pigment, like artificial eye shadow, gives the eye more latitude of expression, increasing the eye's impact. It seems to be more common among females, but does occur at times in men. Ancient Egyptians and modern Arabs use kohl sticks to further darken the area around the eye.

In the midst of deep emotional trauma, the lower lids of human eyes droop and the areas around the lids turn a purple-brown pastel, which exposes the sclera to its highest degree. A sagging lower lid gives the appearance of openness, misery, and sadness — a tight lower lid resignation and toughness. One can even see these differences in lid carriage among Goodall's chimp illustrations, and the corresponding personality differences.

We have produced sagging lower lids among some of our domestic animal strains, and we characterize their behavior anthropomorphically. The woeful-looking basset and bloodhounds with their open "eyes" never fail to elicit emotions of tenderness and compassion from the human observer.

One sees the goggle effect in many forms among other non-human vertebrates. White eye-rings are particularly common. In the spectacled eider these are exaggerated to the point of resembling true spectacles, rims and all. Among mammals, the Indian blackbuck has large eye-rings. The skin around the eyes in many bird species is enlarged and brightly colored (and among some it is erectile), expanding in some lines to form huge eye wattles.

The "shades" effect, on the other hand, is apparent in colored spectacles and silvered sunglasses. There is a gnawing discomfort in talking with someone who is wearing glasses that conceal the eyes. He is transmitting social signals — you know he is transmitting them, but they are obscure. It's kind of like trying to hold a discussion with someone using "double talk." One is ill at ease because the intonation may be a question but the sentence is unintelligible. The possibility exists that the wearer is looking at you with a direct icy stare or ignoring you completely.

It is an interesting study in display paraphernalia to watch a confrontation between demonstrators and police in a black ghetto. The police officer, with his large helmet and silvered lenses, stares across the barricade at the black tough, with his afro and big shades, who stares back — each with his emotional mask concealing a possible "shifty eye" that might reveal weakness.

Sunglasses, like a full beard over the lower face or a complete face mask, are in essence a super poker face — emotionally flat, and, as a consequence, intimidating. The lack of social information in them brings out all our uncertainties as to how to respond.

But we don't have to contrive a special gadget, like sunglasses, to see how the shades effect works among human beings. There are natural organic structures already in existence for that purpose. Heavy eyelid folds cover more of the eye and as a consequence obscure its signal much as wearing shades does. Behaviorally, the "squint" accomplishes the same thing. Note how the squint is complemented by a brows-down gesture. The "mongoloid fold" of the upper eyelid and the one possessed by the African Bushman (which is slightly different anatomically) seem to have arisen as social organs — a reversal back to the cloaked sclera, the hooded eye.

Physical anthropologists refer to these eyelid modifications as *epicanthic folds.* Many have tried, unsuccessfully, to correlate their racial occurrence with temperature, wind, light intensity, and other environmental variables. The tight lid, like the tight lip, carries with it a message of a closed soul, a stoic toughness shutting out free social exchange. Those with big, wide eyes can transform their open signal by a slit-eyed squint, but the full epicanthic folds are an almost fixed signal, like a permanently erected mane, crystallizing their social posture. Such eyes are limited in their ability to reveal weakness.

Orientals in general (also Bushmen and Hottentots) give an appearance of an emotionally "flat" face to the wide-eyed Westerner, who is used to giving and interpreting signals from scleral exposure and eyelid wrinkling. Here we can see an anatomical reversal to an earlier primate strategy, which we might equate with the "hooded eye" of the poker player — a non-revealing strategy. Basically, epicanthic folds hide the stare. Like an eye stripe, these folds allow one to look in the general direction of someone of the same species without revealing dominance or subdominance — i.e., to play social poker.

The heavy "billed" brow of our ancestors may in fact also have provided a form of the shades effect. A gorilla's protruding brow and dark, deepset eyes against his black skin make eye expressions difficult to observe, except at extremely close quarters. A gorilla could look at your naval at 20 yards and it would be impossible to tell he wasn't staring you in the eye.

The eyeshade of the poker player and the turned-down hat brim of the cowboy — or of the zoot-suiter of the 30's and 40's, still used to depict a Humphrey Bogart, tough-guy hood — shade the eye like giant brow ridges and produce the same "shades" effect.

Human eyelashes, unlike brow hair, have the obvious, functional role of protecting the tender membranes of the eye, yet they too are part of the communications repertoire. Long eyelashes, like large eyes, give the adult the appearance of being more juvenile or childlike. Eye and eyelashes of children are almost the same size as those of adults, while their other facial features (e.g., nose, mouth, chin) are considerably smaller. A woman's long artificial eyelashes therefore give her a more childlike appearance.

The blue color in the human iris is not due to a simple reduction of pigment, but to pigment reduction in specific areas. The iris has an inner (retinal) and outer (uveal) portion. When pigment is located only in the inner zone, the pattern of light reflection results in a "Tyndall-blue" phenomenon. Newborn human beings of all races (and many other

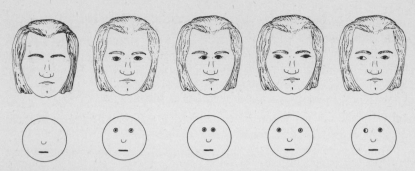

We place value on the relative distance eyes are apart. Compared to the eyeless figure on the left and those changed by putting in eyes the usual distance apart, then narrowing them and spreading them and finally slewing one to the side, the face with eyes wide apart gives a more "transparent" signal since it is easier to triangulate on his direction of stare. Narrowly spaced eyes are tending toward the image of a single eye.

mammals, for that matter) are born without pigment in the uveal portion, so they all have blue eyes. It is difficult to keep from speculating that adult blue eyes are neotenic expressions — an evolutionary regression to a more juvenile appearance. But blue eyes in adults are also associated with an expressive "cold stare," especially if they belong to a dominant who can hold a fixed gaze.

Eckhard Hess and his students have shown that blue-eyed people are capable of more iris dilation (larger and smaller pupils) with changing mood than are brown-eyed people. They have suggested that brown-eyed people, having pupils which are inconspicuous, traditionally depend more heavily than do blue-eyed people, on other body areas for communication subtleties (he used the hand gestures of Mediterraneans as an example).

In accordance with the shades effect, one eye has more threat value than two, possibly because there is a binocular character of a stare with two eyes. It is more difficult to tell if a single eye is looking directly at you or away in another direction. From this fact derives the terrifying aspect of the Cyclops, the one-eyed giant — or, to a lesser degree, of people with a patch over one eye or even a single "goggled" eye in the form of a monocle. Eyes spaced close together function almost the same way as a monocle — the exact direction and character of the stare is more difficult to triangulate. We associate widely spaced eyes with trustfulness and sincerity because it is so easy to interpret their signal. It is largely for that reason that widely spaced eyes, like large eyes, are valued for their beauty.

Human beings appear to see signals in the highlight of the eye. We use such expressions as bright eyes, sparkling eyes, glazed stare, deep pools, twinkling eyes, etc. The major signal of an increased highlight, sharpened by more profuse moist or "lacrimal" secretions, is sorrow or submission. A frequent reaction of someone showing deep emotion of a non-aggressive kind is to have "watery eyes," an involuntary phenomenon. Only a few cultivated actors can produce this artificially, and doubtless most of them do so by deeply involving themselves in the role.

The extreme expression of this condition is "weeping." Here the duct that drains the eye cannot drain rapidly enough to keep the tears from breaking the surface tension and spilling over the rim of the lower lid down onto the cheeks. There seems to be a smooth gradient from a slight lacrimal increase, which creates highlights on through to weeping. Weeping seems to be simply an exaggerated form of the earlier highlight display. Neither weeping nor its auditory counterpart, "crying," is learned.

The most evident example of eye signalling is the stare between potential male-female pairs. There are sexual connotations, but these overtones are derived from the stare as an aggressive signal:

> "Suddenly he lifted his clouded blue eyes. He was startled as well as she. He, too, recoiled a little. March felt the same sly, taunting, knowing spark leap out of his eyes, as he turned his head aside, and fell into her soul, as he had fallen from the dark eyes of the fox."
>
> – D. H. Lawrence, *The Fox*

A poetic expression of the spark of male-female eye contact is a *ping*. One can easily spot someone of the opposite sex who is attracted to him or her by that little flash:

> "Stranger yet he discovered how many girls and younger women were willing to ping-ping their eyes at him – even after they knew who he was. . ."
>
> – E. Hannibal, *Chocolate Days and Popsicle Weeks*

In the literature of comparative ethology there are numerous references to the cross-currents between aggression and courtship or copulation. The aggressive narrowing of the eyelids and slight protruding of the chin accompanying the Mae West stare – the "Why don'cha come up and see me sometime" invitation – are gross sexual signals. Like the soft bite, they are forms of aggression used in a different way, for sexual stimulation.

Recently behavioral experiments on humans have shown that the eye is an important smile releaser between an adult and a small child, strengthen-

Here is a battery of super-heroes and super-villains taken from comic books. They include: the Lone Ranger, the Phantom, Green Arrow, Green Lantern, Captain America, Spiderman, Flash, Captain Marvel, Batman and Robin and many others. Notice how commonly these supermen are given eye masks by cartoonists in their attempt to dramatize strength of character.

ing that bond. This love-gaze between baby and adult has been extended in the form of a love-gaze between adults of the opposite sex.

The cartoonist picks out and stylizes the critical visual elements of human expression to convey an emotion, at the same time deleting the extraneous parts. Probably no cartoon character illustrates the use of eyes as a signal transmitter better than Evil-Eye Fleegle in the comic strip "Li'l Abner" by Al Capp. Evil-Eye uses a "whammy" or even a "double whammy" to zap his opponents. A "whammy" is a form of stare in which the eyes get larger, with more and more concentric rings as they transmit. Little Orphan Annie, who has button spots for eyes, has a forever open, blank expression. On the other hand, the masks of the Lone Ranger, Batman, the Green Hornet, and all the other comic superheroes give the required aloofness of the "shades effect." The language of the eyes runs deep in our culture.

16
THE STIFF UPPER LIP AND THE MOUSTACHE

One little hair patch, the moustache, is a kind of threat device, but belongs in this discussion because of its special power to reveal and conceal.

When one thinks of the moustache of the pre-hirsute era, Clark Gable with his "pencil stripe" comes to mind, or Thomas E. Dewey, or maybe even Adolf Hitler. All these, and most that one sees on the street today, are measly bits compared to the full potential of the pendant, uncut moustaches of middle-aged males. Combined with a beard, they cloak the whole lower face in a mat of thick hair — a half mask or veil. One may catch a glimpse of the pink lower lip, but never of the upper lip.

What a strange ornament the moustache is! Explanations of it in the past have been notably feeble. Some have proposed that hairy upper lips evolved to keep the mouth warm, others have suggested that it may have provided a hair screen to keep insects away from the lips of primitive man.

An interesting twist in the history of moustaches in Western societies is their prevalence among the military — though beards have been generally verboten there. The British army at one time even prohibited its men from shaving the upper lip. In the early bloom of the Anabaptist movement (which later fled Europe and eventually migrated to the United States and Canada), moustaches were so commonly associated with militarism that church doctrine prohibited moustaches among the brethren. The Mennonites and Hutterites, subsects of Anabaptism, to this day do not allow hairy upper lips, though they wear full beards and have tradi-

The moustache is rare among vertebrates and even primates. However, there are some primate species which do have moustache-like hair growths. Pictured from left to right above are the Patas monkey, Allen's monkey, Imperial monkey, Orangutan, Man.

tionalized other elements of dress from the mid- to late 1800's. It is peculiar, on the surface, that the military, who normally try in every other way to erase individual variation among the ranks, should push the moustache custom — which, because of individual hair color variation and growth, adds individuality. It is also noteworthy that during the clean-shaven-upper-lip days of the 1950's, the strongest remaining outpost of the moustache was among the military top brass, who tended to be career soldiers.

Moustaches in the 1800's created some hardware and cosmetics that we wouldn't have without them. There were special mugs made with little bars across the rim, called "moustache lifters." And, of course, moustache wax for those who pulled the moustache to the side in a "Handlebar" effect. With the hair revival in the West, some old French firms are doing a booming business exporting moustache wax in a variety of colors.

A beautiful handlebar moustache is worn by the South American Imperial monkey, but other than that most primates have poorly developed ones. Some orangs and Patas monkeys have a wisp of hair on the upper lip just above each side of the mouth, reminding us of the cartoon version of the Mexican bandido. The Celebes ape has a light-colored try at a "walrus" style. Western man must have the best developed moustache of any primate. But why is it there?

Most of our personal communication is with the mouth. We are most familiar with its sounds, less so with its large visual element. Word meanings are emphasized with mouth positions and can be changed considerably by changes in the visual signal: "Smile when you say that, Buddy." There is also a lot of lip communication without words. Such signals are rather basic to social interaction — a flash of friendship, an opening for social intercourse, a tight-lipped seriousness, the purse of disbelief, the sneer, and so on through a rather complex repertoire.

Optimum strategy of how much information we should reveal or conceal varies with the situation and with social position. Women and children are generally more expressive than men, and more effeminate males are more expressive than those who would be thought of as "locker-room boys." Or is our understanding of femininity and masculinity merely defined by gestures of expressiveness — facial mobility, especially the eyes and mouth, and body movement? In order to promote the dominant image one must not reveal the weak, whining lip of the subordinate. One way is to reduce all emotion — to keep a straight face, a stiff upper lip.

Moustaches — that is, the untrimmed variety — fan sideways and down over the upper lip, blotting out virtually all visual communication by the mouth. They fan out around the edges of the mouth, hiding or at least buffering the signal value of cheek wrinkles and the position of the mouth's corner. An adult male with a full uncut beard and moustache truly wears a mask of stoicism. The stoic face is reversed among males in most societies. The constant "flat" signal transmission in the face of fear, anxiety, tension, or pain promotes an unswerving, persevering, secure image — the image of a high dominant, someone on top of it all.

It's less intimidating to talk to someone behind a screen or over the phone where you can't see his expressions and he can't see yours. We can edit our words better than we can our facial muscle movements. Children learn early to tell oral falsehoods, but mothers also learn to look them straight in the face and ask again, watching the facial patterns for the real story.

As in the case of hair-growth in general, it is ironic that the hippie-mod trends of the late 60's have become symbolized by moustaches (especially the "Fu Manchu" style) and beards, because the lifestyle these trends projected was frank, open, and intimate. But the moustache and beard were better symbols of the mid-1950's, when the lifestyle of social strategy was "play it cool". It may appear a rather arbitrary decision whether to wear a moustache or not, but there is a lot more behind the moustache than appears on the surface. It can be symbolic of either the subscription to or deviation from cultural norms. It changes social posture in a way that traces back to a time when men met with gnashing teeth and strange oaths. It is a reversal to another time, which we shall label "The Montana Face."

17 THE MONTANA FACE

"I was met unexpectedly by the Montana Face. What I had been expecting I do not clearly know; zest, I suppose, naivete, a ruddy and straightforward kind of vigor – perhaps even an honest brutality. What I found seemed at first glance, reticent, sullen, weary – full of self-sufficient stupidity; a little later it appeared simply inarticulate, with all the dumb pathos that cannot declare itself; A face developed not for sociability of feeling but for facing the weather. It had friendly things to say, to be sure, and it meant them, but it had no adequate physical expression for friendliness, and the muscles around the mouth and eyes were obviously unprepared to cope with the demand of any more complicated emotion."

– Leslie Fiedler, *Montana: or the End of Jean Jacques Rousseau.*

Thus a Jersey Jew in Marlboro Country confronts a social face modeled by the natural elements, as Leslie Fiedler so poetically expressed. Our social organs are affected not only by our genetic heritage, but also directly sculptured by our environment. The girl in the Maybelline eye-makeup ad would go blind in the noonday sun of the prairies, but she can let her scleras hang out over the candle-lit tables at Delmonico's.

A. B. Guthrie, Jr., poignantly describes the man from the "Big Sky Country":

"Squinting, he knew why the men he had seen wore the wrinkles of a squint. This country was too bright for the open eye. On all the miles of it the sun glittered. . . A man old but not old. Forty or thereabouts. Weatherworn was better. She imagined he kept a good part of himself unrevealed. . . ."

–Guthrie, *Arfive*

A similar sort of visage is produced at sea, for the sea is similar to the prairies in its ability to weather a man:

"Ericson was a big man, broad and tough; a man to depend on, a man to remember; about forty-two or -three, fair hair going grey, blue eyes as level as a foot rule, with wrinkles at the corners — a product of humor and twenty years' staring at a thousand horizons."
— Monsarrat, *The Cruel Sea*

Few outer organs function in only one way, and a change in one of their functions has repercussions among the others. Nowhere is this more dramatic than in the organs that are also used for social ends. Farmers and other outdoor workers appear to age faster than indoor workers, because the skin changes character in ways that we have come to associate with aging. Blood vessels become more superficial, skin texture more grainy and wrinkled, the follicle pits deeper, and the general tone darker.

If one lives a life exposed to the wind and sun, the "at rest" position of the eyelid becomes a wrinkled squint from continued protection against the elements. But this change carries with it a change in social signal. People accustomed to life continually in the outdoors appear tough to indoor people. Not having spent time required to attain the comfortable squint, we have to wear sunglasses or get headaches from the long exertion of contracted lid muscles.

Lip muscles also tighten against the elements, to keep the mouth closed and to pull the Caucasian's soft pink lip away from the sun. Indoor people take lip balm with them, because they are not tight-lipped from long practice. Our faces are gray-white from the shade, so we must also throw some sunburn lotion into the pack before an extended outing.

Inner and outer weather go together not only in affecting one's spirits of the day, but one's lasting social visage, for there is a large environmental component to social organs. Hair can be bleached blonder by the sun; one's skin and hair texture can be changed by being continually soiled. Size and shoulder breadth are alterable by exercise, as the Charles Atlas advertisements dramatize. Nutrition affects body size and hair luxuriance.

But this particular phenomenon is not limited to human beings. Deer raised on high mineral diets grow larger antlers than do deer raised on minerally deficient diets. Lions in excessively hot areas grow shorter manes than lions in cooler regions. Each population has evolved a potential for social organs depending on the interaction with its surroundings. Deer populations which have lived at low density on highly nutritious browse for millennia maintain their greater potential for developing large antlers even when moved to new habitats. Deer also depend on the wood and soil stain to darken their bony antlers. So, both in the evolution of social paraphernalia and its growth, they are not independent of their surrounding environment.

Our whole evolution as a species has been as an outdoor animal. Our indoor life is a fairly new thing. Our social organs evolved in concert with a plains life and exposure to the weather. The face of the Marlboro Man was the ancestral social face of the dominant. Children's and women's faces were more protected and hence could afford social plasticity. They were the individuals who often remained behind in the shelter when the men were called out to hunt and to war. Coping with noonday elements and scanning distant horizons produced the male's more inflexible social image.

With dominance goes the aloofness that does not reveal weakness or pain. One sees this sort of behavior among dominants of many other species. Whether dominant baboons or dominant dogs, they remain almost statue-like as the young climb over them. It is apparent in carriage and gait as well as in the muscle tone of the face. The posture is relaxed, confident, but still upright, and every gesture is smooth and forthright.

The carriage of the top dog on the block and the top gun in a Western movie are both very lofty. Remember how *Shane* carried himself — slow but deliberate. His sentences were short but direct, he never hesitated when decisions were to be made. John Wayne and Gary Cooper are our heroes because they are the old-time primate "yup" and "nope" men, and not only in their mannerisms. In their tone of voice, which never rises above nor sinks below fairly narrow limits, and especially in their faces — they are Fiedler's Montana faces, bigger than life. They are true grit for the locker-room boys.

Marlboro men can only remain that way in the outback, where new people are not encountered at every turn. Indoor people, cooped up in small enclosures, cannot remain aloof, but must dive into the gabbling, chattering and clucking — the social appeasement of a continual cocktail party, grooming to ease tensions and find social identity. Being strangers forever thrown together, we reveal ourselves like passengers who expect never to meet again. Escalation of emphasis makes us pop our eyes and wobble our mouths — exposing our inner emotions, so intense from all their interactions that they must be vented or die as peptic acids.

In our social dilemma, however, we still spread ourselves along the whole spectrum of the demands for openness and the advantages of concealment. A girl wants a husband who is strong and John-Wayne-like, yet at the same time, someone who is sensitive, open, and expressive. Men's cosmetics, like their cigarettes, are designed to make them feel like products of Marlboro country with pine scents and smells of new leather, in spite of the fact that they might abhor the personality described by Fiedler in the opening quote. We admire sincerity expressed by a freely mobile mouth, yet characterize our stage villains with wobbly, weak mouths.

Certain "villain" faces around Hollywood are saleable because they have features opposite to the Montana face. Their features are usually an odd combination of dominant brows, slit eyes with receding chins, and mobile mouths. And, of course, some men excel because they happened to be born with a particular arrangement of physical features resembling those of the old primate dominant (but delicately): movie actors, executives, bank presidents, politicians, and high administrators in all fields. Politically, of course, the Montana face is a shoo-in, especially when combined with an urbane lucidity — there one gets the best of the entire spectrum — a solid, dominant image to lean on and a sensitivity to the needs of the lower social strata. Politicians have been especially careful about their social faces — with the coming of TV and the decline of radio. The golden voices are losing out to the locker-room boys. Though a man's beliefs about economics, foreign policy, the environment, and population regulation are important in campaigns, we still choose our leaders from gut-level impressions of chins, cheeks, or steadiness of eye and carriage — as our ancestors have always done.

Few subjects are as delicate as skin deformities. One can't help but feel sorry for someone with a purple birthmark over his face, or a messy scar. These may not cause people direct discomfort. They do, however, alter strikingly the subtle social cues our eyes are so accustomed to evaluating. A missing nose, hypertrichosis or hypotrichosis, harelips and many other pathologies obviously affect our stature. That's why they are so emotionally loaded and are sometimes awkward to deal with, whichever end one is on.

It is fascinating to look at peoples around the world and see how their environment has influenced their social postures toward other people. Konrad Lorenz has commented on the geographic differences in traditions of self-revealment in Central Europe. These same differences exist in America as well, where one can more easily trace their possible origins. For example, there are two main centers of social secretiveness in the United States. One is the thinly settled West, particularly the North plains

— Nebraska, Montana, Wyoming, etc. — the type locality for the Montana face. The other area renowned for its self-concealed people is New England for traditionally similar reasons. These are our frontier relics, where the nascent intimacies of forced interdependence have been slow to crack the shell, remnants of early American character, of an inner sensitivity unrevealed.

At the conference table do we misinterpret signals, because physically the social organs are different? In some ways, like a cat trying to communicate with a dog, are the signals similar enough to be grossly recognizable, but the subtle modes of important information exchange so completely different that we have much the same kind of reaction as Fiedler's to the Montana face? The lesson of our body hot spots is that it may be an unwise man who interprets those people to be as different inside as their social organs and mannerisms are on the outside.

PART FIVE: THE SOCIAL ORGANS OF SENIORITY

18
UP AND DOWN
THE AGE SCALE

"For what is man?

First, a child, unable to support itself on its rubbery legs, befouled with its excrement, that howls and laughs by turns, cries for the moon but hushes when it gets its mother's teat; a sleeper, eater, guzzler, howler, laugher, idiot, and a chewer of its toe; a little tender thing all blubbered with its spit, a reacher into fires, a beloved fool.

After that, a boy, hoarse and loud before his companions, but afraid of the dark; will beat the weaker and avoid the stronger; worships strength and savagery, loves tales of war and murder, and violence done to others; joins gangs and hates to be alone; makes heroes out of soldiers, sailors, prizefighters, football players, cowboys, gunmen, and detectives; would rather die than not out-try and out-dare his companions, wants to beat them and always to win, shows his muscle and demands that it be felt, boasts of his victories and will never own defeat.

Then the youth: goes after girls, is foul behind their backs among the drugstore boys, hints at a hundred seductions, but gets pimples on his face; begins to think about his clothes, becomes a fop, greases his hair, smokes cigarettes with a dissipated air, reads novels, and writes poetry on the sly. He sees the world now as a pair of legs and breasts; he knows hate, love, and jealousy; he is cowardly and foolish, he cannot endure to be alone; he lives in a crowd, thinks with the crowd, is afraid to be marked off from his fellows by an eccentricity. He joins clubs and is afraid of ridicule; he is bored and unhappy and wretched most of the time. There is a great cavity in him, he is dull.

Then the man: he is busy, he is full of plans and reasons, he has work. He gets children, buys and sells small packets of everlasting earth, intrigues against his rivals, is exultant when he cheats them. He wastes his little three score years and ten in spendthrift and inglorious living; from his cradle to his grave he scarcely sees the sun or moon or stars; he is unconscious of the immortal sea and earth; he talks of the future and wastes it as it comes. If he is lucky, he saves money. At the end his fat purse buys him flunkies to carry him where his shanks no longer can; he consumes rich food and golden wine that his wretched stomach has no hunger for; his weary and lifeless eyes look out upon the scenery of strange lands for which in youth his heart was panting. Then the slow death, prolonged by costly doctors, and finally the graduate undertakers, the perfumed carrion, the suave ushers with palms outstretched to leftwards, the fast motor hearses, and the earth again."

Though he wouldn't lay claim to being an ethologist, Thomas Wolfe captured the essence of a male's life history in this passage from *You Can't Go Home Again.*

There is a fallacy, in the concept of the individual, which implies unity and permanence. We are not objects as much as processes — not the same today as we were a decade ago, nor even yesterday. The elements that were us a few years ago are mostly dispersed. But most importantly we change socially. Our appearance, tone of voice, carriage, quickness of movement, gait all affect (if not determine) the nature of our social interaction. These changes through time are not just simple artifacts of aging, but are products of our social evolution.

Among the vertebrates as a group, probably no other ingredient of social hierarchy is as important as age. With age there comes increasing experience, strength, and, most importantly, the psychological advantage of being first. You can see this best in herds of hoofed animals, which are led by an old cow or ewe. Even the young, strong males and females in their prime grew up with the image of the old girl as the dominant and carry this through long after they have become her physical superiors.

There are many similar analogies among human beings. No matter how high one rises socially, he will always be subordinate to his elementary school teachers. Fellows two or three years ahead of me in school, whom I knew very well, I still hold in sophomoric awe, though time has obliterated the actual years' difference between us. Second-year girls infrequently date first-year boys, even though their ages overlap so that some sophomore girls are actually younger than many freshmen. This age aspect of social hierarchy always makes for awkward relationships when a younger man is appointed boss or foremen on a construction job, or rises faster among professionals even though it may be widely acknowledged that he is the most capable.

According to the human survivorship curves and our knowledge of peak sexual interests, men logically should marry women slightly older than themselves. But because there is so much status tied up with courtship, it is seldom ever done. The relationships between age and status in our lives are not altogether rational.

Valerius Geist found that mountain sheep of certain age groups were more prone to wandering than others. The very young didn't wander much. It is to their advantage to remain near the protection and experience of older sheep. The ones who wandered most were the mature male sheep who occupied a subordinate place in the community. The more dominant males and most females remained tied to the traditional and familiar areas. The females, the very young, and the dominants had something to lose directly by moving — reproductive potential, their lives, and reproductive license, respectively. But the sexually mature, yet subordinate, males had little to lose and perhaps something to gain by stumbling into a new social situation.

My point is that different social strategies may be selected for during different parts of the ontogeny — the life span. A number of authors have commented on the tendency to have more derring-do or "begeisterung", as Lorenz calls it, during the late teens, and to become more conservative when one gains stature in the community.

As we go about our daily rounds we symbolically move up and down the age scale, depending on our situation. A young woman teacher in her late 20's gets up in the morning, speaks in medium to high tones with her husband, growls in low gutteral tones at the kids — "Get dressed or we'll be late again." At school she assumes an aloof air with her class and speaks in a medium-deep, well-metered and enunciated tone, with head, back, and shoulders erect. But at lunch with the girls her voice rises and her shoulders and hands are mobile as she relates an incident. She has to speak with the county superintendent, however, that afternoon, about an incident relating to student discipline. Her voice is high and soft, brows up, and shoulders slumped slightly forward in the chair.

We all do this, in some form or other, all the time. As children we grew accustomed (conditioned, if you will) to body movements and voice tones varying predictably along the spectrum of authority. As adults we still use those same avenues. We retreat into childhood (our major experience with life as a subordinate) every time something in our adult lives causes our status image to slip. Cecco Angiolieri da Siena said it in a sonnet about 700 years ago:

> "When I behold Becchina in a rage,
> Just like a little lad I trembling stand
> While master tells him to hold out his hand."

Likewise, we race ahead and become wizened patriarchs when our status is given a few boosts.

Looking at the same phenomenon in a different way from the psychodynamics of development, Eric Berne in *Games People Play* proposed:

> "That every individual has had parents (or substitute parents) and that he carries within him a set of ego states that reproduce the ego states of those parents (as he perceived them), and that these parental ego states can be activated under certain circumstances (exteropsychic functioning). Colloquially: "Everyone carries his parents around inside of him."
>
> That every individual was once younger than he is now, and that he carries within him fixated relics from earlier years which will be activated under certain circumstances (archaeopsychic functioning). Colloquially: "Everyone carries a little boy or girl around inside of him."

Psychiatrists rely heavily on where we place ourselves in the age spectrum in relation to others. It is the basis of *Transactional Analysis*. The concept of *regression* in animal behavior also relates, whether in the dilute gestures we have been discussing or in the more extreme pathologies, to a retreat into a more submissive — sometimes a more dependent — social posture.

Our flexibility along the scale of age and status signals is limited to a great extent by the fixed signals of our anatomy, which brings us to another quite different aspect of our ontogenetic social signals. Like many other mammals and especially many other primates, our social posture is reinforced by specific social organs of age.

Gorillas and baboons look to the degree of physical change as a measure of age, because indeed these are more socially important. "Time of puberty" is more socially meaningful than an arbitrary number like eleven years.

Actually, all societies still operate this way. Seldom do we know the age (in years) of many associates and people with whom we deal, but rather react to the organic signals of age. In man and some other species there is an entire, complex program of physical changes in one's social signals, with some parts occurring at different times, at different rates, and with different degrees of precision. There is a rapid change in the development of social organs at puberty (because of the critical change in reproductive status). Other than this, there appears to be a graded sequence throughout the rest of life.

Some of the changes occurring with age are certainly part of the senescence phenomenon. However, many of the changes classified as byproducts of age degeneration seem to be part of the graded changes in social paraphernalia. Balding, graying, voice changes, skin coarsening and

Shown is the continuum of human physical status signals expressed along the age gradient in humans — from puberty to old age. A number of signal combinations are involved, such as neck, nose, beard and eyebrow size, degree of balding, graying and wrinkling. It is difficult to show some others, such as pigmentation, oiliness and odor.

the like, rather than being simply deterioration symptoms, also seem to be important parts of the age-related status shifts, and there is a mechanism to select for these traits.

Among human beings and many other groups, status is not simply a product of fighting ability, nor is net reproductive performance based simply on one's early sexual vigor. Rather, it includes providing for family welfare, correct decision-making based on experience, and continuing to reproduce throughout one's later years. Perhaps in early societies, and surely today, elders have high positions not only because of their accumulated information and experience, but also as a result of longer periods to collect the paraphernalia that symbolize status, and hence privilege. Seniority systems and forms of gerontocracy probably stretch well back into our simian ancestry. Physical changes reinforce a social position that is based directly or indirectly on seniority. If this is so, having organic symbols of age past maturity could increase the total effect of status signalling, resulting in one's likelihood of maintaining a dominant position and an increase in lifespan. A longer life in turn would increase the likelihood of a greater genetic contribution to the next generation (more wives, greater possibility for remarriage in a monogamous situation, prolonged care for offspring and their offspring, and so forth).

In most early human cultures, social position must have had a fairly gross effect on differences in reproductive success. Though modern cultures have blurred these (and in some cases reversed them) it has not been long since they were very real.

Though our lives are a continuum of change, we can speak of the age spectrum in blocks of time which have some physical, physiological, and psychological identities. Presumably they were a product of different selection pressures acting during each period. I have separated the stages of life into six different categories. Admittedly, each could be further subdivided and there is a gradient across almost every limit. Rather than using numbers or names with complex connotations, I have used name-analogies from the life stages of other mammals to freshen our view. In each group I have suggested some of the selection pressures affecting behavior and social anatomy and have drawn a rather subjective curve of the degree of change in social paraphernalia. Just for discussion purposes, I also listed approximate ages in years when the transitions take place; these are somewhat culture- and environment-specific and should only be taken as general figures.

All this is very superficial, of course, but I do believe that as a species we do go through physical and behavioral changes which are adaptive for

Age Class	Age in Years	Changes in Social Paraphernalia	Adaptive Significance of Social Signals
Fawns			Above all must elicit protective response from parents—attention getters with organic appeal.
	6	High pitched voice, soft skin, baby fat, velum fuzz, lighter complexion, greaseless skin, big eyes, no scent glands	Social play—maturing of the social state; but must retain a social profile unoffensive to adults.
Kids			
	13	Male voices deepen, greasy skin, scent glands function, sprouting of body hair, shoulders and hips broaden, facial angles become more pronounced; female breasts enlarge.	Main association and values growing outside the family—formally enter the adult status hierarchy and courtship begins (sexual attractants blossoming).
Spike Bucks and Fillies			Peaking of physical strength—sexual attractants at full bloom, courtship at or just reaching peak, status—very important—but not a dominant.
	20		
Bucks and Does		Darkening of skin, body hair at peak, skin texture coarsens, retreat of scalp line, features sharpen.	Rise to social dominance—sexual attractants strong but declining — family as a status unit.

Age Class	Age in Years	Changes in Social Paraphernalia	Adaptive Significance of Social Signals

40

Bulls and Cows		Graying, balding, coarse skin, voice deeper, eye slit narrows, thin lipped.	Big Poo-Bah, group alliance outside family predominates, sexual attractants past peak—provider and conserver.

50

Mossbacks		White hair, very wrinkled skin, skin quite dark.	Sexual attractant faint—less of physical dominance, but maintains status on experience and accumulations—relies on seniority.

each general age class. The powdered bloom of light smooth skin is replaced by coarse hair and a greasy corncob complexion. The sideburns,
chin and corners of the mouth sprout fur, which eventually develops into
thin wispy cornsilk and later becomes a coarse mat of wire. Foreheads
become higher and greasier, necks thicker, shoulders broader, and appendages hairier.

Among all of these changes in our social organs, there are two evolutionary themes: (1) the incorporation of senescence features into earlier
age groups as symbols of the rank generally associated with seniority and
(2) the incorporation of youthful features into later age groups as attractant
devices, based on our attraction to children. These processes and their
interaction are the subjects of the following chapters.

19
HOARY HEADS
AND
WHITEWALLS

"The bankers were waiting for the cars to take them to luncheon or a conference, perhaps both. The junior men crowded the sidewalks, while the older men stayed inside the shelter of the lobby, hats in their hands, their heads, with their closely brushed hair, an array of shining helmets."

—Helen MacInnes, *The Salzburg Connection*

In Northeast Africa there is a species of baboons known as Hamadryas. Hans Kummer, who has studied them extensively, found that the young are born black and remain in that pelage for the first six months. While they are in this special fur, they have virtually free rein over the group; they can even climb on the snouts of grouchy old males and are generally beloved by all. But at their moult of around six months of age, they turn a dirty brown color, and it is as if a social door had slammed shut. They become social competitors. Similarly, a human grandfather's attitude towards a toddler who spills his best tobacco is mild and protective, but a pimpled adolescent who steals it can expect a much harsher reprimand. The human adolescent no longer carries the baby protection; like the brown baboon, he is entering the world of the adult.

Both male and female juvenile and adolescent Hamadryas baboons are brown. Females tend to lighten slightly with age but remain brown. Males on the other hand continue to lighten so that the old male Hamadryas baboons are almost pure white. Mature males are grizzled gray, and as they age the cheek whiskers lighten first, then the mantle, until finally the only brown remaining is a spot on the lower back, and in very old males even that disappears. The skin of the face and anogenital region remains contrastingly colored (vermilion in the East and gray in the West). The amount of hair-graying is highly correlated with rank. A quick glance gives one a ready estimate of his fellow's position in the age spectrum and hence his social rank.

George Schaller found a similar phenomenon among the mountain gorillas. He categorized mature males into two main social classes: blackbacks and silverbacks. Silverbacks, as the name implies, were so gray that from a distance their bodies appeared silver. Among the gorillas the silverbacks were dominant over blackbacks. The graying process follows a definite pattern. It begins in an area corresponding to the human sideburn. Schaller stated, "With advancing age the flanks, sides, neck, head, and abdomen lighten, until old animals are almost entirely gray, except for the arms which remain black." Like the caribou's white mane, the arms may remain contrastingly colored because of their part in the display arsenal. Female gorillas gray in a slightly different pattern, and like the baboons, tend to be generally browner than the males.

Graying occurs in many mammals besides primates, as most dog owners know. Silvering with age is also prominent in the European badger. That's the frosty hair used in shaving brushes and men's hat decorations.

We can speculate on how graying became connected up with signals of social status. It is in many species a deterioration which accompanies senility. That being so, in situations where either (1) age had definite status connotations, or (2) the graying produced an emphasis of contour which exaggerated the threat-display zones, patterns once senescent in character were pulled into an earlier part of the lifespan. Judging from the uses of graying among the primate species just discussed and its occurrence and location, we can conclude that both of these forces have been at work.

Chimps offer an interesting medium to study the evolution of status graying. Many primates have contrastingly colored snouts, beards, and cheek whiskers. Among some they are white. Some chimps have white hair on the snout from birth and others gray around the mouth with age. So one can witness the results of pressures (though probably not very potent) on a genetic shift of senescent graying back into earlier age groups.

Though we all pretty much know qualitatively the age sequence of graying and the patterns in which it occurs, let's map a little more precisely the various parameters of the graying process.

Like gorillas, chimps, and baboons, we have a characteristic graying pattern. This pattern can best be seen among males in the beard and side-

Humans do not gray randomly, but in a specific pattern. There are three main sites of graying: 1) the lateral tips of the chin; 2) the angle of the jaws; and 3) the temple area around the front and top of the ear. These can occur singly or in combination. People possessing all of these have an alternating varigated swirl of contrasting lines.

burn area. There are three major centers of graying, which vary somewhat in sequence and chronology. These are (1) the chin tip, (2) the angle of the jaw, and (3) the temple area of the sideburn, on a level with the top of the ear. One submodification, the most common one, is for the chin-tip white patch to be bifurcated into two patches, one at each corner of the beard, separated by a streak of beard color. This leaves an alternating variegated pattern. The moustache among virtually all races with well-developed whiskers is the last to gray. The dark (or colored, as it may be) patch between the white patches of the chin and jaw form a Fu-Manchu extension of the moustache color down onto the sides of the face, like a gigantic downturned mouth.

Some people gray mainly in one of the three zones, others in only two. And even among those who gray in all three, one may begin with the temple patch, another with the chin, and still another with the jaw angle patch. The temple and chin patches are most prominent and common, though I have seen one person with only the jaw-angle white patch. No matter what the pattern, these patches continue to expand until the entire beard is white, and eventually the moustache. Finally, the eyebrows whiten, almost always last.

Once the facial hair is far along in graying, the back, shoulder, and chest hair begins to gray. Leg and arm hair, as in the gorilla, usually remains colored, but often there is a tendency to fleck gray.

Why these particular patterns? As I mentioned earlier, chin graying and temple graying are rather typical ape (and, to some extent, general primate) patterns, presumably to emphasize the jaw (the weapon) and to ring the facial rim in white. Gibbons are the best example of the latter. The entire face is white-rimmed. But why the jaw-angle patch? I believe that if contrast is selected for there is a tendency to stripe one line upon another as in the striped tail of the ring-tailed lemur. Once a dark line is contrasted against light, it is easy to make the light color look even sharper by adding another dark line on its other side and so on. That jaw angle spot added to the temple and chin spots by giving contrast to the color in between, and at the same time artificially extended the moustache line across the cheek. This latter phenomenon can be seen in the horn contours of some antelope, being broadcast down upon the face by a black line passing through the eye, for example, in the oryx antelope and roan antelope.

The bifurcation of the chin white spot into two parts seems to be also a result of increased contrast. Having the colored line down the middle gives the white spots added zing. I've been talking about spots because this is how we customarily see them on trimmed beards. But on an untrimmed adult beard they are streamers, ribbons of white separated by contrasting ribbons of color.

In the illustration on pages 147-148, I consolidated the age change in body signals of women and men for simplicity's sake. But now we can see that as in the baboons and gorillas, human sexes have different patterns. Women's status-signalling, viewed by a mature male, changes little until they are in their 30's. Even the signs at puberty are not striking. The body changes at puberty are mainly the addition of copulatory lures — sexual attractants. The man at puberty, like the baboon, is switching over from social protective devices to threat paraphernalia, while the woman continues with much of the "fawn's" attractive protection signals. In the later thirties, her social posture begins to change as well as her social paraphernalia. Skin texture becomes coarse and scalp hair frosty along with the male, for she now has shifted her optimal social strategy away from attracting new sexual partners and immediate care for the family, into extra-familial relationships which reflect back on the family's welfare. Her struggle for stature becomes more intense, because her stature has a direct effect on her offspring's future.

Women probably more than men have borne the tragic social by-products of civilization. A man still carries out the ancient tribal duties, though they are given different names and guises. The male has financial, artistic, professional avenues of self-expression and means of excelling, under some guise of social worth. But the conveniences of the home and baby-sitters have eliminated the traditional fulltime "doe's" duties; she must go into the buck's world to find her social, cultural, or economic worth. This is, of course, what the Women's Liberation movement is basically about.

Later the trauma is even more severe; she has only a slight role in rearing her children, if she has children, and the energy devoted to PTA, the League of Women Voters, or socializing is a much more transparent means of marking time than the husband's. His devotion to getting the final draft of the blueprints for the new bowling alley finished has more apparent worth — though it is probably just a more elaborate time-marker in the final analysis. The post-doe's stature has gained her little and lost her much in the modern world; better she were the less serious, giddy flirt of earlier times, it seems, when things like dates and looks had real meaning. This is the world she retreats into with hair dyes, facelifts, makeup, and rigorous diets. The male does the same thing, but to a lesser degree, because his stature from gray hair and high scalpline is more direct. Yet it, too, is but a shadow of the social regard through which they must have been selected for, generations and generations ago.

The pre-World War II generation in Western societies is essentially beardless, because of cultural vagaries with which we're all familiar. One cannot judge age and stature in this group nearly so easily from the mouth and chin as was the case with our unshaven ancestors. The only gray left exposed is in the temple area, so one can classify "bulls" of that generation into three basic social classes based on graying patterns. In chronological succession these are: (1) salt and pepper, (2) whitewalls, and (3) silver crowns. We react to these three patterns differently, just as we do to the age-class breakdowns outlined earlier. It is easier for a buck to discuss one's illnesses, family life, etc., with a silver crown, for the latter are not his direct competitors and probably have quite a bit of savvy about life. Moreover, they are generally static socially.

I would wager that the bedside manner of older physicians and psychoanalysts could be improved considerably by bleaching their hair pure white. A salt-and-pepper is still up-and-coming; a whitewall is old enough to have made it to some extent.

We can look at our present and historical values about gray hair and see many biological status elements emerging. In Marie Antoinette's time, women wore three feet of hair piled high upon their heads. White wigs done in baroque styles became the fashion of the aristocracy and their associates. The status value of white wigs became traditionalized in positions where an authoritarian demeanor was desired, for example, in court, among parliamentarians, and in jurisprudence. White horsetail hair was the most desirable because the hair was coarse as well as a brilliant white, giving the judge a more masculine image than the fine tendrils of angora hair wigs desired at the time by socialites. Wigs were kept white with powder, and the natural hair as well was powdered white.

The discovery of the uses of hydrogen peroxide in 1867 allowed millions of people to become a beautiful baby blond, but it also allowed people to artificially add stature by graying their hair totally or in streaks or splashes. How many people who depend on their looks professionally have accentuated their sidewalls at the beautician's? Though the usual trend is to dye away gray, it was fashionable several years ago for women to bleach streaks in their hair. A young girl with her hair bleached very white transmits a complex signal. In a way she has the best of two extremes. She has the appeal of the yellow-white-gold human fawn, while at the same time she has the steel-gray-white of the dominant. But in another way this pure platinum has a harsh falseness to it, like the situation when the plastic surgeon overdoes the silicone insertion in breast reformation. The victim of a "supersignal" has a mixed blessing.

Sometimes people are born with a mosaic albinistic patch of skin which produces no pigment in the hair. A high frequency of these patches are near or include the "widow's peak" area. They are generally regarded as attractive and many similar patterns are produced artificially by cosmeticians. I believe our values regarding these white blazes are derived from the basic pattern of whitewalls and white patches elsewhere, as on the chin of a bearded man. Actually, there may have been mild selection pressures in the past to establish this middle streak to complement the whitewalls, for there are other graying patterns in other species in which a similar splotch occurs.

20
NEOTENY
AND
THE NAKED APE

"Her body is young and strong and he knows the smell of her breasts, which are like powdered infant flesh, but all the women turn to cordwood in the town."

—Norman Mailer, *The Naked and the Dead*

A friend of mine, who was balding prematurely, fell in love with a voluptuous little 14-year-old. She ended up marrying a smooth-cheeked army private who, ironically, was about the age of my friend, but looked younger than his years, somehow, more "appropriate." This chapter is about that love affair indirectly, and how it relates to some of our values about our changes in appearance with age.

Our lives from conception to death are a sweeping pattern of changes. This is more apparent in some other species, which are almost separate organisms at different stages of life. To us, who have a relatively determinate growth pattern, the woolly caterpillar winding himself in a cocoon and emerging later as a beautiful airy flier is a miracle. But, in fact, we are the exceptions to the rule, not him. Determinate growth patterns are rarer than indeterminate ones.

Each stage along the life spectrum has its own role and adaptations to the immediate circumstance. The newborn, the juvenile, the larva, the second instar, etc., have evolved as a result of relative success within that age group. One's total evolutionary "worth" represents a complex summation of compromises throughout the life span, and not just differences in adult performances alone. Each stage of our lives has its evolutionary pressures which sculpt our differences in physiology, anatomy, and behavior.

Once this idea is digested and becomes part of one's thinking, several different evolutionary strategies take on a clearer meaning. Though every major evolutionary change has reverberated through one's lifetime, in general there is a "tacking-on" of things in the later stages of life, in an almost additive fashion. In a less common pattern, in which changes throughout one's life are abbreviated by lopping off the later stages, the result is an adult who looks like a juvenile.

This phenomenon, referred to as neoteny, is usually rather extreme. For example, a tadpole may find life as a tadpole much better than a meta-

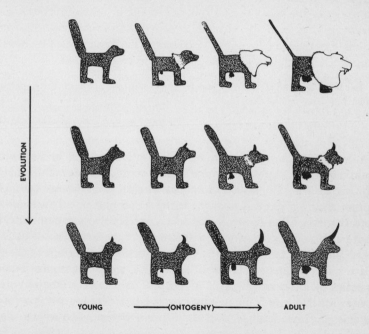

EVOLUTION

YOUNG ———(ONTOGENY)———→ ADULT

Here is a diagram of a hypothetical animal (a booger) to illustrate several different types of evolutionary change. Today they appear as the lower row. The young are small, horned and have no penis hair tuft; adults have large horns and a penis tuft. Earlier in their evolution (top row) the young had bushy tails and no penis tufts or manes while adults had skinny tails and large white manes, big brow ridges, penis tufts and big fangs. Among present day adult boogers (lower right) bushy tails are *neotenic* — having been brought from an earlier stage in the ontogeny into a later one. Manes, fangs and brow ridges have been lost, whereas horns have come into being. The penis tuft remains unchanged.

morphosed adult. Tadpoles who can reproduce, though juvenile in every other respect, sometimes replace adults in that population.

Neoteny is not limited to such gross levels as complete metamorphosis. Moreover, some aspects of an organism can be reverting to an earlier development pattern while others are still accelerating in novel directions; still other characters may be becoming vestigial. Some early evolutionists applied the concept of neoteny to some of the evolutionary changes which have occurred to man. The principle was applied a little too broadly, however, implying that essentially in every trait we represent young anthropoids.

Nonetheless, they did see something rather fundamental. In spite of the fact that lines of the genus *Homo* evolved extremely rapidly off and on throughout the late Pliocene and Pleistocene in novel directions, such as *increased* brain capacity, changes in body posture and their many ramifications — at the same time they also *regressed* in development by becoming more childlike in many characters — that is, more neotenic.

There are two main threads in the fabric of man's neoteny, which often intertangle or even coalesce. The first has to do with the balance of whether to explore (in its widest sense) or to be content with the known. If somebody must rely mostly on learned experience, then he must devote a considerable sum of energy in the early part of life to exploration. But there comes a point when one can best serve his own interests and perhaps those of others if he decreases his exploration and begins to trade off of what he has learned. We face this decision constantly in our everyday lives. Do you hire a very promising outsider to fill a position or promote a solid company man of known performance? Does a fisherman return to his favorite stretch of water where he knows there are some fish or does he look for an even better pool?

In a more primitive life the adult role necessitates a certain conservatism — a reliance on the tested. A child, because he is under parental protection, has little to lose from an exploratory failure and much to gain from a success. For the adult, the price of major change is potentially more severe.

Children must have been the great innovators of early man's lifestyle. It was the children who had the leisure and the social freedom to experiment with new ways of doing things: eating new foods, trying different ways of modifying weapons, playing with new pets from the wild, making noises and music from everyday things, and trying new modes of artistic expression. It is worth noting that the only recorded instance of the wheel in the New World, before white men came, was on a child's toy.

Somewhere along the line it became increasingly advantageous to continue the child's enthusiasm for new experiences on into adult life. Interest in new things is still much greater among the young, but even so, we
are considerably more flexible as adults than are any other organisms or
animals.

A lot has been said about this form of neoteny. Desmond Morris, in his
book *The Naked Ape,* emphasizes the creative-exploratory, childlike adult.
He relates this in particular to a "stimulus struggle": adults no longer
experience the stimulation from a struggle to survive and so extend the
satisfactions and life patterns of the "non-productive" child on into adult
behavior. His general implication is that this is a cultural phenomenon.
But a shift of this magnitude could not have occurred without some genetic
change.

For example, the desirability of having puppy-like behavior and appearance among adult dogs has resulted in a gross genetic change. We have
neotenized all dog breeds, some much more than others. Many dogs
(and cats) never really mature behaviorally, fulfilling to a degree the often-
heard comment, "If they would only remain puppies." Also, our neotenization through selective breeding has affected their anatomy. They retain
the high forehead and rounded contours and loose skin characters of little
puppies. Both Konrad Lorenz and Eibl-Eibesfeldt have pointed out how
much of our physical attraction to young animals is dependent on the
softness and rounded contours that bond us to our own offspring.

The second major kind of neoteny is a much newer concept, which
might be called *social neoteny.* Remember that the common signal of
appeasement is a more youthful or childlike behavior − decreased height,
higher pitched voice, etc. And from appeasement gestures are derived
gestures of friendship. A major difference in our social evolution is that
we are more prone to establish deep friendship alliances − we are more
social.

Where did the psychological machinery for our adult social behavior
come from? Perhaps our childhood behavior is extended into adulthood.
One of the fox's distant relatives, the wolf, illustrates how this can happen.

As wolf puppies mature, instead of leaving and going it alone, they stay
together as a family unit, using those same puppy signals which, in a way,
had preadapted them to a life as social adults. The selection for wolf
social behavior apparently arose from their ability to bring down much
larger prey when cooperating as a pack. Those litters who retained their
puppy sociability were able to last the winter better than those who dispersed and played the fox game. Within some litters, the more aggressive

young left, or were expurged, to hunt alone while the more dependent puppy-like ones stayed behind, aiding parents in the cooperative hunt. So, within the canids, or dog family, interdependence, cooperation, and friendship bonds (that is, *sociability*) seem to be neotentic traits. Likewise, this same prolongation of the sibling and early playmate attachment in man's adult life seems to account for the evolutionary road by which we developed our own social character.

Several anthropologists have pointed out that the human transition, before the Ice Age, from gathering to hunting played an important role in the development of our interdependence. As in the example of the wolf, hunting large game also required cooperation and interdependence within the human group.

At a time in our very distant past as nomadic gatherers with a steep social dominance but weak social bonding, male aggression was closely correlated with who reproduced. But in a very social hunting pack, cooperation is imperative and the group has the power to discriminate against an offensive individual. As it became necessary for male aggression to take on a more subtle expression, the inflexible intimidation organs were selected against — we became the *naked* ape.

A facile way to reduce the adult intimidation organs — the threat paraphernalia — was simply to revert to a more childlike visage. One can picture how this could have functioned, by watching people today. It appears easier for a moderate-to-small, clean-shaven, smooth-skinned, sweet-smelling, neatly-dressed man to make friends than it is for a heavy-browed, dirty, burly, hairy six-and-a-half footer.

The interdependence of the roving band of hunters out alone against the elements, chatting about intimacies by their campfires, began the shift away from the coarse image of the belligerent, rugged despot. This trend continued in the neolithic shift toward agriculture and herding. For unlike the hunting economy, where surplus was sporadic and perhaps infrequent, agriculture standardized surplus and institutionalized leisure. Its main effect on the social structure was in the diversification of labor.

Earlier there had been the hunting males and the homemaking females. Now more specialization was required. And, as in any pattern of class diversity, tasks varied in social value. So the old systems of hierarchy returned but in a quite different way. Instead of a baboon-like reliance on self and immediate associates for status identity, one's social worth was geared to his family and to his class identity — the owner class, the management class, the warrior class, the tiller class, etc.

The most obvious differences between these classes were in such things as the amount of brawn needed, time spent in the sun, and intimacy with the soil. And so these became the foundations for the social signals of class rank. A member of the upper class wore delicately woven finery symbolizing his distance from the soil: white collars, ruffles, gloves, and wide-brimmed hats. Skin whiteness symbolized his lack of necessity to stay out in the sun. But most of all, delicate features and fine bones showed that he did no heavy work — perhaps no work at all. Man's physical weakness was irrelevant to his high dominance, as he owned his own fighters and armies — and one achieved the highest stature not by brute strength but mainly by birthright.

I suspect that this range of physical and behavioral values became traditionalized so that it was part of the cross-class value system. A dark, burly lord gave the appearance of an intruder from a lower class, and a fair, gentle person in the fields appeared as a lord doing commoners' work.

The physical attributes of attractiveness and position in another era — meaty arms, darkened coarse skin, and a hairy body — became symbols of low stature, as they still are in many societies today. Fine bones, an ivory complexion, and soft smooth skin became "highbrow" badges. They are the differences between the Fairchilds and the Smiths.

Undoubtedly the most important social force in human neoteny is the penetration of status and status signals into courtship and sexual attraction. A number of complicated changes in the human mode of life have resulted in a greater and greater emphasis on one's mate as a part of his social state. One's status can be translated into *courtship potential.*

As age is an important element in one's courtship potential, the prime courtship age becomes more and more revered. Crows feet, gray streaks, and bald spots are not dreaded so much for their implications about on-rushing senility, but as signals of reduced courtship appeal. It isn't so much a matter of always wanting to switch mates: it is just that our un-naturally long courtship period, with swarms of potential partners, has conditioned us to respect that period as a source of status.

More juvenile-looking 35-year-old men receive courtship feelers from a wider spectrum of females than do older-looking men of the same age. All else being equal, this phenomenon would surely be an important selection pressure for social neoteny. And it is even greater for women. A thirty-five-year old woman who for some reason or other has gone unmated or desires to remate is usually more attractive to men if she looks much younger. Since there is a considerable genetic variation in "apparent age" among 35-year-old women, one might expect that, throughout recent history, those who looked younger would leave more offspring — hence selecting for younger-looking 35-year-old women.

Through these slightly different avenues we have become more socially neotenic and have brought much of the juvenile social organs into later stages of our lives. Among the more fascinating is our nakedness.

Desmond Morris' and Eibl-Eibesfeldt's theory that nakedness functioned to help cool during hunting activity would suggest that the male should be the less hairy sex. On the other hand, if hairness became socially undesirable, the selection against it would be greater among females. Their inoffensive nakedness would be more critical, so as not to put off the courting male. What misled Morris was the erroneous idea that hair or feather erection in threat evolved from cooling behavior patterns. Hair erection in threat and heat regulation do use the same motor patterns, or at least organs, but for entirely different purposes. When we examine the hair patterns (length, density, and color) of primates, there is a low correlation with thermoregulatory needs, but a high correlation with the animal's social behavior.

It would seem that nakedness is a neotenic character — a youthful characteristic (quite common among what biologists call *altricial* species, those born helpless and dependent). As such, nakedness projects appeasing qualities because of the absence of threat characters. Human nakedness was brought neotenically into the adult stage of development to create a more appealing package. "Baby skin" has become the epitome of female skin beauty.

The term *nakedness* gouges deep into our emotions. It connotes revealment, exposure, submission, because the reduction of our mat of hair — our threat paraphernalia — left us bare to the social eye. The lack of fixed threat devices meant to some degree a sort of fixed submission signal. Clothes, of course, can make for a neutral signal since they are not the intimidating curly hair, yet they conceal our social bareness. But for the most part, clothes replace hair as a social status signal. They are more covert and unlike our former hair are flexible. An executive doesn't have to display his full threat regalia on the weekend as he plays with his kids and putters over hobbies with his pals. He puts on clothes of similar pattern to those he wore as a teenager (or the ones his teenagers wear).

Nudity also has sexual connotations, but these are sometimes inseparable from hierarchy signals. Since, by biological tradition, a female's role in copulation is primarily submissive, her nakedness has a connotation of exposure or a receptive invitation. A male's nakedness on the other hand, is a more aggressive character, since it exposes the tools he uses in his aggressive role in copulation.

Current skin-flicks and girly-mags, that sell mainly on the basis of their sexual stimulation, may be using the wrong strategy in exposing pubic hairs as the ultimate in stimulation. That crotch triangle is one of the many exceptions to our neotenic pattern. Perhaps it is better that they airbrush them away along with the pimples, rough skin, and wisps of moustache hair on their models, to attain that "Lolita attraction" of bare baby bottoms displaced on mature girls.

Smooth skin texture appears to be another example of social neoteny. The other apes have extremely rough skin as adults, but fairly smooth skin when young. If one can judge our ancestral skin textures from a comparison with other living primates (as we earlier judged our hairiness) it looks as if we have become more babylike in skin texture. Only in old male humans is the skin particularly rough. There are major differences between the sexes, with some women maintaining very babylike complexions well past middle age.

Konrad Lorenz has emphasized the importance of rounded contours in the signal of childlikeness. Adults of all species generally have more angular features than their young. This is why we react so readily to young animals with a human "brood care" response: soft little ducklings and puppies are cuddly. The rounded forehead and cheeks of babies have been neotenized into some adult "babes." Many cute girls have that slightly rounded, protruding forehead and peachy cheeks that you could just pinch (the Early Debbie Reynolds syndrome). Eibl-Eibesfeldt has proposed that the bulging cheeks of children have evolved specifically as social organs acting as signalling devices.

I would extend this line of reasoning to its neotenic counterpart in some women: the pink cheek spot. We associate pink cheeks with youth and vigor. They have become a neotenic trait among adult women. Those women who do not come by it naturally often use pigments (rouges) to mimic their lost youth. Some even pinch their cheeks thoroughly before a social performance to enliven the pink spot.

Dimples occur more commonly among babies than adults and more commonly among girls than boys. That little indentation in those round protruding cheeks adds emphasis to the rounded contour in the same manner that a mole (or artificial beauty spot) on a delicate white skin makes the skin appear even whiter.

That girl in the Breck hair shampoo ad is a type-specimen neotenic. The soft, sliky, luxuriant hair of the beautician's ideal is the scalp hair of a prepuberty child.

The Maybelline girl has the eyes of a child, disproportionately large for the size of her face. The sclera is exposed from rim to rim and the irises are larger than most. The lashes are long and curl away from the eye just as they do in a child. Corrections for extreme myopia give a person a "beady-eyed" appearance. In the same way, extreme corrections for farsightedness have an almost startling "bug-eyed" effect, giving the person a childish air.

Chimps are born Caucasian, in a manner of speaking; their skin is a light flesh pink and their eyes a deep blue. But as they begin to mature their skin darkens to a purple-black in some individuals or a rich cinnamon in others. Even in the black-skinned gorilla, the most heavily pigmented of the hominoids, the young are born with very little pigment. This is in essence true of all the apes, including the races of man. Any time the child's physical appearance elicits care and protection from the adult, adults may often profit by mimicking those characters. Crying by adults has a similar effect. For the moment the adult becomes a child to be comforted, pitied, and cared for. Women and girls profited from looking more childlike than men, and whiteness is by extension an effeminate character. Studies in reflectometry have found sexual differences in color among most human racial groups on areas of the body protected from sunlight.

After a baby nurses, its lips are distended and the capillaries engorged with blood from the suction. The outer portion is a crimson red and the inner parts are blanched pale. As I have already mentioned, the nursing suck is an important gesture which we have incorporated into the parent-child bonding ritual, the greeting gesture, male-female bonding, and the development of copulatory behavior. Beneath the superficial role everted lips play in bringing milk into the mouth, they have become cardinal organs of social communication. But their complex role as mobile transmitters and sculptors of sound obscure, to the casual eye, their neotenic signal. The exaggerated everted lip of the lipstick ad model is similar to the Lifebuoy baby-complexion ad — they are "bigger than life" babies. The thin-lipped, square-jawed Montana face is the antithesis of youth; he is the surly, tough, old male carrying a signal of dominance. But that tight-lipped look of the other anthropoids has apparently been on the wane among humans. The everted lip is more prominent among women who desire a baby-like appearance.

Desmond Morris has proposed that the everted red lips of humans are a mimic of the genital labia. It is true that there are behavioral associations between the female genitals and the mouth among different primate groups, and there are colors in common — the blends of blues and pinks. But the major differences in orientation and the lack of eversion of the labia majora suggest that the uniqueness of the adult everted and colored lips is a primarily neotenic trait, with only secondary sexual aspects.

Waxing one's lips bright red, like powdering the face whiter than baby-white, is a form of superstimulus where the original signal is exaggerated to strengthen the response. These are cultural shortcuts paralleling the evolutionary phenomena of social neoteny. Though they are not neoteny, we can use them to analyse how and why social neoteny has taken place.

At different times in history, depending on the spirit of the times, women have capitalized on the clothes of the reproductively immature. The "little girl" look of the late 60's is a good example. Dresses and skirts went up to the upper thigh, like a little girl's dress. Hats, shoes, cut of blouse, lack of obvious makeup, and long scalp hair all took on aspects of children's wear and styles from previous decades. The extreme example was "Twiggy", a skinny, dish-chested, gangly-limbed, early teenage-looking girl.

Neoteny of the human body hasn't been only skin deep. The smooth round contours of the skull (again, particularly in women), the fine lines of the jaw and brow are all in sharp contrast to those of our ancestors a few thousand generations ago. Our hands, feet, and other limb elements have become slender and fragile. There is no reason to believe some of these trends except where limited by other body hot spots, will not continue.

21
LEATHERNECKS, PIMPLES AND SMOOTH BABY BOTTOMS

"Marvelous skin -- oh, marvelous: tender and tanned, not the least blemish . . . But nymphets do not have acne although they gorge themselves on rich food. God, what agony, that silky shimmer above her temples grading into light brown hair . . . the glistening tracery of down on her forearm."

—Nabokov, *Lolita*

In some cultures, retreating hairline or frosty hair are welcomed and viewed with pride, in much the same way a junior-high-schooler in America looks upon his first thin wisps of moustache fuzz. Why?

Stature in most societies depends on accumulated knowledge and refined performance. In a folk society traditions and information are passed on orally and one depends heavily on the slow process of personal experience. Thus, it is the elders who are looked to for their wisdom. We have changed this pattern with our intense formal education system so that a college graduate of 21, for example an engineer, may be placed in charge of guiding the work of many much older men, who earn far less salary and carry much less job prestige.

Though Western cultures have changed their attitudes toward aging to a great degree, our social relationships are still very age-dependent. We still cannot help but absorb the clues of age among our acquaintances and change our social posture accordingly. One of the chief clues our eyes search for is skin texture. The surface texture of ourselves and the people we meet is sort of a numerical social value, as if we wore our age stamped on our cheeks and the backs of our necks, like a quarterback emblazoned with a bright identifying number.

When in a crowd, one's eyes involuntarily skip and scan across the lines of necks, hands, eyelids, mouth corners and foreheads. If you are not accustomed to the seas of moving social information in the downtown area of a large city, people-watching leaves you exhausted in less than two or three hours. In addition to skin texture, you are decoding and piecing together all sorts of other information. Seasoned urbanites, of course, learn to function by filtering out the mass of visual social signals screaming at them from every direction by relegating people to broader classes: sexually interesting, oddies, and ordinaries. The former two are good for a quick glance but most fall into the latter category.

Young animals of many species have different texture from the adult, which gives them a special status. Among human beings it is the smooth silky soft baby skin. It is difficult for an expressive parent to keep from continually nuzzling or caressing a baby's down-soft skin. The soft velum fuzz on it is so fine that individual hairs can only be seen on close inspection. The effect produced by this fine fuzz is an overall, diffuse softness. The skin almost seems so soft that it has no distinct surface but grades imperceptibly into the surroundings. There is no gloss or highlight to the skin, either. The velum produces an eggshell or finely textured matte fabric, which accentuates the skin's smoothness.

The softness isn't just a surface phenomenon, either. The resiliency and patterning of the underlying skin fibers gives the skin an inflated look that is "wrinkle resistant." But the pillowy softness is from the underlying baby fat which is quite pronounced among properly fed babies under all areas of the skin. Thus, when you caress baby skin, not only does the surface have a downy softness, but the whole baby is like one big bundle of down in your arms. Its body is as soft to squeeze as a newly matured breast, for similar reasons.

It is easy to picture how maternal care — the attachment of the female (or parent, guardian, or relative) to the young could have evolved. Under many life-styles (but not all), those who are attracted to their young and care for them well contribute more genetic material to the next generation because of the greater likelihood of rearing their young to maturity. This selects for maternal behavior and it eventually becomes the norm.

Mothers cannot act on the rational basis of the "greater genetic contribution." Her attachment to the young must be more immediate, more organic. Behaviorally, this takes the form of a love identity, a bonding with the child so that it becomes part of herself. She responds to the child's noises and movements as end rewards in themselves and to what, in her own mind, is the inherent beauty and tenderness of the child's appearance. But just as there is a variation in the expression of maternal care, there is a variation in the desirability of children — that soft child beauty which causes a mother to love it so much that her own life would be given to preserve it. One might imagine how children's overall physical appearance could have been enhanced in time past, and still to a degree today, by how much it appealed to the mother. One doesn't have to use infanticide to account for the selection mechanism; just differences in care and attention add important life-lengthening differences.

Well before the teens and sexual maturity, the "baby fat" decreases and the skin tones harshen. The appendage hairs become coarser, but still soft and small. As a human being reaches maturity, the skin has a grainier texture, and later the granular appearance grades into fine wrinkle patterns between the deepening pits that grow into cobbly corrugations among the very old.

The rate of skin wrinkling is affected by race, use patterns, apparently a number of climatic factors (such as amount of exposure to the sun), emotional strain, and probably many other variables. The skin fibers (collagen fibers) that form the fabric of the skin are produced continually and the ones already there are not disassembled and reabsorbed, so that collagen continues to accumulate. This means a reduced resilience of the skin. With age and use, wrinkles tend to become permanently established.

The presence or absence of skin oils tends to emphasize or hide skin texture. Adult skin that is not periodically scrubbed gets an oily, greasy surface that further highlights its coarse texture. This is particularly true of the face and frontal parts of the scalp. A special organ has developed (by sebaceous gland elaboration) in this area as part of the intimidation signal. The stump-tail macaque, like man, has an inordinately well-developed sebaceous organ on the same areas of the face and the frontal part of the scalp. Males of this macaque species have a well developed sebaceous organ and females do not, suggesting that the organ has other functions than keeping the skin from drying out. Also, there is a marked increase in sebaceous activity at puberty. Sebaceous secretions are more abundant in human males than females at puberty and continue that way throughout life. In human beings the onset can be easily mapped by observing one of the more obvious products of this sebaceous increase — the teenage acne problem.

As the skin coarsens it leaves large craters into which the oil glands empty. Dirt and smoke collect in these wells and accentuate the skin texture.

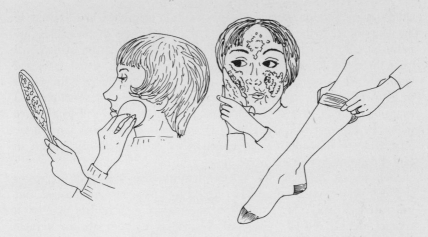

Much of our cosmetic body grooming is done to effect a smooth, more juvenile complexion. We use facial makeup which obscures skin irregularities, wrinkles and general coarseness. Sheer stockings accomplish the same thing on the legs – the sheer nylon gives the legs an appearance of being much smoother than they really are. Degreasing by scrubbing removes the skin highlights and the rough outer layer of dead skin cells making the skin appear more youthful – especially when it is then dusted with powder or talc.

The manner in which people modify their skin texture through cosmetics provides some insights into the social effects of texture. Skin coarseness can be deemphasized by reducing the surface gloss to a "flat" or nonreflective powdered finish. Both men and women apply powder or talc to the newly-washed face to achieve this effect, returning it to the soft, velvety, velum-hair texture of youth. Nylon hose are worn to add to the smooth appearance of the legs by obliterating the irregularities magnified by the skin gloss.

Dirtiness also gives the skin a coarser appearance than when it is scrubbed clean. The dark mineral particles and organics get down in the creases and follicle depressions or "pores", adding contrast, and the large particles break up the surface contours. In many hoofed animals, dirtiness is used as part of the intimidation effect, but there seems to be something quite different involved. These ungulates apparently spread their scent in the mud or dirt which serves as a vehicle to spread it over their own bodies. Elk and dogs, for example, roll in their own urine, or any strong-smelling substance, for that matter.

A very grimy, filth-encrusted child is especially disturbing – rather like a dusty orchid. The contrast is so striking. On a hoary, wrinkled old man, a little dirt doesn't seem to matter so much. Dirtiness, like dark skin, seems to have a deeper social significance than a working-class stigma.

A few years ago, before the "natural look" caught on, many women spent a not insignificant portion of their time going to bed with skin creams, enduring dried clay treatments, and having facial massages in an attempt to get those wrinkles out, or simply to cover them up by laying down a "foundation" cream to give the surface a smooth texture and at the same time putty over the smaller wrinkles.

But for the most part, we are "indoor people" and have only a few skin irregularities. Now and then when we see an old dirt farmer or a picture of a Bushman, we are moved to contemplate how all our ancestors must have looked at our age, unpowdered, unkempt, wrinkled and reddened from the sun, and what gross differences there must have been between people of different ages. An old Hottentot is a study in pigskin leather.

We do, however, have the smoothest complexion of the apes. Orangs have a very knobby facial skin, with lugs like Indian popcorn — especially old males. Chimps, gorillas, and gibbons have dark coarse skin — not just from living in the sun, because neither of the three groups spend much time in the sun. Like human beings they exhibit both age and sexual differences in skin texture.

The values of our body's texture carry on through to our values of fabric and dress, what might be called yard-goods gender. Silks and velvets are feminine, knobby wool tweeds and coarse leather are masculine.

Much of our use of skin texture and color are covert and not obvious. But the baby bottom complexion says more about who a woman is, what she will wear, and where she is going than the social register.

22
REDSKINS, FAIR LADIES AND DARK WENCHES

Few other organs lend themselves to such emotionally charged discussion as the color of the skin. Egalitarians have been quick to accept the recent dogma that skin pigmentation has no biologically social significance; rather, they argue, it is an adaptation to protect us from the sun. In areas where the sun is usually obscured by clouds, people are said to be lightly pigmented to allow more efficient Vitamin D synthesis. This, if true, is nevertheless only part of the story. A sunshade isn't going to cause that much social upheaval. We are uptight about skin color because it is a major organ of communication stretching back hundreds of millions of years through our ancestry. Before examining human skin color, it would be best to take a brief look at the importance of coloration in other species.

Some fish communicate with the skin. They contract miniscule color cells that dramatically create, destroy and recreate other patterns. One second the fish is bright red in threat, the next second it flees and blanches completely silver-white. In one social situation spots or artificial eyes are displayed, in another situation it is striped; each carries a different social signal. Reptiles, especially lizards, also use the skin for communication by varying their color pigments. The little American "chameleon" is an excellent example. Dominant males distend their red throat wattles, raise their skin hackles, and turn black. The subordinate color is a pale, washed-out green.

Many species of fish, amphibians and reptiles use the skin colors to signal mood changes. A species of fish, the chichlid, is shown here in a variety of social colors, each having a certain meaning and used in a certain social context.

Mammals have lost the expandable color cells. With the coming of hair most of the bare skin was covered. But color continued to be of utmost social importance. In addition to direct skin color, pigment was laid down in the hair shafts, but since hair is a dead tissue, its colors must be limited to changes in seasonal moults (it may bleach some with time, but hair "turning white with fright: is an old wives' tale).

A dark coloration seems to have intimidating qualities when one looks across the spectrum of mammalian social coloring. Whenever there is a sexual difference, the dominant sex, the male, is the darker. There are very few exceptions to this, mainly in instances where *contrast* seems to override color, as in the case of the dark bull caribou's white neck mane. In the evolution of some mammals (and birds) the base skin has been exposed and functions as a flexible color signal. Bare skin can be changed rapidly and dramatically, even without the use of special color cells, by flooding the surface capillaries with blood so it becomes a crimson red. The capillaries can be drained and the skin blanches light again. Human reddening in anger functions in this fashion.

Among the other primate groups, skin or pelage color is virtually independent of solar exposure. For example, the mountain gorilla has a deep jet black skin as well as do some South American monkeys, yet both live in deep forests and spend only a small fraction of their time out in the bright sun. The Hamadryas baboon, on the other hand, is exposed to the intense glare of the Ethiopian dry country and has very little skin pigment.

The correlation between skin pigmentation and sun exposure among human groups is also rather poor. No doubt skin pigments do serve some physiological function in screening out damaging sun rays. Skin protection is surely a factor in skin pigment evolution, but it is only one factor – and there are times when its role seems to be minor at best. Some peoples who live in areas where there is intense solar radiation are as light as some living in areas where there is little. Compare, for example, light-skinned Arabs from the desert country with the dark natives in the deep forests of Borneo or the pygmies of the central Congo.

The threat value of dark skin probably has arisen indirectly from its role as a protector for the sensitive generative layer of the skin from ultraviolet excesses. The greater the exposure to ultraviolet, the more the melanin pigment cells proliferate – the darker the skin. Some of this is cumulative, so a person exposed to the sun all his life is darker than his well-tanned stage when young. There is then an age gradient in most groups relating to skin color. And since the social hierarchy corresponds to the age hierarchy the pattern for social color is somewhat inherent.

But there is something more. We are diurnal, that is, daytime, organisms, and we function at night only with an artificial sun — a fire, lantern, or incandescent lamp. Our eyes are daytime eyes and perform poorly at night. Eckhard Hess has suggested that because our pupils are small when we are discouraged or depressed (things "look black") we are actually receiving less light onto the retina. We come to associate darkness then, with bad times and light with good times. There is something mystical, unknown, mysterious about darkness. Black is foreboding, as in "gathering black clouds." The complex mind of man couldn't have helped but make these associations in nature. Black is a synonym for sinister: Black Bart, Bluebeard, the Black Demon, the Black Knight, and the black hats in cowboy movies. Black is aggressive, a Karate belt, and Dracula's cape or even a black nightie. White is submissive, as in a white flag, a white dove, and a wedding dress.

Quite often young or juvenile animals are colored opposite to the adult. In many cases this different coloration gives the young some protection from adult aggression. It is a signal that there is no real threat, even though it is a member of the same species. In many cases the adult must be white for reasons of protective coloration or some other factor, as in white gulls or white beluga whales. Their young are much darker than the adults, unlike the apes, where adults are characteristically dark and the young light. So the uses of a dark pelt as the signal of dominance is not universal among mammals. There are apparently a number of things which can override the threat value of darkness. The chief ones seem to be cases in which the adult must be white for some other, more important reason, say in concealment or cases in which light areas expand over the body due to their contrast value, such as in graying.

The variation in color patterns among the different gibbons, light-limbed brachiating apes from Southeast Asia, provides the best evidence for color changes and their uses within age classes and between sexes. Fooden has concluded that the early gibbons were a homogeneous brown (like the living gibbon species, *Hylobates moloch,* which varies somewhat in shades of brown). From here, he feels, there evolved two color phases of light and dark that were originally not separated according to sex (as in the living species, *H. lar entelloides*). However, the light forms were apparently selected for in the females but selected against in the males (as in the species *H. concolor* and *H. hooloch*) so that all females were cream and all males black. The most extreme form of this apparent trend is in the species *H. lar pileatus,* when young are born paleface and darken with age. The males continue to darken at maturity, whereas the females at maturity revert to the pale phase.

In the Gibbon species, *Hylobates lar pileatus,* whiteness becomes associated with subordinate social stature and carries an obvious signal of rank. It benefits the possessor because it would not provoke the black males. Whiteness in a male of this subspecies would result in his being a "sissy," treated either like a juvenile or a female, which in the rank system of most mammals spells "subordinate".

What has happened, as in the gibbon species *Hylobates lar pileatus,* is that there were pressures to create sharper differences between sexes and the immature and mature. Human beings show these same color differences, only more subtly.

Gilbert and Sullivan should have written, "Only mad dogs and *red* Englishmen go out in the noonday sun". We are conditioned to think of Northwestern European stock as cream colored because they are now an indoor people, and those who work outside wear clothes to shade their bodies and hats to shade their brows. But one can catch snatches of what they must have looked like when they were outdoor people. The row-crop farmers of the midwest wear billed caps, and in late summer it is spectacular to look out over an indoor gathering, where hats are removed. The women are softly tanned from occasional forays to the garden, but the men's faces are studies in contrasts. The lower face from the cheeks on down is a rich rusty brown, but the forehead shines ivory white. There are a few old men who have worked out in the sun year-round all their lives, and they are far from fair.

It's an odd quirk of fate that the white man came to the New World clothed and wearing a broad-brimmed hat; otherwise *he* would have been called the red man. Western Europeans tan a burnished copper red; Orientals, which ancestry the American Indians share, tan a soft brown.

In virtually every society where there are well-developed social classes or castes, and color differences as well, the lower classes are the darker (in the same way that lower classes tend to be hairier); not because these castes are in any way inherently inferior, but because the neotenization process in social ornamentation is more extreme in the higher classes. Hulse has found strong selection pressures for skin color among modern Japanese, along with sexual differences. Japanese have an outspoken admiration for white skin, particularly in women, and they have a long tradition of whitening the skin with powder, as do many Occidental cultures.

In very light-skinned peoples, veins immediately beneath the skin appear bluish through an almost transparent skin, giving rise to the myth that venous blood is blue. I suspect that the combination of light skin being associated with high status and the bluish appearance produced the designation "blueblood" for people of aristocratic birth.

The current slogan "Black is beautiful" really means "Americans of African ancestry are beautiful people" — a legitimate attempt to remold the values of Blacks into realizing they are just as beautiful as all of the white models which have determined American's taste for years. But within a more homogeneous subgroup, saying "black is beautiful" is like saying big beards are beautiful — it all depends on whether and how that society is currently emphasizing the more blatant status signals or the gentility of soft, babyish appearance.

For example, the reversal of the fair-lady mystique after World War II happened as the result of those with leisure being able to swim in the sun or vacation in Miami. A tan symbolized, like white sneakers, crew socks, and polo shirts, that one had the leisure for sports. A brown, svelte swimmer no longer carried the stigma of a dark wench. I suspect that this shift is only temporary perturbation of the whole complex of the human neotenic. Though these changes in our values often appear to be erratic through history I suspect they follow definite patterns. A change in style, cosmetic habit, or the ideal figure, though superficial and arbitrary on the surface, may be deeply tangled in the *zeitgeist* and tied even more deeply in our biological values about appearances.

Skin colors can change rapidly by varying the amount of blood in the skin. There seem to be three themes in the evolution of human communication through flushing the skin with blood. There are (1) the anger flush, (2) the blush, and (3) the sexual flush. The anger flush is an old tradition used today by many non-human primates. It is far from vestigial in humans, but there is considerable variation in its expression among human subgroups and within them. Physicians often refer to flushers and blushers as vascularly unstable. It is part of a syndrome characteristic of the blue-eyed, pink-eared, freckled palm-sweaters of Northern European ancestry. In groups without very dark pigmentation it is common enough to be generally recognized as a signal of internal mood. The more swarthy human subgroups are not as prone to skin flushing with mood changes.

Like the anger flush, there appears to be some within-group and between-group variation among blushers. Daniel Freedman, in his comparative study of small children, found that "The Navajo infants exhibited two outstanding differences from all other groups, a tendency for the entire body to become red when excited and to remain that way for much of the examination . . ."

The third type of reddening is the sexual flush which was emphasized by Masters and Johnson. In the adrenalin peak of the sexual excitement, it is common for many Caucasians to flush red over most of the body: in keeping with an old primate tradition, a splash of red is synonymous with sexual decoration among females.

One might think that these three social signals all employing skin reddening but having quite different meanings and evolutionary histories might become confusing. However, they seldom do. Probably it is because the contexts in which they are used are dramatically different.

It is strange that one could redden both in anger and in subordination and still keep the meanings separate. Yet we've seen that in the submissive grimace among carnivores the teeth are bared to the opponent, almost as they are in a snarl. Differences in situation and pattern keep the meaning of submission and threat quite clear. These signal values are further complicated by the process we discussed earlier of Caucasoid reddening to a new-copper tan with exposure to the sun, which seems to be a more permanent form of anger flush — a badge of dominance (what the rosy cheek is to the subordinative blush). The deeply tanned person loses some flexibility in his social signals and dark-skinned groups have also lost the flexibility to communicate mood with skin color, as the moustached man has lost some visual symbols of his lips.

PART SIX: SOCIAL ANATOMY AND HUMAN VALUES

23 CLOTHES AS SOCIAL ORNAMENTS

"Living in the modern world, clothed and muffled, forced to convey our sense of bodies in terms of remote symbols like walking-sticks and umbrellas and hand-bags, it is easy to lose sight of the immediacy of the human body plan. But when one lives among primitive peoples, where women wear only a pair of little grass aprons . . . and men wear only a very lightly fastened G-string of beaten bark . . . and small babies wear nothing at all, the basic communications between infant, child and adult that are conducted between bodies are very real."

—Margaret Mead, *Male and Female*

We have now had a comparative look at evolutionary themes and how they affect our appearance. How are our attitudes accordingly affected toward the common things in life which go beyond specific social organs — clothes, racial differences, our taboos about dirt and excrement?

One of the universal characteristics of the human animal is our propensity for adornment. Immersed in the midst of traditions and the immediate context of our culture it is difficult to visualize fully the evolutionary role of personal adornment. It is easy to think that clothes simply protect one from the elements and keep one's person clean — but this is not their major function. We use them chiefly as social devices to show station, mood, and class membership. Their chief function is to modify the signal of the natural social organs. As the principles governing the evolution of social ornamentation of other organisms carries through to human beings,

so do the principles regulating our social organs carry through to our
adornment patterns.

The manual dexterity that got us our big brains also provided the
potential for altering our social image. In essence, this ability to dress and
decorate ourselves has allowed our cultural evolution to accelerate rapidly,
for what we have done with dress on a limited time span would have taken
many thousands of years to evolve naturally. We can crop back blatant
signals of status by whacking off beards or covering up intimidating parts
and redoing them in more subtle hues — or we can exaggerate sexual
signals, such as erect lifted breasts, or status clues, such as shoulder pads.

The vagaries of voguery at first glance appear to be almost random, but
only a preliminary analysis shows that we are not being as free as we think
with the way we choose to dress and decorate ourselves. We still follow
those ancient rules of social strategy and physical display. Let's look at
some of the principles in detail. Our decoration and body alterations follow closely the principles already illustrated from our social organs —
threat, sexual allure, apparent age changes, and the continuum of revealment and concealment. The first g-string tab of animal skin covered an
important male threat organ and decreased the sexual invitation of females
in a changing society which demanded a refinement in the coarser signals.
From that point on, adornment began its complex course. Yet our body
signal alterations still focus on the old vertebrate themes of color, texture,
contour, and size.

Generally males are darker than females and adults darker than young.
One theme which disrupts this pattern is the replacement of black by red
— as on the hamadryas baboon face. Many primates use black skin as a
clue to stature. Our feelings about color are carried through to our tastes
in clothes. Black is concealed, defensive but dominant, mourning dress —
Black Panthers' and Hell's Angels' dress — tuxedos, slinky evening gowns,
and mink stoles. White is wedding dress, diapers, soft underwear, formal
gloves, and bulging blouses. Black nighties are suggestively aggressive,
white is naively virgin, as the currents between sex and status intermingle.

Contours are important clues to status, especially weapons and areas
that wield the weaponry. We use clothes to pad and remodel our body
contours to transform our social image. Shoulder padding is probably the
best example. It was exaggerated in the zoot-suiter and de-emphasized
somewhat in the round-shouldered, boyish ivy-league look. We use threat
psychology in sports with shoulder padding. Football shoulder pads extend well out over the shoulder angle, unlike hip and knee pads that con-
form closely to the body contour. We remodel contours to modify sexual

signals with breast harnesses and padding, waist tighteners, butt lifters and stiffeners, and belly flatteners.

Women are understandably concerned with the two main sexual attractant zones, the breast and buttocks. Males keep their hips trim with tight-fitting pants and encourage chest size with several layers of overgarments, including vests. Epaulettes of military uniforms exaggerate shoulder angles and baroque cords; chest plates, medals and cross-straps call attention to the chest area.

In military and sporting outfits the arms and legs are generally emphasized by lateral stripes, circumferential stripes, or barring — one of the important trends in appendage ornamentation among birds and mammals. Appendage movement and position are important elements in most behavioral displays. Hair tufts or tassels are important, with lots of leather and shiny metallic material, many contrast lines, and especially a common identity character of class and team association which is easily recognizable from a distance. We roll the drums and bellow the horns as super-releasers derived from the cries of man-to-man intimidation. In many societies bodies and especially faces are painted in a ferocious design to exaggerate threat. Knights took advantage of many threat principles with their hideous face masks, giant plumes, and helmets adorned with the weaponry of familiar, fearsome beasts, and blue-black armor.

A major in full parade dress is awesome to males in an intimidating way, yet, like the guy in a football captain's uniform, he has considerable allure to females. So, like a strong chin or broad shoulders, threat gestures can be both intimidating or attractive, depending on the social state of the beholder.

Clothing changes seem to correspond to changes in the social *zeitgeist* — using, of course, the basic principles of threat ornamentation, with many added spices and renditions of the particular traditions and themes. "Inward" cultures, like the Athabascans, tend to dress in sombre, concealing colors and patterns, while more "open" cultures, like the Eskimos, prefer flamboyant colors and much ornamentation. Our own return to the "natural" adornment — soft, undone hair, nudity, and child-like clothes with short skirts and sloping shoulders — is consistent with the increased adulation of youth we are experiencing in the 20th century.

The first principle of fashion is the uniformity of class and caste adornment. Looking at the different eras in our own past or photos of other more exotic peoples, there is a definite homogenity of clothing or adornment patterns underlying the superficial individual variations. Generally, the particular theme is not a matter of optimum utility but of social acceptance. The pressures of what to wear or how to decorate oneself are so strong that people end up wearing uniforms which characterize their status in much the same way that military uniforms are rank-specific.

One of the earmarks of feudalism is a strict clan hierarchy in land ownership, costumes, and personal property ownership. There are generally unwritten (sometimes written) edicts as to what a person of such and such station will wear, and how. These are known as sumptuary laws. In such a vertical hierarchy, people literally wore their wealth on their backs. But as laws governing clothing have a way of eroding, gradually there became three major classes in Europe; the aristocracy, the rulers; the middle classes, who did no hard physical labor; and the lower class, who worked with brawn.

As some of the middle class began to be wealthy through business and industry, they could afford to buy the finery of the aristocracy, which destroyed aristocratic dress patterns as symbols of station. At about this time democracy was on the increase and the functional aristocrat was on the decline. So instead of three major classes, two dress strata evolved that were symbols of laborers who engaged in manual toil, and the more leisured class.

The same trend occurred somewhat among women in Western society as it did among men. Women's clothes are moderately inexpensive from the garment factory and differ only subtly from those made up at the custom tailor's and designer's. So the sophisticate in the Rolls Royce wears only very simple jewelry and plain clothes, while the streetwalker and the waiter retain the anachronistic traditions of rouge and diamonds, or white dinner jackets, in an attempt to look "classy."

During the era when there was a distinct class break between gentlemen and commoners, the main signal of class was what J. Laver refers to as the *anti-utility* principle. It has shown up in many forms among numerous cultures and social situations. The long fingernails of the Chinese mandarin are an excellent example.

The major trend in the phenomenon of *gentility* is to show that one is good for nothing but leisure. This has resulted in leisure wear becoming standardized as formal wear — swallowtailed coats and big top hats were once fox-hunting attire, then bowlers, then the brimmed, creased top hat we wear formally today. Presently the European hunting outfit is what we wear in the United States as *sport coat* and tie, and to have European friends come hunting in that getup prompts one to ask, "But why are you dressing up?" when, in fact, it is we who wear hunting clothes to business meetings, church, and other stiff social occasions.

Every time a new sport becomes popular one can almost predict that it will contribute something to the styles of the day. Witness the polo or "T" shirt, tennis shoes, surfer shorts, three-quarter-sleeved football jerseys, high, tight-fitting riding boots, the visored baseball cap, the tennis or cheerleader miniskirt, yachting bellbottoms, safari bush jackets, etc. Laver proposed that at least men's wear follows an inevitable evolutionary pattern: "They are sport clothes, then ordinary town wear, then formal or evening wear, and finally servant's dress, after which they become mere historical curiosities." Notice how the service station attendant gets that classy look with a black bow-tie – something that once was common high class wear.

The henpeck order is nowhere more apparent than in the past history of women's wear. Though there are ways of increasing one's stature over, or attractiveness to men, it seems that women dress mainly for other women, as the old adage contends. It takes a subtle eye to catch the things women observe about one another which are usually missed by the menfolk. Even many fashion shifts are against the male tastes, yet women adhere to them rigorously – tightly cropped hair, flattened chests, and many others that have met with outspoken male criticism.

There have been two main related trends in clothing recently which deserve special attention, because they tell us something very important about our times. One is toward a classless, ideal society, and this takes form in fashion. It could be seen back in the forties with the sloppy bobby-soxer and the dirty white bucks, and in the bluejeans counterpart in the early fifties. The signal was "I don't really care how I look – you have to get to know me to find out something about me." But this was a minor movement at best. In the sixties the theme was carried even further to a "put-on" of established adornment signals – a blatant protest against clothes as status devices. Old army surplus clothes were worn, with beads and flowery materials – anything out of the ordinary. We began (superficially, anyhow) to get away from the clothing status game.

What we had done for centuries, if not for millennia, was to evolve a subtle masking of our natural social organs and a reordering of their signals. Threat signals were covered up (genitalia) and clipped back (hair). Sociosexual signals were modified by additions and coverings of all sorts – we were uniformed into gray flannel "joiners" wearing signals which said we succumbed to a common dogma.

What happened in the 1960's? History will tell us more someday from a distant perspective. It may be that the inevitable hypocrisy of every society came to the surface and the new initiates simply wouldn't buy it. Whether it was Viet Nam, or something more complex, the Western world became a hotbed of dissent with established lifestyles. The counterculture movement symbolized their sentiments in their attire — which has affected the fashions of the decade considerably. The themes of rebellion essentially reverted back to the basic threat theme from our biological ancestry. The "Handy Guide to the Well-dressed Mod Rebel" reads something like this:

1. Color: Black or bright, lots of black as in black motorcycle jackets or reds and blues with paisley prints and striped pants and beads and flowers.
2. Texture: rough, lots of leather, big belts, belt buckles, and watchbands, and high-topped jack boots with lots of chrome and brassy shine.
3. Hair: man, that's where it's at.
4. Nudity: Let it all hang out!
5. Eyes: big specs and tinted lenses.
6. Noise: the louder the better, especially the basses.
7. Cleanliness: What's that?
8. Movement: Be a swinger.
9. Design: military dress when available; Kaiser helmets, army blouses, and epaulets were real camp.
10. Styles: The noble savage, preferably Indian.

An Easy Rider's chopper motorcycle was a biological as well as a cultural phenomenon. There was something more behind the repugnance that sweeps town when the gaudy choppers roar down Shady Lane than mere cultural threat. It was another animal bedecked in every threat releaser we've ever known, the fearsome hordes we've suffered from since the Australopithecines, and here they come, roaring into River City.

What a sad, historical irony in a way: the new pacifistic, eco-religionist movement inadvertently took on the older threat signals by only having the option to go opposite soft white cotton and gray flannel neotenic. Under the roar of the electric guitar and scraggly hair there was supposed to be flowers and love. But we establishmentarians had already become so neotenized with our baby-powder skin, mouthwash, super-chrome-plated razorblades and Ivory soap ideal that becoming flower *children* in appearance was impossible: the niche was filled. The other mode signaled a frightening ghoul, a leather-and-fang troll, all the ogres from our hidden past.

This antiestablishment attire was one of fashion's passing flings and will go the way of the blue suede shoe — but what if it had been something more? Was it an expression of a system of values where individuality is crying to be re-expressed, and attempt to overthrow the tie-clasped Organization Man? I doubt if we could ever have removed the superficial signals of hierarchy and replaced them with inner ones — personal virtue, professional excellence, sincerity; but it would have been a noble experiment. I fear the Age of Aquarius, where love and sympathy abound, was perhaps the dream of older Zions and Utopias dressed in lovebeads and flowers. We are a hierarchical animal and somewhere in our values we have to have expressions of relative worth — exactly where and how is the problem. The real social strategem, I suppose, is to have status accoutrements which do not result in physical or intellectual deprivation, but are "open" in the sense of not having any rigid restrictions on birthright. Whichever route we go, it should be traversed with a knowledge of our biological selves as well as our ideal ones.

Coming from the values of the 60's we can look at the biological significance of one of those vogueries in more detail: dirt.

24
SOCIAL AND PHYSICAL DIRTINESS

"There was much about Gregory Rasputin that was repulsive. He was filthy. He rose and slept and rose again without ever bothering to wash himself or change his clothes. His hands were grimy, his nails black, his beard tangled and encrusted with debris. His hair was long and greasy ... Not surprisingly he gave off a powerful, acrid odor."

—Robert Massie, *Nicholas and Alexandra*

Red deer and wapiti stags wallow in smelly mud pits during rut, and it is possible to tell rutting stags from non-rutting ones at a great distance, as they are covered with mud and peat. The great wallowing pit hollows made by the American bison in the Great Plains are still visible today, almost a century after they ceased to be used.

If we allow our social ornamentation to become fully expressed, the older males become a greasy-haired stinky mess. The "down and outs" of society are intimidating with their stubble beards, wrinkled and dirty clothes, and unkempt hair. I'll bet every time a panhandler approaches you on a lonely street there is a twinge of fear; a lot of it is our cultural categorizations, but some of it is because in your mind he is a desperate, muddy stag still fighting over commodities in limited supply.

As a few people began to "keep" other people, some of these status values began to change. The well groomed individual gives the signal that someone is caring for him, almost like the protective signals given by children — no glandular odors, smooth face, and fresh breath. It has become a posture of social facilitation — of gentlemanliness. These are the signals used as personality clues in psychiatry. A person who has completely let himself go to seed, physically, is someone who has lost his social state — in his own evaluation he has no one below him in the rank order and therefore has no social front to maintain.

A major taboo in most human societies is dirt. Dirt is bad. We rationalize the social stigma of dirt as unsanitary. This is essentially a myth. Coal dust, soil particles, and petroleum grease are for the most part free of pathogens. However, someone who is "dirtied" with them, like the mud-caked red deer, can make bystanders shy away. Dirtiness is the main thing which around the world separates castes and classes.

We think of hands — a child's or a fair lady's — as being very lovely; but seldom beautiful feet, except for baby feet which haven't begun to show use. A beauty queen parades in a bathing suit to reveal the contours of her hips and breasts; however, she covers her feet with shoes — the only object to be covered because it is neutral at best. Big feet in a woman are considered ugly, more masculine. A big "dirty" organ is no asset. The Chinese custom of foot-binding (similar in principle to Western women buying shoes so small they deform the toes) was an attempt to retain the aesthetic foot of the child. Polished shoes, shiny patent leather, or white bucks reveal the wearer as not of the soil — not a *clod*.

In order to give a signal of higher and higher station one had to come up with a classier looking collar and cuffs; in the 18th century collars became so large and ornately ruffled that they impeded function. The same is true of frothy lace cuffs. We have reverted to more practical collars and cuffs, but they are still of light color among the high of stature ("white-collar workers"), and soap ads tell you how to get these important areas "whiter than white". White shoes were a symbol of FDR's upper-class summer wear, which is probably what made the tennis shoe so important in the leisure wear of the 1950's.

Frequent changes of clothing among the well-groomed is another status pattern. A secretary who wears the same skirt and blouse to work every day of the week is not playing the status game with her peers. We don't really "need" a lot of clothes changes.

When one feels "down" there is a sensation of dirtiness about him. Women wash their hair to come out feeling clean and men go to the steam room. Both enjoy a hot tub of water or a sauna after a hard day, especially after one that hasn't gone well and one's status-stat is reading low. We use the terms dirt, dirty, and filthy to refer to other things we dislike: sexual aggression ("that dirty old man" and "filthy pictures"), feces ("were forced to eat their own filth"), ill-earned gains ("filthy lucre"). Most of us treat oily, musky odors with the same repugnance that we treat dirt — garlic, onions, Limburger cheese, and stale cigars.

Most of our table manners are standardized rules of how not to offend your messmates by dirtying yourself. So is the use of different tableware (extra plates, two forks, and two spoons) in formal dining so as not to mix desserts, salads, soups, or tea. We use napkins and finger bowls to keep our person clean. Dinner wear allows you to come to the table looking your cleanest — this was once such an important ritual among the British elite that special dinner dress was taken into the field and used under the harshest extremes in jungle or desert. Cleanliness is an indication of station. The learned and wealthy have often referred to the "others" as the "great unwashed".

The hippie trend of not washing was a way of saying that they were not playing that particular status game (of conspicuous consumption in the form of a large wardrobe, bathing rituals, etc.). It is interesting to see how we mix our values in such statements as "I can see why they wouldn't want to own a lot of clothes, but they could at least stay clean." As conservationists we decry the horrible waste of water, yet spend hundreds of gallons a week flushing our excrement, keeping clean, and washing and rewashing the body scents from our clothes. We fear that dirty clothes and dirty bodies are common indicators of social dirtiness.

The establishment's attitudes toward those who do not participate in this social ritual are particularly hostile, even more than toward uncropped hair or profuse ornamentation. Yet while dirt is an important theme in our social values about appearances and smells, there is one thing far worse — excrement.

25
EXCREMENT
COMMUNICATION

"While the American attended to nature, the soldier stood guard, observing with some interest how a foreigner did it."
— Herman Wouk, *Winds of War*

There is a social drama that goes on daily in almost every public john across the country, which we take so much for granted that it isn't even recognized as a phenomenon. A man picks a urinal far away from one in use, and if a man is next to him, it is forbidden to look at him. He can talk, but he must stare directly ahead at the graffiti or peeled plaster in front of him. Above all, he can't stare down at the other man's running spout.

You can fill in the other elements of the "sociology" of the john. My point is to introduce the way our emotions affect the processes of elimination. Our emotional state is wired into our lower body autonomically and quite intimately. The rules are fairly simple. The more confident, on-top-of-the-situation you are the better control and discipline you have over waste disposal. As you become anxious, you feel you must eliminate. With sustained tension or immediate pressure the process grinds to a halt. But with terrifying experiences one "lets go" or "craps out," as it were. How do we account for this wiring system?

One of the most vivid experiences of inability to urinate comes from run-ins with nurses. For many people, hospitals and clinics are houses of emotional horror, anyway, and one is usually there because of some health worry. But it's always a big put-down to be examined like a lab animal, denuded of your protection of social paraphernalia and told by someone, "Fill this bottle up to here — you can use the little room". We fear, "I know I can't squeeze anything out — I just know it."

Tremendous fear of a terrific emotional upset can cause the urethral sphincters to let fly and one ends up with wet pants. This is a familiar enough pattern, especially during wartime or in earthquake-prone areas.

One could run through the same set of principles about defecation. It is difficult to crap communally — that's what put the two-holer garden castle out of business. Why the privacy of locked-door stalls around public bathroom stools (note that euphemism)? These half-walls don't keep out the stink. They are designed for visual privacy. Some cultures are more private than others about these rituals, but there is still a general theme of privacy.

Having to defecate in the face of mild immediate tension isn't uncommon. Anxiety provokes the peristaltic action of the bowel tract — and blatt, the quick anxiety morning crap. But sustained tension can also be responsible for constipation. (Remember Old Man Portnoy in Philip Roth's *Portnoy's Complaint*). And like urinating under extreme terror, filling one's pants is so widely known that it has become part of the vernacular of expressing great upset: "Oh, he'll shit his pants."

Few things are as taboo as the references to and uses of body excretions. Even "dirty" jokes at the adult level are usually about sexual taboos and not urine and feces. And not even blood and visceral gore are a match for feces when it comes to turning stomachs. Both blood and urine are usually sterile of pathogens — more so than most spring waters. Yet if one had to choose under penalty of death whether to drink blood or urine, people would usually not choose urine. The idea that we have evolved our repugnance of elimination products for reasons of sanitation doesn't hold up entirely, because of the sterile nature of urine. Many other mammals, by the way, have these same emotions toward body wastes; birds, however, do not, except in regard to the physical soiling of feathers. How do we and other mammals come by these social sensitivities to elimination products?

Unlike birds, early mammals saw the world through their noses. Comfort was the smell of home — the smells of good food and of a familiar path or social setting. Discomfort was the smell of a stranger or of a strange place. A person's smell told others something and their smells told him something about them — perhaps their age, sex, where they come from, etc.

But most important, smells were extensions — far extensions — of the self; your smells could be where you weren't. We mammals weren't very social to begin with and running across a turd in the trail meant some*body* had been there. If it was fresh it meant he had *just* been there. Life among fairly asocial creatures isn't relaxed and easy-going. He may be able to encroach into your food resource, take your potential mate, or even kill you.

So it was likewise to your advantage to leave marks behind indicating that you were around, possibly avoiding confrontations which could do you no good. The urine and feces that were left behind in the normal functions were taken over as communication media.

In addition to the natural urine and feces smells, special musk glands evolved in these areas to add further effect. Glands and tufts arose on the penis foreskin or prepuce and special musk glands on many animals developed near the anus to anoint each fecal pellet with their odor.

One late winter day, I walked along an old berm pile on the lower side of our homestead clearing. Natural barriers make good territorial boundries, and a male fox (I could tell by the position of the urine where he had lifted his leg) had urine-marked every thirty yards or so — every time a little prominence like a stick protruded above the snow. He must have eaten a lot of snow to get enough water to do all that marking: however, I imagine it was just a few squirts at each post. Even with my poor human nose in below-zero weather I could catch the musky odor which had accumulated there from repeated sprinklings. Another fox wandering into the area could gather all sorts of information about the fox living there, but the main signal was a repellent: Better get the hell out of here.

When the snow is deep around Fairbanks, one can see which houses have dogs. There are yellow splats (known locally as Alaskan sunflowers) at the entrance to each driveway. The main road is a mixture of community scents, but each driveway is territorially marked and any new dog traveling along the road is forewarned.

The use of urine among dogs (as among many other social creatures) is often accompanied by other signals. It communicates stature, low as well as high. Puppies have a way of urine squirting when petted, or chased by an older dog; it is weak puppy urine without the odors of the adult and hence says, "I'm just a nothing; don't fool with me"; it is submissive urine. Since elimination is a gesture of social meaning, social animals also have special urination and defecation postures. In the dog it is dramatized by a raised leg; but among a pack, only the dominant ones urinate this way — the very subordinate males crouch down and pee like females. Mature dogs will urinate over fresh human urine in their "area," as will many other species.

I propose that our autonomic wiring connecting psyche with bladder and urethral muscles came from our early mammal origins. Tension causes urination because we want to mark — just like a dog when he smells new odors in his yard. When one has a trying day at the office he or she makes more frequent trips to the washroom (not to wash). In situations where we are blatantly in another's area (smelly hospital), it is difficult to urinate because marking foreign turf goes against our ancestral grain.

Despite the fact that we have all the old wiring, it is vestigial for the most part, or tied up with visceral syndromes that relate to other functions. But we still sometimes see these as outward expressions of psychological behavior and even psychological pathologies, as in anal-compulsives. We don't scent our feces or urine with special glands (though the foreskin gland is still there), but we still react to the smell of rancid urea and the bacterial products of feces with an unreasoning nausea. A fart is almost as disgusting as pure feces, yet these bowel gases contain no harmful pathogens.

Like wolves and deer, human beings also have different urinating postures. Postures relate somewhat to anatomy, but interestingly enough, baby boys learn to urinate in the same posture as girls, a defecation posture. After they can do it "standing up," it is exaggerated all out of proportion to the avoidance of urine on the toes. The legs are bowed back, the stomach and sacrum stuck out, shoulders thrown back, and head arched downward to watch the show.

The mara, a South American rodent, even goes so far as to urinate in threat — but on subordinates. So do many rabbit species. Urination on another human is the extreme form of indignation. Spitting on someone seems to be a ritualized form of pissing on them — a ritualization accomplished by males and females alike. And the remark "piss on you, fella," or "shit on you" carries with it unmistakable connotations of rejection, to say the least.

Cultures have contorted and modified the general repugnance humans have for urine and feces. Some cultures tend to build up rigid taboos and others tend to treat it rather lightly. I'm not sure there are any general rules. In our own culture people from rural areas seem to make less of it than urbanites. Maybe we tend to build up stricter taboos as our relationships become more intimate and our populations more dense. Rural blacks and sharecropper whites moving to the city have trouble at times in adapting to the organic aspects of urban ways. Many ghetto tenements (which can more correctly be called first-generation-off-the-farm tenements) reek of urine in the dark foyers, and there are feces piled along the shadows in the back alleys — something which worked on the farm but does not in the heart of Chicago.

But the rural-urban principle doesn't hold up entirely. France, for example, is noted for its forthrightness about bodily functions, yet Paris at least has had one of the longest histories of high density in the Western world. In its pissoirs, a man may leak behind a thin enclosure covering the middle part of his body while he chats with his girl at the same time. Yet all of these are just different subtitles on a theme of the same taboo, for even in France there are couth and uncouth procedures for body elimination that have nothing to do with sanitation.

Though we in the Western world are becoming more and more open about sex and skin exposure, we are becoming more closed about discussing elimination. Some may find this chapter offensive, just because I've had to use some taboo concepts and words in exploring our behavior.

One of the best illustrations of how we are becoming a more closed society is in the evolution of the urinal. First, urinals were simply long troughs. Then in the '40's and '50's separate urinals were used for each person. In the late 50's and early 60's flanges were installed between urinals to separate your privates so the person next door couldn't see if he tried. The next stage, I'll guess, will be complete enclosures.

How does one explain all this? I would guess it's just a sexual facade; we'll really be getting to know each other intimately when a fart is a mild social slip, not a major faux pas. We've come a long way from the two-holer outhouse. Now we feel our privacy encroached upon if a lock on a stall doesn't work. We build several bathrooms for just one family. Not that I would want to go back, necessarily; it's just that our attitudes and physical facilities are probably a clue to our real intimacy, and much of the business about letting it all hang out is just poppycock.

Though it does not have the unmentionable taboo quality of excrement, our next subject, the gross differences among human races, is a tension point in the web of human values — and probably has always been — and may always be.

26
THE
RANK
RACES

In my college years, I began to notice that Jewish girls, who then came into my experience for the first time, had an interesting feature in the upper eyelid. In a casual discussion I mentioned this observation to one of my zoology professors, who misunderstood it as racist in character and promptly berated me, concluding with the remark that the next thing I knew I would be talking about different racial smells. Later I read about racial variations of the quantitative and qualitative production of the axillary (armpit) apocrine glands. We shouldn't be surprised at the extent of our subgroup diversity, for it is one of the features of all living organisms. Purists, incidentally, prefer not to use "race", or "subspecies," for "subgroup" for very unbiological reasons.

Nonetheless, few forces in history have been more potent in their effect on the human condition than the physical differences between human races. And there is no question that these differences are still the main element in modeling attitudes of one class or people toward another. In spite of this deep emotional involvement in modern subgroup physical differences, the precise reasons for their existence are still, at best, poorly understood.

Much of our failure to account objectively for racial differences comes from the fact that we have been relying on functional anatomy to apply its principles of environmental adaptation to what are basically *differences in social ornamentation*. The slant-slit eye of the Cambodian, the coarse, leathery, pebbled skin of a Congo pygmy, the brilliant blue eyes of an Irish colleen, the long graceful neck of an Ethiopian queen, the massive cheekbones of a Plains Indian, and the long penis of a Masai are important *social* tools and have little to do with wind and the rain.

Among other species this pattern is also the rule. Birds differ in toe pattern and bill structure mainly as a result of their habitat and feeding patterns, but the colorful tail patterns, head crests, and breast colors are their social tools and correlate poorly with habitat and food. There are the same strikingly similar racial patterns among other primates that we are accustomed to seeing in human beings. The primate face is the main center of communication and this is where most of the specialized ornamentation is located.

In the face, also, is where one finds rather dramatic variations within species and between species. For example, the faces of African Green Monkeys or South American Saguinus Monkeys vary as much or more than the faces of human beings, in color, whisker patterning, and distribution, eyebrow size and pattern, and eye variations.

Earlier I mentioned the East-West cline in facial coloration of the hamadryas baboon. Eastern animals have a bright vermilion face and Western ones have melanin in the skin which gives the face a dark gray appearance. The drill has a polished jet black face and the mandrill a red and blue face. Most of the other baboons have dark brown to black facial skin. One is tempted to draw parallels between the cline of the hamadryas red to gray from Welshman to East Indian among the Caucasoids. I suspect the differences exist for the same reasons — and It's not just protection from the sun's rays which is the determining factor. One could go on and on with parallel examples; suffice it to say that we are not peculiar in this regard. Any explanation that tries to account for much of the human racial variation must be subject to broader application to other related organisms, and *vice versa*.

In my own mind, there are four fundamental points which account for much of the human racial variation in social organs: (1) the degree of specific and general neotenization (childlikeness); (2) dispersal along the evolutionary spectrum; (3) anatomical displacement among classes or among neighbors; (4) diversity of patterns which are just different ways of doing the same thing.

As we have seen, social neoteny combined the social posture of a juvenile and the physical skill, mental and reproductive wherewithal of an adult. One might expect neoteny to be at its most extreme form where social transparency was at a premium — the society required complete cooperation with and social reliance on one's fellows. There is no one environment nor really any one social situation which one could specify would invariably result in neoteny for social reasons. Eskimos and Bushmen live at low densities in marginal habitats, and they exhibit these qualities in a number of body characters. Their mode of life is such that a single family group would be at a considerable disadvantage as would members of a large populace. The Japanese, another group of social neotenics, however, are just as neotenic, but for different reasons. The combination of insular habitat and moderate to high density creates a forced intimacy. In such a situation one functions best by providing an image of inoffensiveness and interacting freely with many other people.

I suspect monogamous bonds would tend to support the process of male neotenization, especially if a female does much of the process of mate choosing and does not play a very subordinate role in the society. Promiscuity or polygamous bonding with dominant males would tend to select against neotenization in a loose-knit society. However, in a highly organized society (say, feudalistic) dominants usually do not possess the physical rugosity of the working classes and neotenization may be selectively favored on a class basis. Whatever their origin, racial variations seem to involve neoteny. Australoids bald and gray early, while some of the Orientals retain the long torso of youth and hairless body well into adulthood. The potbelly and protruding butt of the adult Hottentot perhaps has some origin in relation to their general childlike body form.

The second theme one finds among group diversity in social paraphernalia represents points along an evolutionary path. Some groups represent earlier conditions of stages through which other contemporary groups have passed. This is a principle on which anatomists have capitalized in their reconstruction of soft-part evolution (organs for which there is no fossil record). Among different living animals one can see a spectrum of, say, heart anatomy that gives one clues as to how the mammalian heart originated.

With some exceptions, this method of reconstruction can be adapted to social organs as well, and it is the process by which ethologists reconstruct evolutionary patterns of behavior. Social behavior and social ornamentation are intimately interrelated, so one must unravel both together. For example, Geist's work with the evolution of horns and hornlike organs: antelope and deer with small simple horns represent early evolutionary patterns of horn development and fighting technique, which in some species have been altered to complex horn or antler structure and highly ritualized fights. Thus, one can conclude that some groups are either evolving more slowly or have stabilized at one point while others have undergoné continual change.

One can discuss these same types of differences among human groups, though virtually all texts about race refuse to do so for fear of being accused of racism. There is an unwarranted assumption that human change is always progress or advancement, and later stages would necessarily represent something "better." For example, ancestors of all human beings had thick, protruding bony brow-ridges. The Australian aborigines have a similar brow, and the Southeast Asian have virtually none — but this doesn't mean one is inherently better than the other. One has simply changed rather dramatically and the other to a lesser degree.

Our early ancestors had massive cheekbones or zygomas. This condition also varies considerably among different racial groups and subgroups. One can go on with other examples: receding foreheads, nose shape, chin size and shape, etc. There are, of course, many features which have no fossil record, but their ubiquitous distribution around the primate world suggests an earlier history such as brown eyes, black hair, and tan skin.

At the same time, ubiquity can be misleading. For example, peoples with considerable body hair are comparatively rare, but judging from other hominoids this must have been an earlier condition, and our slick nakedness is a later product. Again, reversals are probably common, so one would have to be fairly cautious in a judgment as to direction.

The third theme responsible for racial variation in social paraphernalia is a tendency for *anatomical displacement*. It is often disadvantageous for two species that live together to share the same forms of social paraphernalia if they do not compete directly with each other. Moose and caribou never fight in the wild because each species' threat patterns are unique to it. The same is also true for sexual attractants. Also, a similar principle seems to apply along the lines of contact between two adjacent species. The pressure is greater here to recognize the "foreigner."

Among human beings we see similar principles pertaining to castes and neighboring groups. If there are any differences they will tend to be exaggerated. Let's say that there are two neighboring groups, one tall and black and the other short and white; as with all neighbors, there are underlying tensions. To the Short-Whites, being tall and black becomes synonymous with badness, and *vice versa*. But what about the taller, darker *Short-Whites?* They must share a little of the stigma of neighbor hate. The same is true for the shorter and lighter Tall-Blacks. Both of these variants could be expected to leave fewer offspring than more typical members of their groups; hence, the two groups drift farther and farther apart with time, until the Tall-Blacks are really tall and black and the Short-Whites are very short and white.

The same phenomenon seems to occur between castes living together. Since we are more sensitive to physical differences around the "hot spots" of social communication (in humans, the eyes, mouth, skin color, hair patterns, and texture), one might expect these to vary more between castes and human subgroups than most other organs, as indeed they do.

The fourth theme of the diversity of social paraphernalia is probably the most important. There are numerous avenues of change that may effectively accomplish the same thing. There are a number of ways to look more beautiful: baby-doll sex kittens with waterfall curls, or haughty socialites with their hair piled on top of their heads. So also are there various ways to signal status — smelliness, deep voice, graying, balding, big beards, oily skin and so on — various combinations of which may serve a similar function to that of other communication combinations.

But the particular way of changing may occur somewhat at random. Probably some avenues are simply fortuitous — having become culturally traditionalized and selected simply because of some quirk of time and moment. Perhaps the values came from the appearance of a revered leader. We can assume, though, that the form of threat patterns characteristic of animal species is always in compromise with some environmental selection pressures or other social factors. The same must be true among human beings.

A cold-climate animal, like the Rocky Mountain goat, can utilize long, dense fur to cover most of its body, increasing its apparent body mass, while a tropical species is denied this route because of overheating. The more threatening, gaudy individuals of a species that does not depend on visual concealment may leave more offspring than the drab ones, whereas in a species that relies heavily on camouflage, it may be the drab ones who leave more offspring because the gaudy ones live such a short time, though they may consistently gain high social rank. Likewise, human status signals would be expected to take different avenues in different ecological and social settings. The degree of skin pigmentation, body size, relative fragility or robustness, and other physical characteristics may affect one's survival in a number of different environments. Thus, any reproductive advantage conferred by certain status signals may be either complemented or counteracted by their effect on other aspects of the individual's life history.

For instance, the special anatomical features of the penises of some Africans and the artificial extensions used by some islanders in the tropics may have been due to the penis being emphasized by the nudity allowed in warm weather. Farther from the equator the genitals are usually covered by clothing and are not as readily available for continual display.

Not only is there a large ecological component to the direction taken by these social paraphernalia, but there must surely be another large component based on the nature of the particular group's social structure. There are a number of ways social organization could influence social organs: size of the bands, caste system or lack of one, the need for co-operation, courtship patterns, marital arrangement, role of children in the society, the general temperament of openness or freedom of expression, the dominance structure itself, whether linear or class, relative importance of age, social role of women, and many others. All of these indirectly or directly affect the expression of which suite of physical features will be bent in which direction.

The question has often been asked, "Why is there so much variation within a group of human beings?" There is also considerable temperamental heterogeneity among a litter of puppies, and also of wolves. Some are shy, others have blustery daring, some are quiet, others are noisy, some are expressive, others are aloof, and so on. This is not true among foxes. One is stuck by their homogeneity. Adult foxes are asocial, each going his own way, and all adhere to a certain behavioral norm or optimum. But in a social species a number of different social strategies are allowable. Likewise, the social paraphernalia that accompanies behavior exhibits a similar pattern. The throat patches, masks, eye markings, coat color, etc., are extremely variable within a wolf population. This is particularly true among the Northern subspecies, which run in large winter packs and as a consequence are more social than the southern wolf species which occupy a more loner, coyote-like niche.

The extension of this phenomenon to human beings and other social primates is obvious. Gorillas and chimps are extremely variable in their social ornamentation and behavior. Human beings, more than any other primate, are extremely variable within any one group. But if beards are important, why doesn't everybody have beards just alike? A slick chin and strong beard are different social strategies in one continuum; each has its assets and debits. The milieu of a highly social group selects for a broad spectrum of behavior and social paraphernalia.

Pictures of wild African hunting dogs never cease to amaze me. All are mottled in a piebald-skewbald mixture of black, yellow, white, and brown splotches — each with his individual pattern, like a litter of potlicker pups. Somewhat the same is true for Dall sheep; no horn pattern is like any other in size or shape. This is a general principle within human subgroups, whether it is Miamin, Kwakiutl, Turk, or Balinese.

Social identity is based mainly upon variations in social organs — the fullness of the eyebrows, the length and shape of the nose, the color of skin and hair, height, body hair, etc., but I doubt if this diversity has been selected for solely on the basis of creating special identity, as many have proposed. Rather, it seems to be a function of the diversity of social strategies which are selected for in an organized group. An organized group can tolerate (and even function best with) individual specializations and diversity, while loners, like foxes who have only themselves to rely on in the hunt or in encounters with strange foxes, are forced to yield to a narrow range of optimal individual performance.

In comparing modern human subgroups one can piece together some of the history of our social organ development. In some groups a character is only rudimentary, while in others it is fully developed (such as the blue eyes of some racial subgroups being only approximated by lighter brown eyes in others). A well developed social organ in some groups may have been almost lost in others. Also, there are cases of simple divergence: from the original brown skin came both translucent white and blue-black.

Most of us go through life not analyzing rationally all of these differences in our values relating to the social organs of other groups or even ourselves — but there are some who do.

27
THE ART OF PEOPLE WATCHING: THE INFORMED HEART

"The bride came sailing down the long dining room, wheat-colored hair beautifully coiffed . . . cheeks pink with pleasure . . . The white satin, clinging to flanks and breasts like creamy skin, rose demurely to cover her throat. She moved in a cloud of white lace. This blend of white chastity and crude fleshy allure was devastating."

— Herman Wouk, *Winds of War*

Have you ever watched the judges viewing the five-gaited class at a horse show, or attended a bench show for salukis? An untrained eye can see a general difference and assign broad values: but not expert judges — they discern each little line and angle of body and synthesize all these characteristics quickly on a score sheet.

Few of us are expert animal watchers or judges, with one exception: our own species. There is no other animal more engrossing to human beings than ourselves. We're so good that all we need is a flash of a glance and we can tell paragraphs about an individual human. We spend most of our waking hours exercising and refining our skills of human evaluation. You don't see much written about this, because we are orally oriented and think of most communication in terms of words. There is also an egalitarian undertow that discourages us from judging people by things they can't help — weak chins, flat chests, voice quality, crow's feet around the eyes, thin lips, height, and so forth. But we still do internally or even unconsciously. Every time we come into social situations our status-stats are gunning their engines to process all the information; it is so automatic we are hardly conscious of it. We are not alone in this behavior — aardvarks are excellent aardvark watchers, sparrows are great at watching sparrows, crocs at croc watching. As a matter of fact, much of an organism's time is devoted to dealing with his own kind.

But there is a difference between this almost involuntary communication and our ability to identify and sort out what is happening. A good judge at a dog show or an animal breeder has to go beyond this gut-level, involuntary "like" or "dislike" and begin to analyze why one animal looks different from another. Most novelists are artists in this regard, and good novelists possess a special insight into people's subtle signalling because they must be able to recognize it, abstract it, and verbalize it. It is because of this refined ability that I have used excerpts from various authors to illustrate our values about social organs. Cartoonists also can be especially talented people-watchers; and there are many other professions which develop field ethologists at watching people. Psychologists and pyschiatrists are the highest refinement of the art.

The reason behind the threat role of male genitals and beards is not apparent simply by looking at human beings. But that role does fit into an organismic pattern, from which amateur and professional people watchers may perhaps profit. In this way science can assist art, because the identification of different body characters is important in human evaluation. Communication can be enhanced if we know why these characters affect us the way they do.

The biological *why* is just taking reason back one more level from the immediate *why*. One can react to large chins without knowing it. He can react to them and know it is the large chin that he is reacting to. He can react to chins with the experience of an analyst who would understand the status significance of human chins. He could also react to the chin and realize it is a status symbol derived from our evolutionary heritage of exaggerated primate weaponry. These are different levels of understanding of chin signals, and the evolutionary perspective can add dimension to the artist's picture.

Without this historical perspective, the image is two-dimensional — a gesture without origin or heritage. Knowing something about the process of neoteny, one is impressed with the similar esthetics of touching the soft skin of a child with love and stroking the smooth skin of a lovely girl. There is an added depth to the emotion.

A cartoonist must observe different signals and their associated behavior, then eliminate the extraneous lines and reconstruct a purely stylized pic-

ture. Comic books and cartoons should be interesting for physical anthro-
poligists, ethologists, psychologists, and other professional people watchers.
A cartoonist has to be able to show surprise, doubt, vindictive anger, out-
rage, lust and all other forms of human visual signals that will be recognized
as such by all, even the very young. Try drawing some of these emotions
if you don't think it is an art! There's no scientific analysis that the
cartoonist performs, nor a key to which he can refer; it is truly an act of
art — of being a human ethologist — a good people watcher.

A novelist has to describe what is going on, both superficially and in
the minds of his characters. One can get by without being able to describe
such things as the lifting of one brow, the tight-lipped resolve, the sunken
watery eyes of a mourner, and all the other visual clues which help us
build the image in our own mind; but a storyteller without this perception
is severely limited. His characters become faceless puppets who spout
dialogue at one another. What a person says is perhaps the least interesting way to perceive him and live inside his skin.

Actors and actresses must also excel at professional people watching.
To avoid falling into overacting a stereotype, one must be able to give the
subtle but readable clues of character by his motions, carriage, the set of
his face. One can act a homosexual or a business magnate without limp
wrists or belligerent cigar-puffing — just by shifting the tone of voice, the
position of the eyelids, the smoothness of movement, and the carriage of
the head. To put yourself into a role requires some previous knowledge
of how such a person would react, not only in words but in little eye
twitches, whether to flex one's jaw muscles or not, and so on, and the
believability of one's performance will, all else being equal, be equivalent
to his artistic ability and experience at people watching.

The best cosmeticians probably rival cartoonists in having to know
what precise facial features are important and how altering them can
change the person's signal. An eye cosmetician who is good at the art
must know the whole of people's faces and how they affect other people.
Through facial makeup, the jawline can be exaggerated, the cheekbones
made more prominent, and, most important, the texture of the face can
be modeled to revert to a more childlike appearance.

Plastic surgeons capitalize on the cosmetic trade, by removal of a lens
of skin to lighten up an area or pad it with silicone to make it look fuller.
The nose can be shortened, cheekbones made a little more prominent, and
bags under the eyes removed. People will react differently to you, and this
in turn alters your image of yourself. So, a personality change has really
taken place just as surely as if the surgeon had gotten into your cerebrum

and incised or grafted parts.

The rest of us can go through life reacting to these signals at a gut level, never knowing why we feel this or that way about our first impressions or about acquaintances, but I would subscribe to the assumption that the more we understand about what is happening around us, the richer our lives become. At the very least our new understanding satisfies a part of our snoopy nature — a need which we all share — a need to inquire and wonder about things, especially ourselves and our fellows.

Even to us amateur people watching artists, the social processes are more interesting if one can rationally identify the signals he is responding to — even though it may in no way affect one's responses. Witnessing a fashion change from shoulder pads to rounded shoulders or a change in the Hollywood ideal from a high forehead to a low one and being able to comprehend how this interrelated with the changes in the social processes of youth adulation gives it less of a black-box aura. And knowing the evolutionary processes of neoteny that are taking place within our species right now gives our lives a broader meaning and dimension.

By people watching I don't mean just watching others; there is an art in watching oneself. The questions, "Why do I dress a certain way, deodorize, shave, or grow a beard," have psychological, cultural, and biological levels of answers, and it is worth more than fun to ask and see if you can find some rational answers.

Whoever you are, you have all sorts of interesting social organs that differ from mine, and you perform all sorts of organic manipulations to change your social image. Most of these affect your social status, some your closely related sexual attraction. Both men and women continue their seductive ornamentation after marriage (not only for their spouses) because sexual seductiveness is a status symbol.

But I don't want to deny our anti-status acts. As a matter of fact, we go out of our way to hide our status from one another. We place verbal taboos on being a social climber and look down our noses at someone who pushes too hard. Much of our dress and grooming is to remove the blatant signals of threat which our distant ancestors have bequeathed us. Most of these modifications, I feel, are to help us get along better with others. However, the subtle signals of status are still there.

Our descenting, degreasing, and dehairing captialize on the less aggressive response of others to the juveniles we are mimicking. This behavior normally gives the young a semi-sheltered status from the full brunt of adult competition. By reducing one's natural symbols of maturity it is possible to receive a response nearer that received by the immature, easing to some degree the stresses of adult interaction. In spite of the increased rewards of social facilitation and cooperation, there are still advantages in being one up — no, let's say .01 up! Thus the offensive organic threat signals are replaced by considerably altered but more dilute guises. Like our natural status clues, some adornment gives us class identity (e.g., waffle-stompers or a tweed jacket) while others give us personal status (e.g., an original sweater or a genuine elephant's tail-hair bracelet).

We are a very social organism, so people-watching is serious business with us — but it is also a great deal of fun. A judge at a dog show would enjoy himself more and have a greater appreciation of a particular breed if he is aware of its history, the *historical why* of its peculiar variations of behavioral and physical characteristics. The same is true about watchers of people.

Until now I have tried not to attach my own judgment of good and bad to our differences in social organs and the behavior they produce. Now I would like to try.

Biophilosophers who are concerned with environmental and population problems look at man as having evolved for one kind of life, yet now forced to live another for which he is not well adapted. I think the same principle applies to so called "human values".

Within the ancestral, tightly knit group, the social organs were garnishes on intimate personal relations. Social organs and appearances were important but only secondarily so. This is not true today. Our transient mobility and superficiality has put a priority on outward appearances in our values.

This superficiality has caused Western society to rely more and more on courtship potential as a clue to our self-worth. For the most part this has been a bad thing.

During no other time in life are the differences in social stature as susceptible to change than during the early courtship period. As status greatly influences the likelihood of courtship, one's potential mate reflects on one's status.

During courtship, people live in a private world dominated by "feelers" toward courtship. Theoretically, such feelers should cease after mating. But they do not. Due to long courtship periods and a growing uncertainty about status outside ancestral folk society, we continue to employ those same courtship feelers all our lives. In fact, our courtship potential has become the major key to our social state even after mating.

In the Soviet Union, women take a much more active role in initiating courtship than do their Western counterparts. After living there for several weeks and growing accustomed to the continual bombardment of eye-

pings, it was quite an emotional letdown for me to land in Tokyo and return to Fairbanks, being ignored by the opposite sex.

In the last several hundred years our reliance on courtship potential as a reinforcement of our social state has grown out of all proportion. There have been numerous detrimental aspects:

(1) *The overemphasis of appearances.* The dominance of a "courtship potential" status system places a heavy social burden on the ugly and beautiful alike. The ugly live in a world where the inner qualities seldom get a proper showing. The beautiful people, on the other hand, live in an artificial world, where the motivations of friends and lovers can be quite shallow. This overemphasis on appearance has created a preoccupation with "makeup", plastic surgery, voice development, posture, and all the other outside polish, with little emphasis on the inner ones.

(2) *The overemphasis on youth.* As the young have the greatest courtship potential, we give them unwarranted reverence. Likewise, once noble symbols of age have become repugnant. Gray hair, balding, and coarse skin create a fear well prior to the fear of approaching senility. They herald the decline of courtship potential.

(3) *The breakdown of the mating bond.* The heavy reliance on appearance has been devastating to courtship. In a folk society where people's inner persons are almost as well known as their outer ones, a brief courtship may be appropriate. But today mating bonds are fundamentally based on face values. Most are destined to rupture, probably more so than the growing divorce rate illustrates. The search for identity, through signals from the opposite sex, creates the pathologies of the unsatisfied lover who is forever in the quest. We share some of that, in varying degrees, and I would guess that the growing reluctance of many young people to make formal mating commitments stems from our social state being so intimately connected to courtship potential. We are justifiably guarding ourselves from a probable hurt. The failure to subdue courtship feelers after mating has surely eroded the mating bond, and with this failure goes many enjoyments of growing old with someone familiar and loved. All this, for the promise of the brief infatuation of early courtship.

(4) *The overemphasis on sexual performance.* As sexual attraction and competency play a part in courtship performance, they have become exaggerated in the superficial parts of our lives. Advertisements lure us toward sexual happiness with toothpaste and shampoo. Books on esoterica and "little known facts" of copulation are always best sellers. It is seldom said that the best of all is with someone you trust and love deeply.

Sex in Western societies is overplayed, because, I would guess, it is growing less satisfying. Because copulatory satisfactions go beyond outside influences and depend heavily on the inner state, one must feel truly free and trusting for them to provide full satisfaction. In our world of "outside" satisfactions, society is shifting toward the other prostitute end of the scale.

(5) *The loss of personal intimacy.* One wonders if what we now think of as intimate is not just a washed-out shadow of the real potential of human intimacy. We have grown so accustomed to looking for and seeing mainly outsides, that insides are no longer very accessible. Not only are we losing our ability to see beyond the shell, we are developing our ability to build ever thicker shells. I think most of us know this intuitively, but our organized attempts to counteract it through encounter groups, or personal attempts at candidness, are on the whole ineffectual.

It is indeed a tragedy that social organs stand in the way of values about the real inner person — but they do. We are not only very unequal in social organs, but outside differences produce unequal *inside* differences. Maybe we should not struggle to suppress this fact, but rather begin to make some outward acknowledgment of its existence. We have faked equality for a long time, yet know and conceal *deep down* all the intricate rules of our unequal animal signals of physique, visage and color.

We are far from being objective, rational creatures, on a march toward social order. We do not rear our children just from instruction booklets, but from the deep animal attraction — that beautiful anguish one feels towards a fragile, sleeping child. Nor do we choose our mates for the most part, through any cognitive design of kindred spirits, but by that electric lust called love for the opposite sex which so viscerally depends on the animal person. I would contend that the major segment of personal hurt, at least in Western societies today, comes directly or indirectly from our animal persons, our patterns of social organs. These are: the traumas of reaching for adulthood, of courtship and peer stature, of loneliness, of divorce, the anguish of growing old and of being old, and many others. Yet, of all the many things we know about human beings, we know least about the *biology* of our social appearance. The reason for this is that our vested interests are *too* vested. We can even acknowledge behavioral differences for one can change behavior, but we cannot acknowledge the social effects of receding chins, high cheekbones, or coarse skin; they are all too permanent — something we had no role in making, but for which we must bear the important repercussions.

Our lives, for the most part, are not built on rational, objective decisions. There is a spontaneous element — the world of the heart — where we almost unexplainably place values on people with whom we interact. It is difficult to communicate the depth of detail behind our likes and dislikes in this private world; in fact, we have a tendency to suppress them in favor of commonly agreed upon values of the public world. But our private worlds of people values are a real and important part of us and we should be aware of how they work. That awareness may not always (or ever) influence our actions, but we should not be deceived that many of our prejudices, hates, and sparks of charismatic attraction have an organic side which is part of being a human animal.

It is this world of the private, subjective reality in which social organs function. Most of the important things that will happen to us socially will be in greater part products of social organs. This being so, we cannot confine our values about social organs to negatives. Social organs must form the vital seasoning and color behind our social behavior. If we were all identical in appearance, we would be far less human. Something important would be gone. We must learn to savor, appreciate, and understand where our social organs came from and how they function — and to accept their biological diversity.

Most of us involuntarily abstract the world of people about us into some ad agencys' ideal of humanness, but that is a long way from the real world of runts and skinny stilts, pockmarks and pimples, of buckteeth and bald spots. We are a people divided — divided into squat achondroplastic pygmies and proud Masai warriors, peeled-banana Englishwomen, no-ass Athabascans and hairy Ainus. There is ugliness and beauty, repugnance and grace — not somewhere in a magazine or a book, but right there in our neighbor's yard and down at the corner drugstore. In those trim, tapered wool-worsteds is a penis embedded in wiry, black hair, and concealed beneath the Nepalese silks is a gently, honey-colored breast tipped in delicate lilac pink. What a fantastic species we are, the violent, hard eyes and the forlorn, sad ones, the beaks and button noses, the stale crusty aged and cooing babies. We can't be abstract, it's us — you and me. Many of the reasons for our being here, looking the way we do, and feeling the way we feel are sometimes difficult to deal with, because they are dynamically organic. It isn't like talking about a painting or a new model of automobile — we had no creator or assembly line, we got to be ourselves by an erratic organic route steamy with smells, vibrant with colors, and ground with dirt. There were no pre-market consumer surveys, we came as we were and the only compass to give direction was an organic score card for the race from bleeding, pithy afterbirth to when the young were let go on their own. It was a change so subtle none of the players were ever aware of it; they only felt the hurt, love, and excitement in their own time.

All of this doesn't mean it is impossible to look at the evolution of our social selves analytically; we just can't look at it from above, we must see it from within.

I have pursued my interest in the evolutionary biology of our social organs on the assumption that it can give a deeper meaning to my life. I have written this book in the hope that it will do the same for yours. I cannot honestly say that it has grossly changed the day-to-day actions in my life. I don't think my reactions to others have changed all that dramatically, nor their reactions to me. It is in the "accounting for" that makes all the difference. I suspect you will still react in the same way to a big, brassy voice, square chin, and white-walls, but I hope that down inside there is a little smile — not of smugness, but of the satisfaction of savoring the organics of humanness a little more deeply than you did before.

I think these ideas can help us understand our organic selves. A fleck of gray or a receding forehead, a sprouting of pimples or smelly underarm odors, these begin to take on meaning beyond the immediate condition of changing age; they connect us with ancestors who used these organs with the pride of newly-gained identity. Someone with a long nose or short height is wearing a badge of ancestral social strategy — like an organic coat-of-arms from a distant family tree tatooed into one's soul and skin. Such a badge gives us a deeper tradition of kinship than any of us can trace by oral or written genealogies. For somewhere in our background were our ancestors who possessed a bald pate or were diminutive and had other peculiarities like ourselves; they shared the evolutionary cream of their time and participated more fully in life's processes — or else you wouldn't look the way you do today.

The explanation of why you have those particular social organs, which so immensely affect your life, is somewhat unsatisfying if you only know the immediate genetic answer — "your parents carried these genes here, and . . ." It's like someone who is black asking *Why?* It isn't good enough to know that you are black because your kinfolk were black. The explanation of the evolutionary *why* is more satisfying — because you belonged to a distant noble group who once used black skin, as the Scots used their red beards, as status symbols. And that ancient tradition is genetically fixed into your soul. One not only must forever be a part of his immediate tradition of parental, neighbor, and peer relationships — for better or for worse, he must also be an animal with biological heritages that are a part of his life, and he cannot comfortably deny them.

Thus one can begin to make rational sense out of some of his irrational acts — to see through the veil of numb, involuntary rites. For we react almost automatically to tight-lippedness and teardrop-shaped butts. Our responses to people and their personalities are in part a product of how they look — not just how they have their hair done or nails manicured, but the color of their eyes, the size of their cheekbones, and their height and a lot of other things they can't do much about. It's part of our daily lives we have learned to live with, but most of us have yet to consciously acknowledge it completely — professionals as well as amateurs. I would agree with Bruno Bettelheim, the famous child psychologist, that

"no longer can we be satisfied with a life where the heart has its reasons, which reason cannot know. Our hearts must know the world of reason, and reason must be guided by an informed heart."

Real inner emotions come across through visual signals more than through words, which is why it is so important to understand the basic reasons why we react and act the way we do to social organs. That, I suppose, is the message of this book. There are volumes and volumes about the principles of the written and oral word — its rhetoric, linguistics, etc. — but in comparison there is virtually nothing written on the important communication avenues of our social organs: eyelid tonus, dilated pupils, the blush, and so on.

The languages of our social organs, such as genital and eye talk, are so emotionally loaded that it is awkward to commit them to analysis (sort of like the recent physiological descriptions of human copulation). In a sense I have been the analyst, the equivalent of the physiologist in the above analogy, for these few hours of your time. But I don't want to leave you with just a discussion of particulars — the bushy brows and pink nipples. For I am like the physiologist describing copulation ... he doesn't think about epinephrine and sphincter dilations when *he* is flushed with sexual desire. But his kinship with everyman doesn't mean that copulation is less for him — it can be more. The removal of some of the magic, with rational explanations, does remove some of the spiritual wonder, but it is replaced with a deep awe of a different kind.

One of my good friends, having read Masters' and Johnson's description of the physiology of human copulation, became so analytical later that evening that he lost his wonder and rigidity at the same time. So indeed there may be some negatives to the knowledge of our organic functions. Most of our troublesome hangups however, relate in some way or other to these functions, and a better understanding of why we feel these emotions and react the way we do, even if it is no solution to our hangups, can help us be a little more friendly toward them.

I am plagued with being an easy blusher, for example. Though the knowledge of why it's there and any control I am able to exert on this behavior are virtually independent, it does help relieve a lot of inner anxieties to know what's in the black box called blushing, and roughly why. It is essentially an involuntary happening. And as far as I'm concerned, maintaining a wonder of the unknown doesn't compensate for not understanding what is happening to me. Quite the contrary; it gives me a tremendous awe that some of this is an evolutionary product. We're not necessarily a *victim* of it, but it is a part of the natural organic quality of life.

In the beginning I said this was a book about taboo things — the mysteries surrounding the organs we use in our body talk. Most of our important taboo systems are regulators of social action, leaning heavily on our biological heritage. The necessity for cooperation makes flagrant displays of status-seeking repugnant. There is a tone of disapproval in the label "social climber", running through Packard's *The Status Seekers.* The entangling of sex and status produces various blends of sexual taboos. Irrational rejection of urine and genitalia speaks of a tradition of genital and urine signals millions of years old and almost as broad as all mammaldom. We conceal our hairy parts and yet cover our nakedness, which hair was to conceal as well.

I do not mean to tear down those taboos, nor to make delicate things indelicate, nor to confuse one's values of beauty. We can keep our taboos, and should, but it is still fun to call time out, as when we were kids and had to interrupt a game to do something important, to see what the taboos mean. Then we can climb back into our shells and continue with our shell talk and taboo secrets. But, we hope, we will be the richer for that time out.

I wrote this book because somewhere in those pimples, silver flecks, and swinging gait, I feel there was something more than meets the casual eye. We are all deeply involved in the organics of life; the fruity-flower-musky odors, the lilacs and magentas, the satiny smoothness, and the whispery hoarseness. In a way this was meant to be an expose designed not to scandalize our self-view, but to provoke a disturbance which would heal into a more pleasant way of seeing ourselves. I will have had some satisfaction if I know that tomorrow, at your customary grooming session, you see something different in the mirror, or reflect for a moment when you squirt your armpits with deodorant, or even on occasion acknowledge the wild-eyed, combat-booted streaker in yourself if you happen on him. Then back to the game of living — time in!

REFERENCES

Altmann, Stuart A. (ed.) 1967. Social Communication among Primates. Chicago and London, University of Chicago Press.

Andrew, R.J. 1964. The displays of primates. *In* Evolutionary and Genetic Biology of Primates: Vol. 2 (J. Buettner-Janusch, ed.) p. 227-309. New York and London Academic Press.

Andrew, R.J. 1963. Evolution of facial expression. *Science* **142**:1034-1041.

Andrew, R.J. 1963. The displays of primates. *In* Evolutionary and Genetic Biology of Primates (J. Buettner-Janusch, ed.). New York, Academic Press.

Andrew, R.J. 1963. The origin and evolution of the calls and facial expressions of the primates. *Behav.* **20**:1-110.

Anthoney, T.R. 1968. The ontogeny of greeting, grooming, and sexual motor patterns in captive baboons (Superspecies *Papio cynocephalus*). *Behav.* **31**:358-372.

Argyle, M. and J. Dean. 1965. Eye contact, distance and affiliation. *Sociomet.,* **28**:289-304.

Barbara, P.A. 1956. The value of non-verbal communication in personality understanding. *J. Nerv. Ment. Dis.* **123**:286-291.

Barlow, G.W. 1972. The attitude of fish eye-lines in relation to body shape and to stripes and bars. *Copeia No.* **1**:4-12.

Bartholomew, G.A. and N.E. Collias. 1962. The role of vocalization in the social behavior of the northern elephant seal. *Anim. Behav.* **10**:7-14.

Bastian, J. 1965. Primate signaling systems and human languages. *In* Primate Behavior: Field Studies of Monkeys and Apes. (I. Devore, ed.). New York, Holt, Rinehart & Winston.

Bastock, M. 1967. Courtship: An Ethological Study. Chicago, Aldine Publishing.

Benedict, B. 1969. Role analysis in animals and men. *Man* **4**(2):203-214.

Bernstein, I.S. 1970. Primate status hierarchies. *In* Primate Behavior, Vol. 1, New York, Academic Press.

Blest, A.D. 1961. The concept of "ritualization". *In* Current Problems in Animal Behaviour (Thorpe and Zangwill, eds.). Cambridge, Cambridge University Press.

Blurton-Jones, N.G. 1972. Non-verbal communication in children. *In* Non-Verbal Communication (R.A. Hinde, ed.). Cambridge Univ. Press.

Blurton-Jones, N.G. 1967. An ethnological study of some aspects of social behavior of children in nursery schools. *In* Primate Ethology (D. Morris, ed.). Chicago, Aldine Publishing Company.

Bolwig, N. 1964. Facial expressions in primates with remarks on a parallel development in certain carnivores. *Behaviour* 22:167-192.

Brannigan, C. and D. Humphries. 1969. I see what you mean . . .*New Scientist,* May 22, pp. 406-408 (also in *Time,* June 13, 1969, p. 48).

Brown, J.C. 1963. Aggressiveness, dominance and social organization in the steller jay. *Condor* 65:460-484.

Buechner, H.K. and R. Scholeth. 1965. Ceremonial mating behavior in Uganda kob (*Adenota kob thomasi* Newmann). *Zeit. f. Tierpsychol.* 22:209-225.

Burgers, J.M. 1966. Curiosity and play. *Science* 154:1680-1681.

Cannon, W.B. 1963. Bodily Changes in Pain, Hunger, Fear and Rage. (2nd edition; orig. 1915). New York, Harper and Row.

Chance, M.R.A. 1967. Attention structure as the basis of primate rank orders. *Man* 2:503-518.

Chance, M.R.A. 1962. An interpretation of some agonistic postures: the role of "cut-off" acts and postures. *Symp. Zool. Soc. Lond.* 8:71-89.

Christian, J.J. 1970. Social subordination, population density, and mammalian evolution. *Science* 168:84-90.

Coghill, G.E. 1964. Anatomy and the Problem of Behaviour. New York and London, Hafner.

Comfort, A. 1971. Communication may be odorous. *New Scientist and Sci. J.* 412-414.

Coon, C.S. 1966. The Living Races of Man. New York, Knopf.

Craig, J.V., L.L. Ortman and A.M. Guhl. 1965. Genetic selection for social dominance ability in chickens. *Animal Behaviour* 13:114-131.

Crombie, D.L. 1971. The group system of man and paedomorphosis. *Am. Anthrop.* 12:147-170.

Cullen, J.M. 1966. Reduction of ambiguity through ritualization. *Phil. Trans. Roy. Soc. Lond.* 251:363-374.

Daanje, A. 1950. On the locomotory movements in birds and the intention movements derived from it. *Behavior* 3:48-98.

Damon, A. and R.B. Thomas. 1967. Fertility and physique – height, weight and ponderal index. *Human Biol.* 39:5-13.

Dart, R.A. 1937. Physical characteristics of the khoumani Bushman. *In* Bushmen of the Southern Kalahari (D.J. Reinhart-Jones and C.M. Doke, eds.). Johannesburg, Univ. of Waterstand Press.

Darwin, C. 1904. The Expression of Emotions in Man and Animals. Popular edition, John Murray, London.

Dittman, A.T. 1962. Relationship between body movements and moods in interviews. *J. Consult. Clin. Psychol.* 26:480.

Douglas, J.W.B., J.M. Ross, and H.R. Simpson. 1966. The relationship between height and measured educational ability in school children of the same social class, family size, and stage of sexual development. *Human Biol.* 37:178-186.

DuBrul, L.E. and H. Sicher. 1956. The Adaptive Chin. Springfield, Illinois, Charles C. Thomas, Publishers.

Duncan, S. 1969. Nonverbal communication. *Psychological Bull.* 72(2):118-137.

Dundes, A. 1970. The eyes have it or seeing is believing: worldview in American folk speech. *AAA Preliminary Program and Abstracts, Bull.* 3(3):44.

Ehrlich, P. and J. Freedman. 1971. Population, crowding and human behavior. *Scientist and Science J.,* April 1, pp. 10-14.

Eibl-Eibesfeldt, I. 1970. Ethology, The Biology of Behavior. Intraspecific Aggression pp. 306-334. New York, Holt, Rinehart and Winston.

Eibl-Eibesfeldt, I. 1970. Ethology, The Biology of Behavior. Chapt. 18, The Ethology of Man, pp. 398-465. New York, Rinehart and Winston.

Eibl-Eibesfeldt, I. 1967. Concepts of ethology and their significance in the study of human behavior. *In* Early Behavior (H. W. Stevenson, E. H. Hess and H. L. Rheingold, eds.). New York, Wiley.

Eibl-Eibesfeldt, I. and H. Haas. 1967. Film studies in human ethology. *Am. Anthrop.* 8:477-479.

Eisenberg, P. 1937. Expressive movements related to feeling of dominance. *Arch. Psychol.* 30:5-72.

Eisenberg, P. and E. Zalowitz. 1938. Judging expressive movement: III. Judgments of dominance feeling from phonograph records of voice. *J. Appl. Psychol.,* 22:620-631.

Ekman, P. 1972. Facial affect scoring technique: A first validity study. Semiotica.

Ekman, P. 1969. Pan-cultural elements in facial displays of emotion. *Science* 164: 86-88.

Ekman, P. 1957. A methodological discussion of nonverbal behavior. *Psychol.* 43:141-149.

Ekman, P. and P. Ellsworth. 1971. Emotion in the Human Face: Guidelines for Research and A Review of Findings. New York, Pergamon Press.

Ekman, P. and W.V. Friesen. 1971. Constants across cultures in the face and emotion. *J. Per. Soc. Psych.* 17(2):124-129.

Ekman, P. and Friesen, W.V. 1969. The repertoire of non-verbal behavior: Categories, origins, usage and coding. *Semiotica* 49-98.

Ekman, P. and W.V. Friesen. 1969. Nonverbal leakage and clues to deception. *Psychiatry* 32(1):88-106.

Ekman, P., E.R. Sorenson, and W.V. Friesen. 1969. Pan-cultural elements in facial displays of emotion. *Science* 164:86-8.

Ellis, R.A. and W. Montagna. 1962. The skin of primates. VI. The skin of the gorilla (*Gorilla gorilla*). *Amer. J. Phys. Anthrop.* 20:79-93.

Emanuel, S. 1938. Mechanisms of sebum secretion. *Acta Dermato.-Vener.* (Stockholm) 19:1-15.

Estes, R.D. 1969. Territorial behavior of the Wildebeest (*Connochaetes taurinus* Burchell, 1923). *Zeit. f. Tierpsychol.* 26:284-370.

Every, R.G. 1965. The teeth as weapons, their influence on behavior. *The Lancet* 11:685-688.

Ewer, R.F. 1968. Ethology of Mammals. Logos Press, Bristol. pp. 418.

Fast, J. 1971. Body Language. New York: Pocket Books.

Fox, M. 1972. The social significance of genital licking in the wolf, *Canis lupus*. *Jour. Mamm.* **53**:637-641.

Fox, M.W. 1969. A comparative study of the development of facial expressions in canids: wolf, coyote and foxes. *Behavior* **34**:49-73.

Fox, M.W. 1969. The anatomy of aggression and its ritualization in Canidae: a developmental and comparative study. *Behaviour* **35**:242-258.

Fox, M.W. 1965. Canine Behavior. Springfield, Charles C. Thomas.

Freedman, D.G. 1964. A biological view of man's social behavior. *In* Social Behavior from Fish to Man. Phoenix Books, University of Chicago Press, W. Etkin (ed.).

Freedman, D.G. 1964. Smiling in blind infants and the issue of innate vs. acquired. *J. Child Psychol. Psychiat.* **5**:171-184.

Freedman, D.G. 1961. The infants's fear of strangers and the flight response. *J. Child Psychol. Psychiatry* **1**:242-248.

Freedman, L.A. and A. Roe. 1958. Evolution and human behavior. *In* Behavior and Evolution. A. Roe and G. Simpson (eds.). New Haven and London: Yale University Press.

Garn, S.M., S. Shelby and M.R. Crawford. 1956. Skin reflectance studies in children and adults. *Amer. J. Phys. Anthrop.* **14**:101-117.

Geist, V. 1972. Mountain Sheep Behavior. University of Chicago Press.

Geist, V. 1966. The evolution of horn-like organs. *Behavior* **27**:175-214.

Geist, V. 1963. On the behavior of the North American moose (*Alces alces andersoni*, Peterson) in British Columbia. *Behavior* **20**:377.

Ginsburg, B.E. 1966. All mice are not created equal: recent findings on genes and behavior. *Soc. Serv. Rev.* **40**:121-134.

Ginsberg, B.E. and Alle, W.C. 1942. Some effects of conditioning on social dominance and subordination in inbred strains of mice. *Physiological Zoology* **15**:485-506.

Glass, B. 1966. Evolution of hairlessness in man. *Science* **152**:294.

Goffman, E. On face-work. *Psychiat.* **18**:213-231.

Goodhart, C.B. 1960. The evolutionary significance of human hair patterns and skin coloring. *Advance. Sci.* **17**:53-59.

Grant, E.C. 1969. Human facial expression. *Man* **4**:525-536, Plates 1a-12b.

Grant, E.C. 1968. An ethological description of non-verbal behavior during interviews. *Br. J. Med. Psychol.* **41**:177-184.

Grasse, P.P. 1955. *Traite de zoologie,* 17 (fascicule a).

Grizimek, B. 1965. Wild Animal White Man. London, Thames and Hudson.

Grombrich, E.H. 1972. Action and Expression in Western Art in Non-verbal Communication. R.A. Heinde (ed.). Cambridge University Press, London.

Guthrie, R.D. 1971. A new theory of mammalian rump patch evolution. *Behavior* **38**:132-145.

Guthrie, R.D. 1970. Evolution of human threat display organs. *Evolutionary Biology* **4**:257-302.

Guthrie, R.D. 1971. Evolutionary significance of the cervid labial spot. *Jour. Mammalogy* **52**:209-212.

Guthrie, R.D. 1969. Senescence as an adaptive trait. *Perspect. Biol. Med.* **12**:313-324.

Guthrie, R.D. and Petocz, R. 1970. Weapon automimicry among mammals. *Amer. Nat.* **104**:585-588.

Hall, E.T. 1969. The language of space. *J. Amer. Inst. Arch.* Feb.

Hall, E.T. 1966. The Hidden Dimension. New York, Doubleday.

Hall, E.T. 1964. Silent assumptions in social communication. *Am. Anthrop.* **66**: 154-163.

Hall, E.T. 1955. The anthropology of manners. *Sci. Amer.*, April 84-90.

Hall, K.R.L. 1963. Tool-using performances as indicators of behavioral adaptability. *Curr. Anthrop.* **4**:479-487.

Hall, K.R.L., R.C. Boelkins and M.J. Gaswell. 1965. Behavior of the patas monkey (*Erythrocebus patas*) in captivity, with notes on the natural habitat. *Folia Primat.* (Basel) **3**:22-49.

Hamburg, D. 1968. Evolution of emotional responses: Evidence from recent research on nonhuman primates. *Sci. and Psychoanal.* **12.**

Hamburg, D. 1963. Emotions in the perspective of human evolution. *In* Expression of the Emotions in Man. P.H. Knapp, New York, International University Press.

Harlow, H.F. 1963. The maternal affectional system. *In* Determinants of Infant Behavior II. B.M. Foss (ed.). London, Methuen.

Harlow, H.F. 1958. The nature of love. *American Psychologist* **13**:673-685.

Hediger, H. 1965. Man as a social partner of animals and vice-versa. *In* Social Organization of Animal Communities, pp. 29-314. *Symp. Zool. Soc.,* London No. 14.

Hediger, H. and F. Zweifel. 1962. Primaten-ethologische Schnappschusse aus dem Zurcher Zoo. *Bibl. Primat.* **1**:252-276.

Heider, K.G. 1970. The Dugumdani. New York, Viking Foundation Press, No. 49:244-247.

Hershkovitz, P. 1968. Metachromism or the principle of evolutionary change in mammalian tegumentary colors. *Evolution* **22**:556-575.

Hess, E.H. 1965. Attitude and pupil size. *Sci. Amer.* **212**:46-54.

Hess, E.H. and Polt, J.M. 1960. Pupil size as related to interest value of visual stimuli. *Science,* New York **132**:349-350.

Hess, E.H. 1975. The Tell-Tale Eye. New York, Van Nostrand Reinhold.

Hewes, G.W. 1966. The domain posture. *Anthropological Linguist* **8**:106-122.

Hewes, G.W. 1957. The anthropology of posture. *Sci. Amer.* **196**:123-132.

Hewes, G.W. 1955. World distribution of certain postural habits. *Am. Anthropol.* **57**:231-244.

Hinde, R.A. 1972. Non-Verbal Communication. Cambridge University Press.

Hooton, E. 1946. Man's Poor Relations. New York, Doubleday and Company, Inc.

Huber, E. 1931. Evolution of Facial Musculature and Facial Expression. Baltimore, Johns Hopkins Press.

Hulse, F.S. 1967. Selection for skin color among the Japanese. *Amer. J. Phys. Anthrop.* **27**:143-155.

Hurley, H.J. and W.B. Shelley. 1960. The Human Sweat Gland in Health and Disease. Springfield, Illinois, Charles C. Thomas, Publishers.

Hutt, C. and Ounsted, C. 1966. The biological significance of infantile autism. *Behav. Sci.* **II**:346-356.

Izard, D. 1968. Cross-cultural research findings on development in recognition of facial behavior. *Proc. Amer. Psychol. Assoc. Convent.* **3**:727.

James, W.T. 1932. A study of the expressions of body posture. *J. Genet. Psychol.* **7**:405-437.

Jolly, A. 1966. Lemur Behavior. Univ. of Chicago Press, Chicago, pp. 187.

Jones, F.P., F.E. Gray, *et al.* 1959. An experimental study of the effect of head balance on patterns of posture and movement in man. *J. Psychol.* 47:247-258.

Jones, M.R. 1943. Studies in nervous movements II. The effect of inhibition of micturition on the frequency and patterning of movements. *J. Gen. Psychol.* 47:247-258.

Kahneman, D. and J. Beatty. 1966. Pupil diameter and load on memory. *Science* 154:1583-1585.

Kastle, W. 1967. Soziale Verhaltenweisen von Chamaleonen aus der pumiluo und bitaeniatus - Gruppe. *Zeit. f. Tierpsychol.* 24:313-341.

Keller, C., S. Ridgway, L. Lipscomb and E. Fromm. 1968. The genetics of adrenal size and tameness in colorphase foxes. *Heredity* 59:82-84.

Kendon, A. 1970. Movement coordination in social interaction. *Acta Psychol.* 32:100-125.

Kendon, A. 1970. Some relationships between body motion and speech. *In* Studies in Dyadic Interaction. New York, Pergamon.

Kendon, A. 1967. Some functions of gaze-direction in social interaction. *Acta Psychol* 26:22-63.

Key, M. 1962. Gestures and responses: A preliminary study among some Indian tribes of Bolivia. *Studies in Linguistics* 16:92-99.

Khatchadourian, H. 1966. Gestures as expression in the middle east. *ETC* 23: 358-361.

King, W.S. 1949. Hand gestures. *Western Folklore* 8:263-264.

Knapp, P.H. (ed.). 1963. Expression of the Emotions in Man. New York, International Universities Press.

Korn, N. and F. Thompson (eds.). 1967. Human Evolution: Readings in Physical Anthropology. New York, Holt, Rinehart and Winston.

Kramer, E. 1963. The judgement of personal characteristics and emotions from non-verbal properties of speech. *Psychol. Bull.* 60:408-420.

Krout, M.H. 1954. An experimental attempt to determine the significance of unconscious manual symbolic movements. *J. Gen. Psychol.* 51:121-151.

Krout, M.H. 1935. Artistic gestures: An experimental study in symbolic movement. *Psychol. Monogr.* 46.

Kummer, Hans. 1968. Social Organization of Hamadryas Baboons. Basel and New York, Karger.

Kummer, H. 1957. Sociales Verhalten einer Mantelparvian-Gruppe. *Schweiz. Z. Psychol.,* Beiheft 33.

LaBarre, W. 1947. The cultural basis of emotions and gestures. *J. Person.* 16:49-68.

Lack, D. 1968. Ecological Adaptations for Breeding in Birds. London, Methuen and Co., Ltd.

Laver, J. 1964. Costume as a means of social aggression. *In* The Natural History of Aggression, J.D. Carthy and F.J. Ebling (eds.). New York, Academic Press, Inc.

Lawick-Goodall, J.A. 1968. A preliminary report on expressive movements and communications in Gombe Stream Chimpanzees. *In* Primates: Studies in Adaptation and Variability. Phyllis C. Jay (ed.). pp. 313-374. New York, Holt, Rinehart and Winston.

Lawick-Goodall, 1967. My Friends the Wild Chimpanzees. Washington, D.C. National Geographic Society.

Lawick-Goodall, J.A. 1965. Chimpanzees of the Gombe Stream Reserve. *In* Primate Behavior. (I. DeVore, ed.) pp. 425-473. New York, Holt, Rinehart and Winston.

LeBoeuf and R.S. Peterson. 1969. Social status and mating activity in elephant seals. *Science* 163:91-93.

Lent, P.C. 1966. Calving and related social behavior in the barren-ground caribou. *Zeit. f. Tierpsychol.* 23:701-756.

Leuthold, W. 1966. Variations in territorial behavior of Uganda kob *Adenota kob Thomasi* (Neumann, 1896). *Behaviour* 27:215-58.

Lewis, T.H. 1942. Biology of the Negro. Chicago, University of Chicago Press.

Leyhausen, P. 1956. Verhaltensstudien bei Katzen. *Zeit. f. Tierpsychol.* Beihoft 2.

Lorenz, K. 1966. On Aggression. London, Methuen.

Lorenz, K. 1964. Ritualized fighting. *In* The Natural History of Aggression. J.D. Carthy and F.J. Ebling (eds.) London and New York, Academic Press.

Lorenz, K. 1962. The function of color in coral reef fishes. *Proc. Royal Inst. of Great Britain* 39:282-296.

Lorenz, K. 1955. Morphology and behavior patterns in closely allied species. *In* Group processes, Transactions of the First Conference. B. Schaffner (ed.) pp. 168-220. New York, Josiah Macy, Jr. Found.

MacCoby, E. 1966. The Development of Sex Differences. Stanford, Stanford University Press.

Mackworth, N.H. and M.H. Bagshaw. 1970. Eye catching in adults, children and monkeys: Some experiments of orienting and observing responses. *Res. Pub. Ass. Res. Nerv. Ment. Dis.* 48:201-213.

MacLean, P.D. 1969. The paranoid streak in man. *In* Beyond Reductionism. A. Koestler and J.R. Smythies (ed.). London, Hutchinson.

MacLean, P.D. 1962. New findings relevant to the evolution of psychosexual functions of the brain. *J. Nerv. Ment. Dis.* 135:289-301.

Maginnis, M. 1958. Gesture and status. *Group Psychother.* 11:105-109.

Martin, R. and K. Saller. 1962. Lehrbuch der Anthropologie. Vol. 4. Stuttgart, G. Fischer.

Maslow, A.H., H. Rand and S. Newman. 1960. Some parallels between sexual and dominance behavior of nonhuman primates: Vol. 2. A.M. Schrier, H.F. Harlow and F. Stollnitz (eds.). pp. 335-364.

Maslow, A.H., H. Rand and S. Newman. 1960. Some parallels between sexual and dominance behaviour of infra-human primates and the fantasies of patients in psychotherapy. *J. of Nerv. and Men. Dis.* 131:202-212.

Masters, W.H. and V.E. Johnson. 1966. The Human Sexual Response. Boston, Little, Brown and Company.

Matthiessen, P. 1962. Under the Mountain Wall. New York, Ballantine books, 1969 edition.

McBride, G., M.G. King and J.W. James. 1965. Social proximity effects on galvanic skin responses in adult humans. *J. Psychol.* 61:153-157.

Meggitt, M.H. 1962. The Desert People. Angus and Robertson, p. 262 (printed in the U.S.A. by University of Chicago Press).

Michael, G. and F.N. Willis. 1968. The development of gestures as a function of social class, education and sex. *Psychological Record* 18:515.

Milne, A.H. 1955. The humps of East African cattle. *The Empire J. of Experimental Agriculture*. Vol. 23, Nos. 91-92.

Mitchell, J.C. 1968. Dermatological aspects of displacement activity: Attention to the body surface as a substitute for flight or fight. *Canad. Med. Ass. J.* 98:962-964.

Montagna, W. 1963. The phylogenetic significance of the skin of man. *Arch. Derm.* (Chicago) 38:53-71.

Montagna, W. and R.A. Ellis. 1963. New approaches to the skin of primates. *In* Evolutionary and Genetic Biology of Primates, Vol. 1. J. Buettner-Janusch (ed.). New York, Academic Press, Inc., pp. 179-195.

Montagna, W. and J.S. Yun. 1963. The skin of primates. XV. The skin of the chimpanzee *(Pan satyrus)*. *Amer. J. Phys. Anthrop.* 21:189-203.

Montagna, W., H. Machida, and E. Perkins. 1966. The skin of primates. XXVIII. The stump-tailed macaque *(Macaca speciosa)*. *Amer. J. Phys. Anthrop.* 24: 71-86.

Morris, D. (ed.) 1970. Primate Ethology. New York, Doubleday and Co.

Morris, D. 1969. The Human Zoo. New York, Dell Publishing Co.

Morris, D. 1967. The Naked Ape. London, Cape.

Morris, D. 1957. "Typical intensity" and its relation to the problem of ritualization. *Behavior* 11:1-12.

Morris, D. 1956. The feather postures of birds and the problem of the origin of social signals. *Behaviour* 9:75-113.

Moss, H. A. 1967. Sex, age and state as determinants of mother-infant interactions. Merrill-Palmer Quart. 13.

Moynihan, M. 1955. Remarks on the original sources of displays. *Auk* 72:240-246.

Murphy, R.F. 1964. Social distance and the veil. *Am. Anthrop.* 66:1257-1274.

Myrberg, A.A. 1965. A descriptive analysis of the behavior of the African cichlid fish, *Pelmatochromis guentheri* (Savage). *Animal Behavior* 13:312-329.

Napier, J.R. and P.H. Napier. 1967. A Handbook of Living Primates. New York, Academic Press, Inc.

Oppenheimer, A.M. 1968. Behavioral novelty — An evolutionary force. *Am. Anthrop.* 70:562-563.

Osgood, C.E. 1966. Dimensionality of the semantic space for communication via facial expressions. *Scand. J. Psychol.* 7:1-30.

Perutz, K. 1970. Beyond the Looking Glass; America's Beauty Culture. New York, Morrow.

Pittman, A.T., M. B. Parloff and D.S. Boomer. 1965. Facial and bodily expression: A study of receptivity of emotional cues. *Psychiat.* 28:239-244.

Price, J. 1967. The dominance hierarchy and the evolution of mental illness. *Lancet* 2:243-246, July 29.

Price, J. 1968. Neurotic and endogenous depression: A phylogenetic view. *Brit. J. Psychiat. Soc. Work* 114:119-126.

Pruitt, W.O. 1960. Behavior of the Barren-Ground Caribou. Biological Papers, University of Alaska No. 3.

Quackenbos, H.M. 1945. Archetype postures. *Psychiat. Quart.* 19:589-591.

Quay, W.B. and D. Muller-Schwarze. 1970. Functional histology of integumentary glandular regions in black-tailed deer *(Odocoileus hemionus columbianus)*. *Jour. Mamm.* 51:675-674.

Rasa, O.A.E. 1968. Territoriality and the establishment of dominance by means of visual clues in Pomacentrus jenkinsi (Pisces: Promcentridae). *Zeit. f. Tierpsychol.* **26**:825-845.

Reich, W. 1947. The Function of the Orgasm: Muscular Attitude and Bodily Expressions. New York, Orgone Institute Press.

Robson, L.S. 1967. The role of eye to eye contact in maternal-infant attachment. *J. Child. Psychol.* **8**:13-25.

Robson, L., F. Pederson, and H.A. Moss. 1969. Developmental observations of diadic gazing in relation to the fear of strangers and social approach behavior. *Child Develop.* **40**:619-627.

Rosenberg, B.G. and J. Langer. 1965. A study of postural-gestural communication. *J. Personal. Soc. Psychol.* **2**:593-597.

Rosenfeld, H.M. 1966. Instrumental affiliation functions of facial and gestural expressions. *J. Personal Soc. Psychol.* **4**:65-72.

Rue, L.L. 1962. The World of the White-Tailed Deer. New York, Lippincott.

Saitz, R.L. and E.J. Cervenka. 1962. Colombian and North American gestures, a Contrastive Inventory. Bogota, Centro-Colombo-Americana, 90 pp.

Schaller, G.B. 1963. The Mountain Gorilla. University of Chicago Press.

Scheflen, A.E. 1964. The significance of posture in communication systems. *Psychiatry* **27**(4):316-331.

Sebeok, T.A. 1962. Coding in the evolution of signaling behavior. *Behav. Sci.* **7**: 430-442.

Sebeok, T.A. and A. Ramsey (eds.). 1969. Approaches to Animal Communication. The Hague, Netherlands, Mouton.

Seltzer, C.C. 1946. Body disproportions and dominant personality traits. *Psychosom. Med.* **8**:75-97.

Sharman, G.B. and J.H. Calby. 1964. Reproductive behavior in the red kangaroo, *Megaleia rufa,* in captivity. C.S.I.R.O. Wildl. Res. **9**:58-85.

Spuhler, J.N. (ed.). 1967. Genetic Diversity and Human Behavior. Chicago, Aldine Publishing Co.

Stonor, C.R. 1940. Courtship and display among birds. London.

Strohmayer, W. 1937. Die Vererbung des Hapsburger Familientypus. *Nova Acta Leopoldina* **5**:219-296.

Struhsaker, T.T. 1967. Behavior of elk (*Cervus canadensis*) during the rut. *Zeit. f. Tierpsychol.* **24**:80-114.

Sudoff, R.L. 1966. On the nature of crying and weeping. *Psychiat. Quart.* **40**: (3): 490-503.

Thoday, J.M. and J.B. Gibson. 1970. Environmental and genetical contributions to class difference: a model experiment. *Science* **167**:990-992.

Thompson, D.F. and L. Metzger. 1964. Communication of emotional intent by facial expression. *J. Abnorm. Soc. Psychol.* **68**:129-135.

Thompson, T.I. 1964. Visual reinforcement in fighting cocks. *J. Exp. Anal. Behav.* **7**:45-49.

Thompson, T.I. 1963. Visual reinforcement in Siamese fighting fish. *Science* **141**: 55-57.

Thornton, G.R. 1944. The effect of wearing glasses on judgments of persons seen briefly. *Jour. Appl. Psychol.* **28**:203-207.

Tiger, L. 1970. Dominance in human societies. *Annual Review of Ecology and Systematics* **1**:287-305.

Tiger L. and R. Fox. 1966. The zoological perspective in social science. *Man* 1:1.

Tinbergen, N. 1968. On war and peace in animals and man: *Science* 160:1411-1418.

Tinbergen, N. 1964. The evolution of signaling devices. *In* Social Behavior and Organization among Vertebrates. W. Etkin (ed.). Chicago and London, University of Chicago Press.

Tinbergen, N., E. Ennion, and H. Falkus. 1970. Signals for Survival. Oxford, The Clarendon Press.

Tinbergen, N. and M. Moynihan. 1952. Head flagging in the black-headed gull, its function and origin. *Britain Birds* 45:19-22.

Tomkins, S.S. 1963. Affect, Imagery, Consciousness. Vol. II, The Negative Affects. New York, Springer.

Tomkins, S.S. 1962. Affect, Imagery Consciousness. Vol. I, The Positive Affects. New York, Springer.

Tomkins, S.S. and McCarter, R. 1964. What and where are the primary affects? Some evidence for a theory. Perceptual and Motor Skills, 18:119-158.

Trivers, R. 1971. The evolution of recriprocal altruism. Quart. Rev. Bio., March, p. 35.

van Hoof, J.A.R.A.M. 1967. The facial displays of catarrhine monkeys and apes. *In* Primate Ethologie (D. Morris, ed.), pp. 7-68. Wiedenfield and Nicholson, London.

van Hoof, J.A.R.A.M. 1962. Facial expression in higher primates. *Symp. Zool. Soc. London* 8:97-125.

Vine, I. 1970. Communication by facial-visual signals. *In* Social Behavior in Birds and Mammals. J.H. Cook (ed.) pp. 279-236. Academic Press, New York.

Wall, G.V. 1942. The vertebrate eye and its adaptive radiation. Cranbrook Inst. of Sci. Bloomfield Hills, Michigan.

Walters, J., D. Pearce and L. Dahms. 1957. Affectional and aggressive behavior of preschool children. *Child Develop.* 28:15-26.

Walther, F. 1958. Zum Kampf- und paarungsverhalten einiger Antilopen. *Zeit. f. Tierpsychol.* 15:350-380.

Washburn, S.L. Behavior and the origin of man. (Huxley Lecture delivered November 9, 1967 at the Royal Anthropological Institute of Great Britain and Ireland, London).

Washburn, S.L. 1963. Comment on tool-using performances as indicators of behavioral adaptability by K.R.L. Hall. *Curr. Anthrop.* 4:492.

Webb, W.W., *et al.* 1963. Eye movements as a paradigm of approach and avoidance behavior. *Percept. Motor Skills* 16:341-347.

Wickler, W. 1967. Socio-sexual signals and their intra-specific imitation among primates. *In* Primate Ethology, pp. 69-147. D. Morris (ed.). Aldine, Chicago.

Wickler, W. 1966. Mimicry. McGraw-Hill Co., New York 255 pp.

Williams, F. and J. Tolch. 1965. Communication by facial expression. *J. Commun.* 15:17-27.

Wilson, P.R. 1968. Perceptual distortion of height as a function of ascribed academic status. *J. Soc. Psychol.* 74:97-102.

Winick, C. 1962. Eye and face movements as nonverbal communication in group psychotherapy. *J. Hillside Hosp.* 9:67-69. (See also *Amer. J. Psychoth.* 15:56-62 *Psychiat.* 24:171-182, 1961).

Wolf, A.P. 1970. Childhood association and sexual attraction: A further test of the Westermarck hypothesis. *Am. Anthrop.* 72:503-515.

Wolf, A.P. 1966. Childhood association, sexual attraction, and the incest taboo: A Chinese case. *Am. Anthrop.* 68:883-898.

Woolpy, J.H. 1968. The social organization of wolves. *Nat. His.* 77:46-55.

Zajonc, R.B. 1965. Social facilitation. *Science* 149:269-274.

Zumpe, D. 1965. Laboratory observations on the aggressive behavior of some butterfly fishes (*Chaetodentidae*). *Zeit. f. Tierpsychol.* 22:226-244.

INDEX